It's Been Said Before

It's Been Said Before

A Guide to the Use and Abuse of Clichés

Orin Hargraves

OXFORD
UNIVERSITY PRESS

OXFORD
UNIVERSITY PRESS

Oxford University Press is a department of the
University of Oxford. It furthers the University's objective
of excellence in research, scholarship, and education
by publishing worldwide.

Oxford   New York
Auckland   Cape Town   Dar es Salaam   Hong Kong   Karachi
Kuala Lumpur   Madrid   Melbourne   Mexico City   Nairobi
New Delhi   Shanghai   Taipei   Toronto

With offices in
Argentina   Austria   Brazil   Chile   Czech Republic   France   Greece
Guatemala   Hungary   Italy   Japan   Poland   Portugal   Singapore
South Korea   Switzerland   Thailand   Turkey   Ukraine   Vietnam

Oxford is a registered trade mark of Oxford University Press
in the UK and certain other countries.

Published in the United States of America by
Oxford University Press
198 Madison Avenue, New York, NY 10016

© Oxford University Press 2014

Library of Congress Cataloging-in-Publication Data

Hargraves, Orin.
It's been said before : a guide to the use and abuse of clichés / Orin Hargraves.
pages   cm
Summary: "This book provides a concise and lively guide to the most abused phrases
in the English language today"—Provided by publisher.
ISBN 978-0-19-931573-4 (hardback)—ISBN 978-0-19-931574-1 (ebook)—
ISBN 978-0-19-931575-8 (ebook)
1. Clichés.   2. English language—Terms and phrases.   3. English language—Usage.
4. English language—Humor.   I. Title.
PE1442.H37   2014
428'.1—dc23   2013047098

9 8 7 6 5 4 3 2 1

Printed in the United States of America
on acid-free paper

This book is dedicated to my mother, Barbara Magness,
whose unwavering belief in me has been
a foundation of every good thing I have done.

Acknowledgments

Many conversations with friends and colleagues over the past couple of years have been helpful to me in writing this book, especially those that took place at the University of Colorado where I have a day job. In particular I would like to thank Steve Bethard, Jim Martin, Martha Palmer, and Will Styler. I am also grateful to my colleagues Paul Cook of the University of Melbourne and Graeme Hirst of the University of Toronto for fruitful exchanges. Hallie Stebbins, my editor at OUP, made useful suggestions that greatly improved the first draft of the manuscript.

The research for the book, which I believe has turned up hundreds of interesting facts about what people do with clichés, would have involved effort far beyond what one mortal could achieve in a lifetime if not for Sketch Engine, the software developed by my friend and colleague Adam Kilgarriff for querying corpora. I—and every lexicographer who has had the benefit of using Sketch Engine—owe him a huge debt of gratitude. Finally I would like to thank the many lexicographers whose kindness, camaraderie, enthusiasm, and dedication have been an inspiration to me since I began investigating the behavior of words many years ago: particularly Faye Carney, David Jost, Sidney Landau, and Erin McKean.

Contents

Introduction

Everyone thinks they know a cliché when they see one, but in a given piece of text, it's unlikely that any two readers will agree on how many clichés are present and which expressions are in fact clichés. A phrase might be considered a cliché in one context, while seeming to be a model of clarity and effectiveness in another. In other words, not all expressions deemed familiar enough to be called clichés at one time or another are to be unequivocally shunned. While it is true that a vast number of expressions have become tired through overuse, there is an opportunity to make even the most worn expressions striking and powerful. How do we decide which among many such expressions may be just right for the occasion, or just wrong?

This book seeks to answer that question. I discuss the problems that arise from the use of clichés, when their use is not problematic, and how problems arising from the use of clichés can be avoided. I clarify the degree to which misapplication of various common phrases results in their being labeled as clichés, supporting the identification of clichés with actual data about usage. From this data emerges a picture of the very high degree to which context determines whether a familiar expression successfully captures an intended meaning or fails to do so and falls into the well-worn rut of cliché.

The book is intended to be a helpful guide and to provide an understanding of how certain phrases come to be thought of—negatively, in nearly all cases—as clichés. It is not, however, intended to be a dictionary of clichés, a catalog of clichés, or a definitive list of clichés. There are many clichés in the wild that have yet to be catalogued, and there may well be phrases in this book that you personally do not think of as clichés. If you use the index of this book as a checklist to ensure that your writing does not contain any clichés you will have missed its point, as well as missing out on many opportunities in which you might aptly deploy a cliché in your speech or writing.

The standard treatment of clichés in book-length form is to compile a dictionary of them; there are three or four of these currently in print in English, and historically, half a dozen more. I have consulted these books, but I don't fully understand their point, and it is not my intention here to continue their tradition. What purpose does a dictionary of clichés serve? Would you use it to check that you'd scrubbed your own writing of all clichés? To catalog the clichés in someone else's work as a means of disparaging it? In all of the published dictionaries of clichés I find a superfluity of entries that appear to have been included simply to bulk out the book, and many of the entries in cliché dictionaries are not clichés at all; they are idioms, a distinction that I address in greater detail in chapter 1.

It is my hope that you will read this book with an open mind and consult the individual entries, either by browsing or by looking them up in the index, as a way of familiarizing yourself with the role that clichés play in language, the ways in which they can be useful, and the times, surely considerable in number, when they should be avoided. I also provide you with tools to investigate for yourself whether a given form of words falls into the disparaging category that people call "cliché," and if it does, whether it is prudent for you to use it. You can then proceed with the confidence that you have made peace with clichés through greater understanding and that you have established a relationship with them that will serve your interests when you write and speak.

Orin Hargraves
Niwot, Colorado
March 2014

It's Been Said Before

1
What Is a Cliché?

A breath of fresh air. Few and far between. At the end of the day. Most of us immediately recognize these as clichés, whether we use them or not. Most of us also agree that English is suffused with expressions that are widely considered to be clichés, even if we can't arrive at a consensus about just which of many expressions deserve the label "cliché" or, for that matter, how cliché should be defined.

Dictionaries, of course, have a say in the matter. The word *cliché* comes to English from French. Its original, literal denotation thoroughly informs its meaning today: a cliché was a convenience of printing, specifically a stereotype block bearing text that was used to produce multiple printed copies. From this meaning arose the idea of an invariable and reusable expression. Dictionary definitions of *cliché* all share some common features. Here are a few examples:

- a phrase or opinion that is overused and betrays a lack of original thought

- a trite phrase or expression
- a sentence or phrase, usually expressing a popular or common thought or idea, that has lost originality, ingenuity, and impact by long overuse

The difficulty that arises in the very definition of cliché is that its principal characteristics—overuse and ineffectiveness—are not objectively measurable. What, exactly, constitutes overuse? Who is to be the judge of effectiveness? You will hardly find a definition of cliché that does not include these ideas, but it is difficult, if not impossible, to find an objective standard by which to gauge them.

Any judgment about whether a form of words is overused was necessarily subjective or speculative before it was possible to gather accurate statistics about language use. Nearly all judgments about what constitutes a cliché have traditionally relied on consensus: if enough people think a form of words is overused, or if a person who is perceived as having some authority about language declares such a thing, then the word or phrase becomes a cliché. The result of this haphazard process is that many phrases are designated clichés without there being evidence of their frequent use. That is, infrequently used words and phrases may be deemed clichés, simply because a large number of people, or a small number of influential people, find them annoying or designate them as clichés for some other reason. When asked to produce a cliché, many speakers simply produce an idiom. Idioms, looked at in isolation, are not necessarily clichés. Yet hundreds of these idioms fill up the pages of dictionaries of clichés, with little justification for their inclusion according to the very criteria that the compilers of these dictionaries enumerate. My research, on the other hand, has identified hundreds of phrases that are frequently used—indeed, surely overused—in English and that I think readers will agree are clichés, even though many of them have not traditionally been treated as clichés in popular or scholarly literature.

Today, lexicographers and other language researchers have a tool that makes the study of language much easier and more evidence-based than ever before: the corpus. A corpus (plural: corpora) is a collection of natural language in machine-readable form, assembled for the purpose of linguistic research. Most corpora are put together with careful attention toward achieving balance, so that the corpus as a whole is as much as possible a representative sample of contemporary or historical language drawn from a wide range of genres, often capturing both published texts and transcriptions of speech. In looking at language for the purpose of studying clichés, corpora have given me an excellent tool for determining how often, and in what contexts, a particular phrase or form of words is used. This makes it very easy to put to the test the question of whether a given way of expressing something may be, in fact, "overused." While there can be no level of frequency that officially constitutes overuse of a word or phrase, statistics are very revealing about how often words are used in particular groupings.

Working with a corpus it is possible, with a few keystrokes, to call up a dozen or a hundred or a thousand instances of a word or a phrase in the context of actual speech or writing. Other items in the lexicographic toolbox provide statistics on the frequency of words and phrases in relation to other words, or as a percentage of English generally. From these statistics emerge portraits of the life of words, their mating habits, their abuses, their triumphs and failings, in a much clearer and more comprehensive light than can be gleaned from casual reading or listening; it is a portrait that is far more dependable than the one that results from merely consulting your intuition about how often a form of words is used or whether people use it consistently, aptly, or inappropriately. Modern computational lexicography makes it possible to learn at a glance which pairs or groups of words are getting together far more often than their overall frequency in the language suggests that they would. Such pairings of words are called collocations and may include typical combinations representing several different parts of speech, such as adjective + noun (like *abject poverty*), noun + noun (like *software download*), or adverb + verb (like *virtually guarantee*). Figure 1 shows the way word combinations of extremely high frequency appear in a statistical format as extracted from a corpus. Here you see an index of the uses of the noun *stamp* when it precedes a prepositional phrase beginning with *of*. In other words, the illustration provides statistical information from the corpus about the phrases *stamp of approval*, *stamp of authenticity*, *stamp of legitimacy*, and so forth. The second column in the table is a raw count of the number of instances of the various combinations; the third column is a statistical construct that reflects the likelihood of such a combination occurring, based on the frequency of the words in the language considered separately. As you can see, the combination *stamp of approval* is many dozens of times more frequent than any other such combination—and in my view, the only phrase in the form *stamp of* _____ that might be considered a cliché.

N*of-i N	1991	1.3
☐ approval	885	7.74
☐ legitimacy	21	4.37
☐ credibility	20	3.48
☐ authenticity	19	4.96
☐ personality	11	1.55
		>>

As for the effectiveness of a given form of words: this is impossible to put to an objective test because the arbiter of the effectiveness of language is its hearer or its reader. We all have access to the common lexicon of English that may alert us when we encounter an overworked form of words, but its particular effect on us will depend on subjective and individual facts, such as the breadth and depth of our reading habits. A phrase regarded as a cliché in one context may pass unobtrusively in another, where it is credited with quietly or even cleverly doing its job. Complicating matters further, everyone works with a rather fuzzy mental definition of what a cliché is. A very broad definition of *cliché* (which is not the basis of this book) takes in expressions that some people would regard mainly as idioms, proverbs, or both.

Thousands of expressions in English have a necessary but not always sufficient identifying characteristic of a cliché: they express a common idea that requires frequent expression. Yet many of these expressions are not normally considered clichés because, despite extremely frequent use, they do not lose their effectiveness. Consider, for example, *the day after tomorrow*. What else are you going to call it? Though it is a rather long phrase syllabically, English (unlike some other languages) does not have a sparer formula to express this idea, and so we readily accept the expression as a unit and we neither grow weary of hearing or seeing it nor feel that speakers and writers use it too often and should perhaps find some other way of expressing the idea behind it. In a similar way, many idioms gain extremely high frequencies in English because they express very succinctly an idea that would take many more syllables if expressed in a literal way. *Shed light on* is a good example of this; it's an entry in some dictionaries of clichés, but I do not think its inclusion is merited. I do not know of anyone who would declare that *shed light on* is not effective; it expresses efficiently to most people the idea "make known certain facts about," and it is certainly preferable to the longer, more literal form. Some short idioms—such as *bottom line*—may go through a period in which they may be considered clichés but they eventually achieve the status of standalone entries in dictionaries because English has found no more efficient way of expressing the ideas behind them. These, to my mind, do not usually constitute clichés unless they are seriously and frequently misapplied.

What then, are the factors that are likely to nudge an expression from mere frequency in the language to perception as a cliché? What I have found in looking at hundreds of common expressions and collocations is that misuse, or at least infelicitous use, is very often the culprit that contributes to the perception of both overuse and ineffectiveness of a given form of words. In other words, it is often misapplication, rather than frequency of application, that leads to the perception of a phrase as a cliché. An expression is much more likely to be regarded as a cliché if it has typical or frequent use in contexts where it doesn't apply very well (by being imprecise, misleading, or inaccurate, for example). Take the noun phrase *best-kept secret*. *Best-kept*, as an adjective, has few uses in English other than to precede the word *secret*, and discounting the adjective *dark*, *best-kept* is the adjective most likely to be found preceding *secret* in nearly every genre of writing. But as a few examples will show, things that are dubbed *best-kept secrets* are in fact often not secret at all, and it is rarely specified, sometimes not even implied, in what sense they are "kept." This, in effect, makes both parts of this compound expression not very meaningful. It is also the case that the *best-kept secret* is found preponderantly in journalism, a medium that is by its nature contrary to the idea of "secret."

> Dr. Eng has dubbed the often overlooked family health history as "the best kept secret in health care."
> Community colleges are no longer the "best-kept secret" in higher education.
> Hilary Weston and Nicole Eaton featured them in their book In a Canadian Garden, and Reader's Digest once referred to them as "Canada's best kept secret."

Usages like these very easily evoke a response that we are hearing about more best-kept secrets than we need to, and it is only a short step from this perception to declare that the form of words is a cliché. This phenomenon has its analog in the physical world: a tool used for the wrong purpose will be much more likely to show signs of wear than one used properly. If you use a saw as a hammer, you'll not only fail to get the job done, but you'll inflict signs of wear on the saw that may compromise its proper use for a more suitable purpose.

With that as background, let me lay out what is not a cliché as treated in this book so that readers will have a clearer understanding of its scope. The first distinction I will draw, mentioned in passing above, is between *idiom* and *cliché*. Many clichés are idioms, and many idioms are clichés, but they are not the same thing. Both idioms and clichés are expressions that typically have two common elements: first, familiarity, in that they are known to nearly all fluent native speakers; second, noncompositionality, which means that you cannot necessarily or easily infer the meaning of the expression by looking at the meanings of its constituent parts and composing them. All idioms are noncompositional: that quality is included in the definition of an idiom, although it should probably be noted that an educated native speaker can often make a good guess about the meaning of an unfamiliar idiom on the basis of its components and from its context. Many clichés are also noncompositional, such as *elephant in the room*; *lock, stock, and barrel*; and *on the same page*. Other clichés, however, do not meet this criterion, such as *quick to point out*; *in any way, shape, or form*; and *a whole new level*.

Published dictionaries of clichés contain many expressions that are clearly idioms but that I do not consider to be clichés in most of their usages. Numerous of these common expressions are not, to my mind, clichés, because they do not meet the criterion of ineffectiveness, despite their great frequency of use. This is particularly the case with idiomatic expressions that have a very specific meaning, the more literal equivalents of which are lengthy and unwieldy. Expressions in this category include, among many others, *as the crow flies*, *get out of Dodge*, *out of pocket*, *test the waters*, *shed light on* (already mentioned above), *a bone to pick*, and *catch red-handed*. While obviously noncompositional, these expressions lack one of the core qualities of cliché: ineffectiveness. All of these expressions have considerable frequency in English because they convey a specific idea efficiently and effectively. I do not find evidence that they are overused or misused, and therefore it does not seem sensible to classify them as clichés. The economy of *shed light on* is discussed above. *Catch red-handed* is similarly economical and vivid and is used in all contexts except extremely formal ones because it succinctly conveys an idea that is more cumbersome when expressed literally. Additionally, and like *a bone to pick*, it calls a vivid image to the mind that is based on sense data, and any expression is made more vivid and effective by having an element that is derived from input through one of the senses.

I would also distinguish clichés from what I call formulas because there is sometimes a close relationship between the two. By *formula* I mean a fixed order of words that has a particular and sometimes technical meaning in a specific domain or genre. Examples include *null and void* in law and *growing body of evidence* in scientific literature. When formulas come unmoored from their genres, as they often do, they are likely to become clichés because of their more general, imprecise, or inaccurate application in more or in broader genres of writing, particularly in journalism.

In choosing which clichés to examine in detail in this book I have considered frequency as a core determining factor, since it is after all overuse that often leads to an expression being deemed a cliché. Expressions that I examined and found to have a frequency of less than .1 per million words are not included. On this basis, I excluded some familiar expressions such as *rare window*, *get off the couch*, *lay down a marker,* and *at daggers drawn* that, if used more frequently, might well attract the label *cliché*. A fuller explanation of the frequency of clichés and the way that frequency is presented in this book can be found below in the section titled "Metrics."

Having determined that a given expression met the core criterion of frequency, I then examined dozens or hundreds of instances of usage of each expression. Those that I have found to be used widely in contexts where they do not apply very well, or whose usage in particular contexts is problematic, I deem clichés and I treat in this book.

The least quantifiable quality of clichés—and in fact the feature of expressions that leads people to call them clichés—is that they are often annoying. But they are never annoying in equal measure, to the same people, in the same contexts, and for the same reasons. As a natural language user and producer I am not immune to the irritation factor and I'm sure that it has influenced a few of my choices for inclusion in deciding where to draw the line between frequent expression and cliché, but I have never let this be a main determining factor, because of its subjective nature.

There are two other terms I would distinguish from clichés that are not treated in this book: *proverbs* and *fillers*. Both are frequent in English but do not meet the criteria of cliché, for reasons detailed below.

A proverb is a full sentence that expresses a general truth or that imparts a piece of advice, such as *A stitch in time saves nine* or *Too many cooks spoil the broth*. Proverbs may share with clichés the quality of being frequent and familiar; many of them are also not compositional. However, since they are generally taken to be true and effective in expression, they are essentially in conflict with one of the core ideas of cliché—namely, that of being trite or ineffective. Additionally, proverbs, being full sentences, do not fulfill a straightforward grammatical function, which is a feature of most of the clichés I treat in this book.

A filler is a word or sound inserted into speech that does not necessarily perform a grammatical function and that can be eliminated without changing the meaning of the text. Speakers use fillers to fill a pause, perhaps while they take time to think or simply out of habit. Common fillers in English are *you know*, *like*, *well*, *uh*, *I mean*, *sort of*, and *basically*. Some other fillers can be attached syntactically and are problematic cases because this feature would make them candidates for treatment as clichés, since they already fill the other criteria of frequency and ineffectiveness. Good examples of this border area of fillers are *of course*—which I do not treat in this book, though it is frequently used to no purpose—and *once again*—which I do treat, partly because it so easily bounds across the irritation line. But my guiding principle in the case of borderline fillers has been whether the expression represents a genuine intention on the part of the speaker. This feature, like some others about clichés, is one that cannot be determined with scientific certainty but that examination of instances of usage has allowed me to make informed judgments about.

HOW DO CLICHÉS LIVE?

All clichés have a revenant lifestyle: they flutter to life briefly, vainly, whenever they are thoughtlessly disgorged from the mouths, pens, or fingertips of speakers and writers. And though they are often dead on arrival at their destination—the intended audience of the speech or writing—clichés have a viruslike ability to infect their recipients. Listeners to and readers of clichés, if they do not take precaution in the form of attentiveness to their own speech and writing, will find themselves the unwitting vectors of these forms of words when they write and speak. The clichés then continue to spread through the torrent of English, so many obstacles in a fast-moving stream, discouraging anyone who would navigate the stream deftly and slowing down the progress of effective and efficient communication.

A quality of clichés that is typically overlooked when people are disparaging them is that many of them are really very clever and original. Or rather, they were very clever and original the first time they appeared. So much so, in fact, that they immediately attracted hundreds and thousands of imitators: speakers and writers who were perhaps so eager to use the newly coined form of words that they applied it willy-nilly, or simply created a context in which they could use it so as to appear as original as the coiner had been. So, in this sense, clichés are very often a victim of their own early success. Just as a joke loses its ability to shock or amuse on subsequent hearings after the first, so it is with the ability of a clever phrase to seem particularly eloquent and apt.

An earlier draft version of this book was titled "The Graveyard of Dire Clichés." The inspiration for that title was the naïve idea that it might be possible to actually put many old and tired clichés out of their misery by naming and shaming them. Following more extensive study and discussions with many friends and colleagues, however, I realized that most clichés will never die. All speakers find them extremely useful to smooth the steady flow of speech. Many, perhaps most, writers must resort to cliché from time to time in order to connect with their readers in a way that formal language, often barren of cliché, does not allow them to do.

So while I have scaled back my ambition as a cliché-killer, I have persisted in my attempt to stop some clichés in their flight, capture and anesthetize them, splay their dull wings, pin them to the specimen board, and make them visible for all to see, so that they may be revealed in their true lack of color. My intention is to make speakers and writers more aware of the occasions when they are using clichés or when they think that they need to—for it must surely be the case that clichés are largely used mindlessly, given their viral proliferation. An increased awareness of clichés and the detriment that they typically represent to effective communication should serve as a motive for language users to consider alternatives to them.

WHERE DO CLICHÉS LIVE?

A number of genres are included in the main corpus I used in my research, the Oxford English Corpus. These include news journalism; lifestyle or "soft" journalism; blogs; writing on agriculture, sports, law, arts, the military, business, technology, medicine; other scholarly and scientific writing; and fiction. No genre of speech or writing is free of clichés, and it has been one of the many fascinating results of my research to discover the ways in which particular clichés are concentrated in different genres. Of all genres, however, none is more cliché-burdened today than journalism. Journalism has been historically and continues to be the true home of the cliché. The majority of clichés treated in this book are found in greater numbers, and in greater proportion, in journalism than in any other genre of writing. Many phrases originate in genres outside of journalism and continue to have a specific or technical meaning in their place of origin: *matter of fact* in law, for example, or *exhibit a tendency* in scientific writing. Once an expression has made a home in the fertile and supportive soil of journalism, however, it thrives and grows in thick patches, often losing its particular semantic characteristics.

There are many reasons to believe that journalism today is even more cliché-ridden than ever before. First of all, there is simply more of it: the barrier to entry that used to be represented by paper publication no longer exists, and today it takes nothing more than a web server and an Internet address to establish a presence behind a shingle that is effectively indistinguishable from much longer-established journalistic enterprises. Additionally, and lamentably, the resources that were formerly devoted to copyediting in journalism are no longer available or affordable to the purveyors of news stories. News items must be rushed to publication by fewer journalists doing more work than ever before, and much journalistic prose gets only the lightest or possibly no going-over by a senior editor who in former times might have been able to consider whether the reporter's draft might be improved by the removal of numerous fixed phrases.

Another genre that is particularly rich in cliché today is the blogosphere. Blog posts, often even those carried by well-established and funded concerns, do not typically receive editing attention from anyone other than the writer. All writers can attest to the influence that reading exercises on their own writing. If a writer of a particular blog spends appreciable time reading other people's blogs, the viral capacity of clichés finds yet another vector and clichés continue to proliferate unchecked.

WHY PICK ON CLICHÉS?

The anticliché tone that has prevailed thus far in this discussion may give the impression that I oppose the use of clichés at all times, in all places. Far from it! Make no mistake! Let me be perfectly clear! All natural speakers, and most writers, use clichés from time to time, and language would be a very different and unwieldy medium for communication if we did not have clichés at our disposal to perform a number of mundane tasks. Clichés are often the readiest and most effective tool available for quickly introducing informality into a discourse when the time is right for doing so. They may also help to establish confidence in an audience by introducing to them a note of familiarity from speakers or writers who are dealing with a difficult or daunting subject, or with an unfamiliar audience. From a pragmatic perspective, clichés can establish trust by giving assurance that the writer speaks the reader's language. None of these judicious uses of cliché, if kept in check, is objectionable.

No writer can or should avoid clichés altogether, all the time—any more than a cook should strive to serve completely novel and unfamiliar dishes at every meal. That would be a needless burden on the cook and an unrewarding experience for the diner. We all look for some degree of familiarity and pattern in our experience, and this applies equally to our experience of reading and listening. The judicious writer and speaker will take the reader or listener on a journey that is grounded in familiarity but that leads to areas unknown and unexplored. On this road, familiar landmarks provide confidence for the travelers; but too many familiar landmarks quickly suggest that no one is going anywhere. Thus, cliché-ridden language is offputting to readers and listeners because it very quickly gives the impression that there is nothing to be learned from it—that the speaker or writer is simply rehearsing something that has been heard or read before, giving expression to things already well known rather than to things never before revealed. Effective writing and speaking is nearly always a matter of invention, and cliché is the opposite of invention; it is repetition, and thus a missed opportunity to exercise creativity or invention. Truly dire cliché is speaking and writing that puts its audience on automatic pilot, because of its overfamiliarity and imprecision; it suggests to its audience that nothing is being said or written that merits attention.

Clichés, like the poor, will always be among us; but like the poor, their constant presence is not a justification for ignoring them, and their constant presence should not lead to the conclusion that they are intractable. Today, readers and listeners are probably subject to more clichés than ever before: we have the opportunity, if we wish to seize it, of listening to an unending stream of unedited chatter on television, radio, and online, much of which consists almost entirely of clichés, variously divided and reassembled. The Internet makes it possible for writing to be placed in the public eye a second after it has exited the writer's mind—often without judicious inspection by the writer, let alone by an editor who might suggest repairs for faulty or ineffective expressions. The result is that clichés become even more overused, but unfortunately no less virulent.

It is easy to assemble an argument that we have now entered a perilous era in which clichés threaten to overtake language completely because of the declining quality of writing and education, the increasing exposure of everyone to poorer models of language, and the greater cultural influence of celebrities and others whose accomplishments rarely include their ability to model language cleverly and intelligently. This idea, however, is not new. The British scholar and critic Christopher Ricks, in his essay "Clichés" from the late 1970s, wrote "the feeling lately has been that we live in an unprecedented inescapability from clichés. All around us is a rising tide of them; we shall drown and no one will save us."

He mentions "multimedia" as a factor in this development, at a time when the Internet, blogging, texting, YouTube, and Twitter had not even entered people's imaginations.

Readers who have taken up this book with the hope that it will guide them to words and phrases they might use in the place of worn clichés may be disappointed. I have purposefully avoided suggesting alternatives to clichés in most cases for two reasons: (1) an alternative way of expressing the idea behind a cliché is often itself another cliché and (2) by suggesting that a particular form of words is a workable alternative to a cliché, I would simply be laying the groundwork for another cliché to develop. Clichés are the sterile offspring of a mind that is not engaged in creativity, and following the advice of an authority is surely the opposite of creativity. So rather than propose alternatives, I would direct the reader to George Orwell's admonition to be wary of letting ready-made phrases do the work of expressing what you want to say:

> They will construct your sentences for you—even think your thoughts for you, to a certain extent—and at need they will perform the important service of partially concealing your meaning even from yourself.

The best way to free your speech and writing of unneeded and detrimental clichés is to construct it thoughtfully, paying close attention to the common tendency to insert a ready form of words in a place where it easily fits. Does it really say what you mean to say? Or can you commandeer words from the vast store of English to do the job for you more effectively, by building up the expression of your ideas from smaller pieces? A writer and speaker who dimly illuminates his subjects with formulaic expressions, while also using such formulas to bind his thoughts together, unwittingly telegraphs to his audience that there is no need for them to pay attention because nothing is being said that they have not heard before.

ORGANIZATION OF THIS BOOK

Except when they are the result of mindless chatter, when the speaker or writer is hardly aware of what he is saying or writing, a cliché normally has an intention behind it—which is to say, the writer or speaker is usually trying to accomplish some communicative, grammatical, or semantic function when employing a cliché. For this reason, it is sensible to organize clichés with reference to their grammatical or semantic status, and that is the approach I have taken here. You will get the general idea of this by looking at the table of contents, and the beginning of each chapter gives more information on the particular sorts of clichés grouped within it.

The first four chapters of the book are organized around grammatical concepts. Each contains clichés whose usual function in a sentence is that of a noun, adjective, adverb, or predicate. Three subsequent chapters are organized on a principle outside of the grammatical rubric: "Framing Devices," "Modifier Fatigue," and "Clichés in Tandem." The clichés treated in these three chapters are mainly classifiable under one of the main grammatical heads and could thus be inserted in another chapter but I thought it important to distinguish them on the basis of the principal feature that makes them clichés. The end of each of the first four chapters lists any clichés found in other chapters that fulfill the role of that chapter's theme clichés.

Within each chapter, clichés are alphabetized by the first invariable nonfunction word. What exactly does that mean? If a cliché contains a variable or an optional element, that element is not considered for alphabetical order. Thus, *(so) richly deserve* is alphabetized at *richly*, not at *so*, which is an optional element—as indicated by its enclosure in parentheses. *Double/two-edged sword* is alphabetized at *sword* because the initial element is variable. The function words that are disregarded for purposes of alphabetization within chapters include the following:

- articles (*a, an, the*)
- pronouns (personal *one, I, you, he, they*, etc., as well as *someone* and *something*)
- two- and three-letter prepositions (e.g., *at, in of, for*; longer prepositions such as *after, beneath,* and *with* are alphabetized as content words)
- demonstratives (*this, that, these, those*)
- the conjunctions *and, or, but* (*if* is alphabetized, being integral to the clichés it occurs in)

The practical result of this organization is that the first invariable noun, nonlinking verb, adverb, or adjective in a cliché is the one that is alphabetized. The index of all clichés in the back of the book is, by contrast, simply a machine-sorted index that lists all the clichés in the book in their canonical form alphabetically. It is my hope that by offering these eclectic and varied organizational tools readers will have at least some success in finding an entry they are seeking right away, and no one will always be able to do so without finding something else of interest along the way.

Within each entry, organization is as follows:

---

most typical form of the cliché, in bold
☛ *a gloss of the cliché's meaning, if this is not obvious or if it is not talked about in the discussion below the examples*
Two or more examples of the cliché, taken from the Oxford English Corpus or, in a few cases, from online news sources or blogs. Examples are in italic and indented.

Following the exemplified cliché is a short discussion about the cliché aimed at helping the reader understand what problems may arise from its use. Where appropriate, details about the cliché's history, distribution, or meaning may be discussed. A few entries contain cross-references to other entries in the book that are related or are of interest.

I have not considered any single words to be idioms. Many single words do in fact meet the general criteria I use here—namely, great frequency and inapt use—but single words are well treated in dictionaries, which normally have comprehensive coverage of all the uses of single words, including the ones that are widely disparaged by language authorities. I have, however, considered a few word combinations as clichés in which one word invariably contributes to the cliché status of the combination, such as the word *literally*. These clichés can be found in the chapter titled "Modifier Fatigue." Except for a small number of the framing devices, I have not considered any complete sentences as clichés. Here the exclusion is more problematic because there are in fact many complete sentences that are fixed in form, trite, overused, and ineffective in most cases, such as *Here today, gone tomorrow, Is the Pope Catholic?*, or *What goes around comes around*. These overworked expressions are more complicated semantically than the clichés that I have analyzed and they deserve treatment as clichés, from the perspective of pragmatics, in a work of larger scope than this one.

A continuing challenge in identifying clichés is to determine their exact boundaries. Clichés and idioms, though consisting of multiple words, often behave as single words in context, and one thing that single words do is to form enduring associations with other words. Idioms and clichés do this as well, teaming up with other words and sometimes with other clichés to form strings. So we find, for example, that each of the following chunks of text occurs frequently enough to be examined as a possible cliché. Which, if any of them, actually is a cliché? And does it make sense to treat more than one of them as a cliché?

- personal stamp
- a personal stamp on something
- put a personal stamp on something
- put your (own) personal stamp on something

In this particular case, after examining hundreds of instances, I decided on the last of the bulleted items as the form to include. This is not to say that the shorter formulas are not clichés, simply that the fullest form provides the best opportunity to illustrate information about the use of the cliché. The problem can also be seen with *take* _____ *by storm*. Many individual fillers of the blank occur with sufficient frequency to be treated as clichés: *take the Internet by storm*, *take the world by storm*, *take the music world by storm*, *take New York by storm*, and so forth. For clichés of this kind I have simply considered the canonical form as containing a blank, whose fillers are examined at the entry for the cliché.

METRICS

You will find the clichés in this book marked with a score between 1 and 5. 5 indicates clichés with the greatest frequency, 1 with the least frequency. This is a measure of their frequency and use across a broad spectrum of English in the Oxford English Corpus (OEC), as discussed above. This marking system simplifies and generalizes the actual frequency of phrases, but in a useful way: the frequency of a given phrase is never the same in different dialects of English, or in different genres of speech and writing, and to give a precise statistical picture of the use of various phrases would be very difficult, quite lengthy, subject to dispute, and not very helpful. The aim here is to provide some guidance about which, among clichés, are the mildest and the worst offenders in terms of frequency of usage.

Where do these numbers come from? I have used the OEC, a colossal database that contains two-and-a-half-billion instances of words in context, drawn from a very wide selection of English speech and writing. This massive database is used by scholars and researchers in a number of ways, and it reveals many interesting facts about the language. With the software used to query the corpus it is possible to generate numerous statistics about words and phrases and their frequency. Take, as an example, the word *work*, including all of its inflections (as noun and verb). *Work* is the eighty-seventh most common word in English; it occurs more than 3 million times in the OEC, or proportionally, a little more than 1,200 times per million words. The phrase *the day after tomorrow*, which I mentioned above, occurs 420 times in the corpus, or about .15 times per million words. Though that's a tiny figure compared to the frequency of a single word, it's quite high for a four-word phrase. If *the day after tomorrow* were considered a cliché, it would score a 2 in my one-to-five scale of noun clichés.

Some classes of clichés are overall more frequent than others—for example, framing devices as a class are proportionally more frequent than adjectival clichés—so in order to arrive at the frequency scores for clichés within each category, I compared frequencies only with clichés of the same type. The clichés within each category—adverbials, let's say—are effectively divided into fifths in terms of frequency. This gives the reader the opportunity to assess how frequent a cliché is in comparison to other clichés of the same type.

Is greater frequency of a cliché really an indication of its diminished effectiveness or of its widespread abuse? Considered in isolation, I don't think it is because some clichés simply express ideas that require more frequent expression than others. As an example, *silver bullet* is about ten times more frequent than *the blind leading the blind*, but the former is not therefore a worse cliché than the latter; it's simply that writers find more situations that they wish to characterize with reference to silver bullets than they find for the blind leading the blind. This fact may lead the reader to ask, why bother with noting the frequencies of clichés at all? I believe the numbers are helpful to alert language users to the pervasiveness of some clichés relative to others, and the relative frequency with which speakers and writers resort to a particular fixed form of words to express a recurring idea.

What then should readers take away from the frequency numbering system? Mainly, an awareness of how likely it is for a given form of words to be perceived as overused, tired, and ineffective. Every cliché runs the risk of being dead on arrival for its audience, especially in writing. A common idea—a stereotype, in many cases—that is expressed with a boilerplate expression—that is, with the cliché that comes to mind most immediately to express the idea—is not likely to stir anyone from a word-scanning slumber in which the mind is not sufficiently stimulated to attend to input from the eyes or ears. For clichés numbered 1 or 2, you may simply want to give some thought to whether this ready form of words really expresses what you want to say. Clichés with a score of 3 are typical in frequency and will probably strike their audience as much for their use as cliché as for the idea that they express. This is almost surely not what you would wish to do as a writer, and so it behooves you to consider whether an alternative would do greater justice to the message or idea at hand. Clichés with scores of 4 or 5 are often dire and may serve little purpose other than to batter the eardrums of listeners or dull the attention of readers. Unless you are using clichés with these numbers in a notably original way, chances are that the main message your audience will take away is that you reached into your bag of tricks and pulled out the first shopworn item, without even looking at it.

As noted in the template entry above, I have not defined (that is, provided a gloss for) clichés whose meaning is self-evident to native speakers or whose meaning is covered in the discussion of the cliché that follows the examples. If neither of these things is true, a symbol, ☞, precedes a gloss of a cliché. Two abbreviations are used for the clichés as they appear at the beginning of entries: *sb* for someone/somebody, and *sth* for something. These abbreviations are standard in many Oxford reference works. Most examples that I have used to illustrate the use of clichés are drawn from the OEC and are taken mainly from American, British, and Canadian English. I have occasionally taken sentences from other sources, notably from Google News, from blogs, or that I have come across in my reading and listening while writing this book. When a cliché is limited to or found in particularly high proportion in certain genres, this information is given at its entry. I have not identified the writers of any illustrative text I have used, and no aspersions about the style, intelligence, or word choices of any author are intended. Obvious spelling, grammatical, and punctuation errors have been corrected in the illustrative examples but I have not Americanized the spelling of examples taken from other dialects of English.

In the chapters that follow you will find many expressions that strike you immediately as being fully credentialed members of the genre of cliché, and you may nod your head sagely as you read the examples from speakers and writers who took the easy way out of expressing an idea. But you will probably also see many familiar expressions that you might not have considered as clichés—perhaps because you use them yourself all the time, or because they do not conform to your idea of what constitutes a cliché. It is my hope that the experience of reading this book will give you an opportunity to examine the ways in which you express your own ideas in speech and writing and to become aware of the pitfalls that arise simultaneously with the inclination to express an idea in that same way that everyone else seems to express it.

2
Clichés That
Name Things

The clichés in this chapter are noun phrases. They can substitute for the name of a person, place, object, activity, event, or other abstraction. The motivation to use a cliché, rather than a literal description or the actual name of a thing where one exists, is sometimes to characterize or categorize the thing in a flattering or disparaging way. Many such noun phrases in English are frequent but do not strike most speakers as clichés because they uniquely identify a thing, abstraction, or concept with a shorthand phrase: a *near miss*, for example, or a *whiz kid*. There are many others that some would consider to be clichés on the basis of frequency but that I do not treat here because they do not fulfill other criteria that I discussed in the first chapter. *Ball and chain*, for example, is likely to be more effective in most contexts than "burdensome restraint" and *the lap of luxury*, though frequent, has the appeal of alliteration, vivid imagery, and a connotation of excess that would be hard to convey in fewer syllables.

Characterizations like these are subject to descent into clichédom when they are used in contexts that don't fully support the baggage that the expressions carry with them. Take, for example, a *damsel in distress*. The phrase accounts for nearly 20 percent of the use of *damsel* in modern English, having taken a sudden and unexplained upturn in usage around 1970. Now it's widely applied to females of all sorts without a claim to damselhood, in situations that most people would not consider distress. In addition, the phrase carries a connotation that there is an opportunity for chivalry but it is used often today when no such association is appropriate. Thus is a cliché born. As a contrast, *an ax to grind* is much more frequent than *a damsel in distress* but I don't count it a cliché on the basis of its usage, which shows it to be used nearly always in an apt and efficient way, to characterize someone with a private agenda or ulterior, selfish purpose.

Many noun phrase clichés have no particular characterizing function: they are simply a collocation of adjective + noun or noun + noun that writers (usually journalists) conceive as a unit and scoop up in tandem from their lexicons, as if the pair were inseparable. Surely many nouns benefit by the addition of a modifier that adds some nuance of meaning. Not many nouns, however, benefit from modification by the same adjective or noun a great proportion of the time. Examples of this kind include *close-knit community*, *deafening silence*, and *seamless integration*. This category is probably the most open-ended of all and readers should regard the ones in this chapter as a representative sample rather than an exhaustive list. I hope that the effect of studying the examples offered will be to impart to the reader a sense that such frequently collocating pairs are not inseparable and that new opportunities for communication arise when a noun has an opportunity to choose its adornment from a well-stocked wardrobe, rather than grabbing the usual ready-to-wear.

A few clichés in this chapter would be classified as predicate clichés but for the variety of verbs that introduce them. For example, *the weight of the world on your shoulders*. It's nearly always in a predicate after verbs such as *have*, *carry*, *support*, or *bear*—but it is effectively a single cliché and so is alphabetized in this chapter under its invariable part. I have prefaced clichés with "a" or "an" if they occur overwhelmingly in the singular and with the article, and with "the" if used overwhelmingly with the definite article, even though variants may occur occasionally: *his ace in the hole*, *several aces in the hole*, along with *an ace in the hole*.

Noun clichés are numerous, second only to predicate clichés in this book. Their range of frequencies as a class is comparable to that of adjectival clichés. Glosses are supplied for many noun clichés, which as a group are less literal than those in any other class. In general I have not included epithetic compounds that journalists frequently use for variation (*the Big Apple*, *the nation's capital*, *Islam's holiest shrine*, and many others).

an accident waiting to happen   3

*We've heard reports that there were complaints that went up the chain of
command potentially about this being a soft target, an accident waiting to
happen.*

*After a set of pullovers, he absentmindedly left a dumbbell dangling off the
edge of a flat bench—an accident waiting to happen.*

*This festival is an accident waiting to happen and if the inevitable occurs
then those members of the licensing committee who voted in favour of
granting the licence should be held responsible.*

News media find regular employment for this cliché for the vividness of
its imagery. In fairness to journalists, they are often simply quoting inter-
viewees who use the phrase in attempts to call attention to what they
think is pressing; thus its frequency can be partly attributed to the wide
genre of news stories whose theme is "why doesn't someone do something
about this?"

an ace in the hole   1

*North Korea appears to appreciate that nuclear capability is an ace in the
hole that will cause "the new Rome" to falter.*

*"But our ace in the hole is the Internet," he said. "It has democratized
communications."*

*But we have an ace in the hole. We can learn to do better. Here are some quick
time-savers you can implement immediately.*

Calculating the exact odds of having an ace in the whole is not a straightforward task, but it's an advantage that is surely less rare than the figurative
aces that people seem to enjoy. *Ace in the hole* is an effective way to characterize a unique and reserved advantage, as in the first example above. When
these conditions are not met—for example, in talking about a small advantage or one available to anyone—the cliché is stretched beyond its limits.

acid test   3

☞ **a definitive test of the value or success of something**

*The acid test of any piece of legislation is the interpretation given to it in the
courts.*

*But the sine qua non, the acid test for Gary Condit is the lingering impression
is that he's failed to answer some important questions.*

*The Extreme Chicken Club was packed with fresh lettuce and tomatoes. The
lettuce was crisp, which is the acid test.*

When used correctly, as in the first example above, *acid test* is a succinct expression for the idea of establishing genuineness. When used less precisely or unclearly (as in the other examples) the expression falls off the cliché cliff. A genuine acid test should be something that has happened, or could happen, and the context should make it clear what it is a test of in order for the expression to be effective.

all and sundry   5
☞ *everyone*
It is blindingly obvious to all and sundry that Harry loves Erica and that they
will eventually get together.
During his lifetime he made his ballets available to all and sundry on
extraordinarily generous terms.

When might it be preferable to characterize "everyone" as *all and sundry*? The cliché imparts an air of folksiness to any sentence it appears in but doesn't have any other obvious redeeming quality. In the two examples above, "to" along with the cliché that follows it, could be eliminated altogether without any loss of meaning. See also *various and sundry* in the adjectival clichés.

the almighty dollar   1
Media outlets are filled with ads, commercial plugs, and vapid or corrosive
content, leaving the impression that gifted artists sell out to the almighty
dollar sooner or later.
I cannot believe there is no company in this country that can outfit our own
Olympic team. This is about national pride and not the almighty dollar.
"Some men pursue the almighty dollar at all costs, spending their health to
gain wealth," says clinical psychologist Dan Baker.

This cliché has persisted historically through the many vicissitudes of the actual dollar and does not show any sign of losing ground now, despite the expected decline of the role of the US economy internationally. The expression is often used to stand for wealth or mammon generally, a job for which it is increasingly not well suited.

ample opportunity   5
The Claimant had had ample opportunity to comply with the order in relation
to service of experts' reports had it wished.
Everyone in Britain has had ample opportunity to learn that the BNP is a
neo-Nazi party and a pretty useless neo-Nazi party at that.

Capricorn: This week offers ample opportunities for tying off some of those
   dangling threads of unfinished biz that have been lingering on for yonks.

This cliché is unusually frequent in legal writing, where it usually carries a barb: an implication or accusation that someone failed to take advantage of such an opportunity. Its leakage into mainstream discourse does not always seem justified: many of its uses with singular *opportunity* can be omitted, and with the plural *opportunities* it doesn't necessarily to a better job than *many* or *several*.

the apple of sb's eye   1

☞ **one regarded with great affection or worth**

Then the police got to our bookstore, which I had been guarding as the apple
   of my eye because it was such an excellent screen for all our illegal work.
He returned to Italy to marry the apple of his eye, Pierina Mosna, who was
   born in Romagnano, Austria, in 1881.

This cliché got established in English via translation of biblical passages and has now settled down mainly as a colloquialism. It seems incongruous when the *apple* is not a person (first example) but is otherwise hard to argue against as a representation of "favorite" or "cherished one."

back-of-the-envelope calculation   1

Based on my back-of-the-envelope calculations, of 4,743 people registered on
   WeddingChannel.com that Match had surveyed, 395 met online.
Solomon offered some quick back-of-the-envelope calculations showing that
   the man would probably be highly placed in the Forbes 400 by the time he
   was seventy.
A back-of-the-envelope calculation reveals that Iraq quenches less than
   6 percent of America's Black Gold cravings.

Envelopes provide adequate space for many sorts of calculations, resulting in this cliché being used for a range of figures from extremely vague to precise. The mid-twentieth-century novelty of the expression is now faded and most sentences that feature it would do as well with "approximate," "quick," or some other succinct formula.

a bed of roses   2

☞ **a comfortable and easy situation**

Acting is no bed of roses at the best of times, but those early years can be
   particularly hazardous.

Marriage is not a bed of roses, but is built on trust and forgiveness.
Nothing in life is a bed of roses, but picnics are certainly very relaxing.

Writers who wish to go straight for the jugular will state the cliché in its full canonical form: "Life is not a bed of roses." Short of that, there are many variations on the bed of roses theme, which is nearly always accompanied by a negation. The cliché is a minor offender and most often serves to remind an audience that life doesn't usually support unusually optimistic expectations. After "life," the situation most likely to be characterized as unrosebed-like is marriage.

a bee in your bonnet 1
☛ *obsessive preoccupation*
Our bee in the bonnet is costs, insurance, and wages.
Society seems to always have a bee in its bonnet, to always be facing yet another moral crisis.
There is a bee in his bonnet, but what species of bee? And what strange bonnet?

This lively cliché often does more good than harm, injecting a note of liveliness into the idea of obsession. In that respect it is probably preferable to the phrase *obsessively preoccupied* in most contexts but it is not very effective for characterizing a problem that requires action, as in the first example. The third example uses the cliché originally and effectively by calling on the reader to examine its parts rather than swallow them whole.

bells and whistles 5
☛ *attractive and sometimes superfluous features*
We get caught up in the bells and whistles of site-specific farming and lose focus on the real objective: to increase net income for the stakeholders.
With all the bells and whistles in this thing, it's pretty hard to pass up, whether it's an upgrade or a new system.
Instead of the complete solution with all the bells and whistles, I opted for functionality.

This cliché is most frequent in literature about computers—not surprisingly, since they are the products most likely to be distinguished by or marketed on the basis of various special features. *All the bells and whistles* accounts for more than a quarter of the cliché's use and is often a sign that some disparagement is intended, the *bells and whistles* being by implication a poor substitute for underlying substance.

best-kept secret   3

One of the best-kept secrets about creating one's own cable TV show is that no experience is required.

One of the best-kept medical secrets is the incorporation of soya into the day-to-day diet.

QB Jon Kitna has his moments and WR Chad Johnson is one of the best-kept secrets in football.

Lifestyle journalists and sportswriters are chiefly responsible for springing best-kept secrets on the public. There would be fewer of them if the cliché were used of things that were genuinely secret, as opposed to little-known, not factual, or just not very interesting. The cliché got a foothold in the mid-twentieth century and is still in sharp ascendancy.

sb's better half   3

My better half brought it home from the DVD place last night and it's sitting atop my TV as I type, waiting to be this evening's main event.

So, your better half has begun asking about quality time, and you want to find just the right thing, which means something you also like to do.

Both myself and Tony's better half, in an effort to shed some excess weight, signed on for a month-long stint with the good folks behind RejuvaSlim.

The more informal the context, the less objectionable this whimsical and much-overused epithet for one's spouse. It is frequent in blogs and soft journalism in which those with spouses are addressing others similarly attached. When these conditions don't prevail this term rarely contributes meaningfully to the text.

bitter irony   2

In a bitter irony for long-suffering passengers who have put up with delays and cancellations by Arriva, the dispute has been prompted by a pay deal designed to ensure that the company could run a better service.

And now the final bitter irony is that straight society has proved itself actually more able to find the mote in its own eye, to put its house in order, than hip society has.

If this happened the pact would yield its most bitter irony of all: rendering the euro unattractive by application of a measure designed to preserve its attractiveness.

Irony comes in many flavors and gradations. After *great*, *bitter* is the most common in usage, and not from any bitterness actually associated with the irony but from writers' mindless attachment of the adjective to the noun. The term is useful when bitterness—the figurative kind, of course—may either result from or be associated with the ironic situation, as in the first example above. The cliché would regain some of its force if writers reflected for a moment on what specific species of *irony* they are reporting on and labeled it accordingly.

the blind leading the blind   1

The fact is, the entire basis of Slashdot's rating system is flawed—the blind leading the blind, as it were.

Except for those few people who understand the horrors of unchecked government, it has been a long and dreary episode of the blind leading the blind.

Prof. Jeremy Siegel of the Wharton School of Finance has recently declared on CNBC that the bear market is over—a brilliant case of the blind leading the blind!

In religious writing, where this allusion (Matthew 15:14) is still frequent, there is often an attempt to conform to the original context, which is suggestive of the need to question or at least be cautious of authority. In other genres there is generally no awareness of the original context and the intention is simply to disparage authority by way of a clipped quotation that has become a cliché.

a bone of contention   4
☛ *a subject of dispute or disagreement*

The only negative bone of contention in terms of the technical presentation regards the subtitles, which are heavily truncated.

The declaration stated that Ukraine had no outstanding debts to Russian export monopoly Gazprom—a central bone of contention between the two countries.

The main bone of contention for the activists is the fact that Shannon airport continues to be used by coalition forces to transport troops to and from Iraq.

Bones of contention are offered plain or modified. The chief varieties are *main*, *major*, *big*, and *real*. They are mainly brought to the attention of the public by news reporters. The first example above shows an infelicitous use since the writer is talking only about something unfortunate, not contentious. The other two examples are standard news jargon, where the cliché is generally preferred to the simpler "dispute."

a breath of fresh air   5

☞ *a welcome and refreshing change*

With the lack of new and innovative ideas in the field of nursing and patient
  care, this book serves as a welcome breath of fresh air.
Coventry's rise to the top division brought a breath of fresh air to English
  football.
Given the dearth of real alternatives in today's political landscape, Negri's
  perspective offers a much-needed breath of fresh air.

Like many clichés that consist of monosyllables, this one is often preferable
to a more literal formulation of the idea it expresses. It becomes clichéish
only when accompanied by the superfluous *welcome* or *much-needed*; it is a
rare breath of fresh air that does not have these attributes inherently.

---

a (fertile) breeding ground for _____   4

As with any communications medium, the Internet has become a fertile
  breeding ground for rumours and misconceptions.
Failed states like prewar Afghanistan may provide a breeding ground for
  Islamic extremism.
Our schools have become breeding grounds for gangsterism and drug dealers.

The boundaries of this cliché are expandable from the core idea of *breeding
ground* outward. *Become a* _____ *breeding ground* is frequent, as is *a breeding ground for terrorism*. The phrase is an example of one of the formulas that
the news media uses to interpret current events for their consumers, perhaps unhelpfully providing the rather shallow pigeonholes in which information about the modern world is to be sorted. Equally frequent with
the clichéd use of this phrase are literal fertile breeding grounds for mosqui-
toes and bacteria.

---

the calm before the storm   1

The long reign of Antoninus Pious has been described as the calm before the
  storm, a storm that would plague the reign of his successor, Marcus
  Aurelius.
There was complete silence. It was unnerving, like the calm before the storm.
It's very much the calm before the storm now. The riders are moments away
  from starting the climb up to Courchevel.

This cliché is most effective when accompanied by convincing characterizations of both the calm and the storm, with some indication of the significance of the change of state. The first example does this. It is not necessary

as filler to simply describe a change of state. Such changes are ordinary and for that reason are not good candidates for the particular characterization this phrase provides.

a headless chicken   2
a chicken with its head cut off   1

He was running around like a chicken with his head cut off, and stressing over all of the little details.

The way the discussion of bird flu is heading, we won't need an actual outbreak of bird flu to start running like headless chickens.

But when he gets out, the rest of the batsmen nowadays bat like headless chickens and totally lose the plot.

British English gets credit at least for preferring the shorter version of this unwieldy, unpleasant, and unflattering cliché that is used to characterize chaotic movement and behavior. The longer American version almost never justifies its polysyllabic requirements.

close-knit (_____) community   3

Though not as strict in rejecting the trappings of modern life as the Amish, his close-knit Mennonite community was founded on frequent church attendance.

Many homes are well-maintained, mostly by the senior residents who have lived in this traditionally close-knit community all their lives.

The shooting sent tremors through a section of Rego Park that has attracted a close-knit community of Jewish immigrants from Russia.

The rules by which journalists are obliged to characterize a community as *close-knit* can be deduced from examples of usage. Is the community an ethnic minority? Are they immigrants? Has some newsworthy and unfortunate thing befallen them recently? If the answer is "yes" to all three, it seems likely that an editor would supply the adjective for any maverick writer daring enough to have omitted it.

a commanding lead   4

The company enjoys a commanding lead as the biggest maker of programmable DSPs.

The second game was a very low-key affair as Mayo took a commanding lead to win 21–3.

It appears that Democratic presidential candidate Howard Dean tonight has taken a commanding lead in the race for his party's presidential nomination.

This phrase occurs primarily in journalism, where it characterizes political races and economic competition, and in sports writing, where it applies to athletic competition. It is accurate and descriptive for characterizing a lead that entails prerogative or victory but falls into cliché, often retrospectively, when used to characterize someone who merely pulls ahead.

corridors of power   4

The next-worst movie, Secret Things, *concerns two beautiful young women who graduate from a strip club to the corridors of corporate power.*

Investigations by this newspaper demonstrate that this is no remote political row confined to the corridors of power in Whitehall.

The woman who would be America's first Hispanic supreme court justice was walking the corridors of Washington power on crutches today after tripping at a New York airport on the way to scheduled meetings with senators.

An unknown mid-twentieth-century writer seems to have coined this combination metonym-meronym and it is now standard journalese for centers of government. It's particularly popular when contrasted with a starkly different venue, as in the first example above. The third example is a clever enlivening of the phrase that gets double value out of *corridors.* The second example is mere cliché, where the meaning intended is sufficiently conveyed by "Whitehall" alone.

a damsel in distress   3

To our Western minds, reared on the Hollywood version of so much history, the Crusades mean noble knights rescuing damsels in distress.

Male rapists look for the weak and fearful damsel in distress.

Male exiles from the faith do not seem to attract the same sympathetic open-armed treatment as the damsel in distress who has liberated herself from the shackles.

Damsel in distress is in effect a cliché that names a cliché, and when it is doing that (as in the first example) it's not a cliché, but rather a descriptive term. In the other two examples, however, it doesn't improve considerably on "woman" and needn't be used.

deafening silence   3

Despite the importance placed by all on a healthy financial sector, the deafening silence of the banking association on matters related to crime fighting makes it appear that it is really not interested in fighting crime.

Should the country interpret the prime minister's deafening silence yesterday
    in relation to tax cuts as further evidence that her government's priority
    remains spending ever-increasing amounts of taxpayer dollars?

This clever (when new) coinage has been gaining momentum since the early twentieth century and is now a staple in opinion journalism to obliquely shame someone, often an authority who forgoes an obligation to speak. Perhaps the deafening effects of the many silences so characterized prevent reporters hearing from underused adjectives in their lexicons that might provide relief.

dreamlike quality   1

By abstracting natural forms, the architect creates a fundamental ambiguity
    in his imagery that contributes a dreamlike quality to the house.
The blurring effects produce hauntingly beautiful photographs, which exude a
    dream-like quality that is meditatively magnetic and invites a closer look.
The shimmering beauty of "Can't Explain," with its heartfelt lyrics and
    pensive, brooding style, is lent an almost dream-like quality by Ulrich
    Schnauss's epic remix.

The charitable excuse for this cliché is that writers use it to avoid using *dreamy*, because of the ambiguity of that adjective. The examples of usage, however, indicate that it is the refuge of critics whose powers of discernment have simply gone home for the day. *Dreamlike quality* appears in writing on the arts more than twice as often as in any other genre. What quality of dreams is alluded to? The context rarely makes this clear and the reader is usually left with a vague notion of "not strictly representational."

the elephant in the room   3

It's easy to see how that loss of Englishness could use a visible minority as a
    scapegoat. This insecurity is the elephant in the room in the identity
    debate.
Both sides consistently neglect one important aspect of the debate: the cost of
    keeping Terri Schiavo alive. It may seem cold-hearted to bring up money
    but money is already the elephant in the room.
Our writers routinely ignore the obvious elephant in the room: that America,
    from the land grab of Texas and California, from Mexico to the imperial
    policies of Manifest Destiny, has long been an imperial power.

Counting only the elephants people talk about in specific locations, elephants in rooms outnumber elephants in Africa by nearly twenty to one, a rather shocking statistic for this cliché that only gained currency in the late twentieth century. *The elephant in the room* presents an apt image of a thing everyone can't help being aware of. At present the usage of the cliché is still increasing and writers seem eager for opportunities to trot it out, sometimes in circumstances that don't really require an elephant. It works best to characterize a straightforward situation in which something that ought to be talked about is being ignored, as in the third example above.

end of an era 5

This is without a doubt the end of an era and the start of a period of
uncertainty, as he (Arafat) has not designated anyone to replace him.
While members can still take their grain crops to other mills nearby, the
closure marks the end of an era for the area.
It was the end of an era at Sligo Railway Station recently as five of its
employees hung up their railway hats for the last time.

Era participates in numerous clichés and none is so numerous as this one. Journalism accounts for nearly half of the instances of the cliché: the designation of a period as an era is also the de facto fashioning of a news hook. Eras' ends are probably more reliably perceived than their beginnings because of the benefit of hindsight but all readers would probably be better served if eras were judged with even greater hindsight and not brought into existence at the moment of their demise. See also *herald a new era* and *enter a new era* in the predicate clichés, and *beginning/dawn of an era*, below.

every nook and cranny 3

Blame it on Venezuela and commie gym teachers from Cuba who are
infiltrating every nook and cranny in Caracus.
The university professor's case indicates that politicians do not have a
monopoly on corruption and that scandal can be found in every nook and
cranny of our society.
Perhaps surprisingly, contemporary London isn't as festooned with billboards
as it was in the Victorian era, when advertising pervaded every nook and
cranny.

The meaning of this cliché is usually different from its plural form, *nooks and crannies*, which is treated below. The core idea behind *every nook and cranny* is thorough penetration or saturation, often in a pernicious or unstoppable way. Verbs likely to precede *every nook and cranny* are *explore, find, fill, infest, infiltrate*. Though somewhat informal the cliché is welcome in most contexts and doesn't present confusion with the plural form to native speakers, though it may be unclear in learners' or in computational contexts.

fevered speculation   1

JJB Sports, Matalan, and Woolworths are all the subjects of fevered speculation.

The media is awash with fevered speculation about what to do about crime and violence.

Fevered conspiratorial speculation last week suggested that this was some kind of oblique attack on the Liberal Democrats.

This cliché seems to have been handily invented by the news media for its own use; it occurs four times more often in news than in any other genre. It is not unusual for the cliché to appear in stories in which one sector of the media is simply reporting on another that is speculating feverishly. Thus the phrase itself and the activity it reports on are effectively self-perpetuating enterprises of the news media. See also *fuel speculation* in the predicate clichés.

a fish out of water   3

But the film itself is a fish out of water as well, with modern euphemisms sprinkled through the dialogue and rock and roll playing as part of the musical score.

Arjun is the classic innocent abroad, the fish out of water, making for moments both slapstick and poignant.

I felt somewhat like a fish out of water at Beaver Creek—a diehard Nordic skier in the middle of one of the largest, swankiest alpine ski resorts in America.

The vivid image presented by this cliché makes it a suitable metaphor for anyone or anything struggling against unsuitable or unsupportive surroundings, as in the second example. It is not the best choice when all that is meant is "anomaly." *Fish out of water* is unusually popular in writing about the arts, perhaps reflecting the fact that fish out of water are engaging subjects (or are they clichés?) for depiction in film and fiction. *Fish out of water* is also unusually frequent with a first-person subject, which may be due to speakers wishing to convey something more colorful about themselves than "out of place" or "alienated."

flesh and blood   5

It just felt so wrong to give up her own flesh or blood or even have an abortion.

Faith is not revealed to us by flesh and blood: no one can communicate it to himself or to any one else.

The Australian people know their leaders are just flesh and blood and not a species without sin.

A surprising number of instances of this phrase are literal ("Who would not rather have a joint of flesh and blood than one of titanium and polyethylene?"). It appears more in religious writing than in any other genre, perhaps reflecting its scriptural origin. In figurative contexts *flesh and blood* emphasizes human frailty, vulnerability, and relatedness. It is in the last context where it is most likely to slip into cliché, and indeed, *one's own flesh and blood* is frequent enough to merit the red flag of cliché by itself. It should be used with caution in referring routinely to one's relatives, without the intention of one of the particular associations above.

flotsam and jetsam   2

Embedded in the glass is colorful flotsam and jetsam, such as coins, bits of crushed soda cans, toys, bottle caps, etc.

They were modernist, Marxist, and anti-Stalinist, despised by communists and ignored by conservatives, the international flotsam and jetsam of the Age of Ideology.

He was not the terrorists' third in command but a middle-ranker derided by one source as "among the flotsam and jetsam" of the organisation.

Neither of the technical words forming this expression is used often in a literal sense and the combination of the two makes up more than a quarter of the instances of *flotsam*, well over half of the instances of *jetsam*. The cliché nearly always characterizes people in a negative way but is kinder to inanimate or abstract things, where it is up to the reader to decide if any disparagement is intended. This distinction makes the expression problematic for computers or learners; dictionary treatments of the phrase and its components are usually cursory and not helpful.

a force of nature   3

The central character is a force of nature, whose chief features are a violent attractiveness to men and an equally violent independence.

As a force of nature, his will cannot be crossed, and so we don't see a lot of whatever internal change brings him to finally free his slaves.

"Newt is a man of ideas and he is a force of nature," said one GOP official who leans in favor of making Gingrich RNC boss.

This phrase is always a cliché when used to characterize a person and is most common in writing about the arts, especially cinema, suggesting that actors and film characters who can be characterized as *a force of nature* are themselves a cliché, described with another one. Descriptions of the marvelous traits that make someone *a force of nature* are often alone usually sufficient to convey the idea of a strong and forceful personality or performance, making the cliché superfluous.

a foregone conclusion   5

It is not a foregone conclusion that the Green Party will run a candidate for president in 2016.

A statistician, they say, is someone trained to draw a mathematically precise line from an unwarranted assumption to a foregone conclusion.

It's pretty much a foregone conclusion that organic is better, hands down, for the soil and the environment.

This cliché has impeccable credentials from having appeared first in Shakespeare. That does not prevent its abuse, which usually comes in the form of imprecise and incorrect use. Its more modern meaning, an inevitable conclusion or result (first example), has pushed out the earlier one—a conclusion reached before argument or examination (second example). Some writers seem discontent with only two meanings and have introduced a third, "perfectly obvious" or "indisputable," as in the third example above.

a game changer   2

☞ *something or someone that causes a shift in the current way of thinking about or doing something*

Out of twenty different technology firms, they're the only one that in my opinion was a game changer.

While Mr. Wu didn't offer any thoughts on market share gains, he did say that Boot Camp potentially could be a significant game changer.

The Florida primary could very well be a game changer in this topsy turvy Republican race for president.

When clichés have offspring it's reasonable to assume that the apple will not fall far from the tree, and so it is here: *game changer* is conceivably a bastard child of *a whole new ball game*. Though *game changer* originated in sports, where it still has a somewhat literal meaning, the cliché is found today most often in news and business journalism. It is helpful when context makes clear exactly what figurative game is being affected, as in the third example above.

a game of two halves   2

Eastway Rovers crashed to a 2–1 defeat against Harchester as fallen idol Jack
Ferguson had a game of two halves on his debut at Lea Road on Saturday.
And so it proved in a classic game of two halves with the home side on top in
the first period and Trojans hammering away incessantly for the second
45 minutes.
But it was a game of two halves. In the first half of the year, sales were up
52 per cent on 2000, but in the second half, turnover fell 8 per cent on the
same period last year.

This cliché grew out of soccer and doesn't yet have any traction in American English. In British and Irish English it is the favorite resort of the sportswriter in need of a thumbnail to characterize a game with sharply contrasting features. Outside of sports, the cliché doesn't add any obviously helpful associations to the subjects that journalists attach it to.

(you,) gentle reader   3

This country, dear and gentle reader, is rotten to the core
I can confess to you, gentle reader, that it drives me nuts when I get fired.
I am here to tell you, gentle readers, that not only does something deeper
than mere love exist—it lives inside me now.

Writers who use this early-nineteenth-century conceit sometimes intend a humorous effect and sometimes smite their readers with it in dead seriousness, like a slap in the face with a dead fish, rarely with good results. It is popular in lifestyle journalism and among bloggers who employ it as a means, straightforward or ironic, of engaging their readers directly. It usually prefaces opinions that are as easily expressed and recognizable without the direct second-person baggage.

grand old man   2
grand old dame/lady/woman   1

Enter Richard Serra, the grand old man of American sculpture, although he
still looks as if he could throw a mean punch.
I asked Alan Campbell about it also. He is one of the grand old men of phage biology.
The grand old dame of the former Austro-Hungarian empire, Budapest has a
stunning location on both banks of the Danube.

The only real problematic use of this cliché is the masculine singular because it usually involves the writer nominating someone arbitrarily to a position of eminence that others may dispute, as in the first example. When used in the plural it simply locates a man, however tritely, among a group of esteemed peers. The feminine form of the cliché is used as often of buildings and institutions as of women.

grave concern   5

This is an area of grave concern to ice cream manufacturers and we urge you to implement a program of mandatory reporting for inventories immediately.

The Tribunal had not found Ms. Harrison to have been dishonest in the past but they clearly had the gravest possible concerns about her ability to run a solicitor's practice.

A series of accidents and other incidents in the armed forces have raised grave concern among the people over the suspected slackening of discipline.

Concerns come in a number of large sizes—*major, serious, great, big,* and *deep*—all of which can have a hackneyed ring in some contexts. *Grave concerns* outnumber all other things *grave*, making them not well geared to waken readers to their intended seriousness. The collocation often imparts an alarmist tone where none is needed, perhaps borrowing from the associations of *grave danger* and *grave threat*. *A matter of grave concern* accounts for about 10 percent of instances and is itself a cliché.

grist for/to the mill   3

☛ *something turned to good use or profit*

Students in both sociology and economics who are searching for viable dissertation topics will find grist for their mills on these pages.

There's so much grist for the mill in the Gospel lesson, have you ever reflected with your congregation on Daniel or Ephesians?

Somare and Howard had a one-to-one meeting that is still regular grist to the Port Moresby rumour mill.

This cliché is admittedly livelier than the more straightforward text that it might replace, such as "useful material." It's not very effective in characterizing something that would be expected by its nature to be useful or profitable (second example). Specification of whose or what mill (third example) enhances the effect of the cliché.

a growing body of evidence   3

A small but growing body of evidence supports the interpretation that predatory lenders consciously target African-American communities.

These results add to the growing body of evidence of adverse respiratory effects of diesel exposure on the lung.

There is, however, a growing body of circumstantial evidence which Eric King, the naturalist who oversees the park, is happy to discuss.

This cliché is found overwhelmingly in medical and scientific literature, where it should perhaps be regarded as a formula and not a cliché. When used in news media, the phrase is often rhetorical and without supporting context, simply supplying a handy substitute for reporting specific facts. To quote George Orwell: "When there is a gap between one's real and one's declared aims, one turns as it were instinctively to long words and exhausted idioms, like a cuttlefish spurting out ink." This phrase, if used at all, is best employed as a preface to details that justify the use of a formulaic introduction.

hard-fought battle   1
Junior officers led the army back to Cremona, near which in a hard-fought battle the Vitellian forces were defeated.

APA waged a hard-fought battle for inclusion of psychologists in GME for years.

Hard-fought has limited work in English, to characterize contests and victories (never losses, despite how valiantly losers may have fought). Conflicts surely don't rise to the designation *battle* without vigorous engagement and the modifier *hard-fought* only serves to alert the reader that the writer has heard the cliché before and did not hesitate to spurt it out.

heavy lifting   4
Milman lets the songs do the heavy lifting, with her rich, lustrous alto alternating between intense focus and brassy playfulness.

The search engine was easy to use and generated lots of cash for affiliates without much heavy lifting.

The author cautions that America does not necessarily have to do all the heavy lifting and provides examples of other nations' involvement on the continent.

More than a quarter of the instances of this noun phrase follow *do*, making *do the heavy lifting* a predicate cliché unto itself. What is the heavy lifting? The context doesn't always make this clear, which is one of the problems with this cliché besides its overuse. The intention seems to be to convey some sense of effort or accomplishment that in many contexts writers would do well to flesh out.

a hive of activity   3

The deck was a hive of activity, with couples locked in passionate embraces
*   scattered all over it.*

Windhoek Agriculture Show will be a hive of activities with 532 cattle and
*   1,006 small stock taking part in various competitions.*

The segment has been a hive of activity in recent months, with Symantec, F5,
*   and NetScreen buying into the segment.*

The effectiveness of this cliché is compromised by one of its most frequent
uses: to characterize a situation in which a number of people (or other
agents) are all doing the same thing. In such cases it is hard to see what advantage the phrase has over "busy." The most apt use may be in sentences
like the second example above, in which a number of different activities are
related to a common purpose, as in a hive.

---

hop, skip, and a jump   1

The real reason I love our new place is that it is barely a hop, skip, or jump
*   from one of New York's best cupcake joints.*

Both scientists note that the military is already turning to semi-autonomous
*   weapons and cyber-assisted soldiers to fight battles. From there it's only*
*   an intellectual hop, skip, and a jump to cyborgs.*

So, Jonathan, this actually means that we're just a hop, skip, and a jump
*   away from knowing the name of the winning city.*

This cliché whimsically denotes a short distance (sometimes a figurative
one) in sentences where some construction using "near" or "not far" would
give an acceptably equivalent meaning. It is evenly distributed across informal genres and journalism. Users' preference for it suggests their intention to make it clear they are treating their subject in a lighthearted way,
and it is only jarring if previous context would make this incongruous.

---

hot-button issue   4

☛ *a controversial issue*

Hot-button issues like same-sex marriage and stem-cell research in particular
*   took center stage.*

Indeed, calcium is a hot-button issue, as just 10 percent of girls and
*   25 percent of boys between the ages of nine and seventeen receive the*
*   recommended daily intake.*

Another hot-button issue under debate is a proposal to allow future immigrants
*   to come to the US to work under a so-called guest worker program.*

Usage of this cliché is evenly divided between singular and plural, suggesting that controversies like to keep company. A point to note by those intent on using it is that *hot button* alone, as a noun, conveys the entire idea. But in fact *issue* alone also does all the work that is required, making it especially unfortunate that journalists find this cliché so irresistible.

iconic image   3

The most iconic image of course is the commander-in-chief as intrepid naval aviator, bathed in the evening glow of the sun, strutting across the deck of the carrier USS Abraham Lincoln *in his full naval jump suit with its swelling codpiece accentuated.*

The Scream is an iconic image and the decision to take another version of the painting seized ten years ago helped to ensure that the recent crime received international attention.

Speaking after the meeting, Cllr Cooke said a casino shaped like Mayflower would give the city its iconic image.

Icons are images. Images that are also icons might be called iconic images, though writers cannot be faulted for referring to such images merely as icons. The first example above is a worthy example of the phrase that addresses the degree of iconicity in a particular image. The other examples seem to slot in the cliché because it was there for the taking, though other modifiers of *image* would probably have told a more accurate story.

an ignominious end   1

It was an ignominious end for the grandson of a Scottish bricklayer who became prime minister and fought valiantly for black rights in Zimbabwe.

As is often the case, an ignominious end appears to have brought Jeffrey a more enduring remembrance than many of his peers.

The slightly alliterative quality of this cliché has kept it in circulation for centuries. It is typically used to characterize a fall from grace, as in the examples given. When applied to abstractions—"Netscape's ignominious end"—it sometimes oversteps its boundaries and cheapens the idea of ignominy.

a raging/blazing inferno   1

I looked out to discover that to get out this way we'd have to jump a story down and about 20 feet across a raging inferno.

A teenager has thanked fire crews who saved his life by rescuing him from a blazing inferno.

She works herself up into a raging inferno, stirring in repeated refrains of
"Where am I?"

An unwritten rule of modern prose writing seems to be that *inferno* cannot be used without an accompanying modifier, of which the most popular choices are *raging* and *blazing*. The cliché is surprisingly popular in online fiction for describing both people and mental states (*the raging inferno inside my head*). "Fire" is often an adequate substitute for the whole compound.

the ins and outs (of sth)   5
☛ *characteristics, intricacies, particulars, details, or peculiarities*
Once you know the ins and outs of spirals, you can take your bracelet
technique and adapt it to most anything.
Each platform has its own ins and outs and no two match up on strengths.

The broad meaning of this cliché, combined with its brevity, make it hard to find any objectionable use. Context usually makes clear which of its associated meanings should apply and it is not typically used in contexts where precision is required. It may seem incongruously applied to things that seem too simple to have ins and outs; on the other hand, simply saying that ins and outs are present may give a thing the degree of complexity that the phrase implies.

kith and kin   2
Of all groups of kith and kin, wives were the least likely to abandon their
husbands emotionally.
It was no surprise, several years ago, that he moved his kith and kin to
St. Helena, to open a couple of restaurants.
First episode: Mum of son leaves when boy is aged two, step-mum raises boy
as her own kith and kin.

Many dictionaries now allow a definition of "relatives" for this phrase, though its literal meaning is broader, encompassing friends, neighbors, acquaintances, and relatives. Its use to designate this broad group in the first example above is an efficient and felicitous use. The third example batters the phrase into cliché-shape: "child" would express the meaning better.

the lady of the house   2
It was the lady of the house, standing at the window, completely oblivious to
the testosterone-fuelled turmoil she was about to cause down below.

Eddie finds himself with loads of time on his hands and falls in love with
  Marion, the melancholy lady of the house, who is temporarily separated
  from her husband.
These parties were held in private homes and the lady of the house got a
  commission for hosting.

This phrase is attested in Old English and is firmly established as one way to designate a female head of household. Now in the twenty-first century, writers would do well to consider whether the popular thousand-year-old formulation is always the best one. The designation has been in slow decline since the mid-nineteenth century but is still frequent in soft journalism and unedited web text. It seems to work best today in historical contexts.

the land of the living   1
The market is back in the land of the living and real companies with real
  earnings are leading the rally.
As I write these words, it is unclear whether Saddam is still in the land of the living.
If once-active recipients have stopped opening your emails, those recipients
  are no longer in the land of the living, according to SubscriberMail.

A third of the instances of this cliché are preceded by the preposition *in* and constitute a seven-syllable substitute for the adjective *alive*. Other uses are nearly always preceded by a different preposition (*to, from, into*) as a way for writers to avoid simpler expressions while signaling a note of informality.

leading light   5
☞ *a prominent or influential person*
Another leading light of the spaghetti western subgenre was director Sergio
  Corbucci.
Even the leading lights of our environmental movement cannot help
  inadvertently underscoring what really is, for them, an inconvenient truth.
One of Wandsworth Tories' leading lights has returned to her native
  Staffordshire after more than thirty years.

Writers—particularly British journalists—use this formulation profusely as a complimentary way of designating an influential person in a particular sphere who may not be an official leader. Plural use outnumbers singular, suggesting that the distinction is usually shared. It is most effective when associated with an undertaking that actually benefits from leadership, and for that reason it often co-occurs with *movement* and *party*.

leafy suburb   3

When the busloads of children turned up to see the Christmas from around the World show in the leafy Miami suburb of Coconut Grove in early December, they found the doors of the venue locked and Ellisor nowhere to be found.

It's a bright morning in Woodland Hills, California, a leafy Los Angeles suburb filled with sprawling office parks.

Second only to adjectives denoting the main points of the compass, *leafy* is the chief characterizer of suburbs in print media. The original intent of *leafy suburb* (attested in the nineteenth century) seems to have been to note contrast with the urban environment. Its frequent use now has reduced *leafy* to the status of filler.

---

a lethal cocktail   1

  ☞ **a harmful or fatal combination**

What happened in the Eircom issue is that you had a lethal cocktail of greed and ignorance.

Scorned love made for a lethal cocktail of violence, and both of them couldn't wait for the fight to start.

This lethal cocktail of toxic fumes soon overpowers the cooking smells, nullifying your appetite.

This cliché seems to have emerged in the 1950s and has increased steadily in usage since then. In its quasiliteral use it is not a cliché (*a lethal cocktail of drugs in excessive doses*) but writers use it willy-nilly to characterize a number of things that lack any valid comparison with a cocktail—for example, things that are not actually being compounded, as in the second example.

---

light at the end of the tunnel   5

  ☞ **an indication that long hardship or difficulty may be rewarded or relieved**

While there seems to be a never-ending supply of stories warning of an overweight generation permanently affixed to devices, perhaps there's a light at the end of the tunnel.

Do you see the light at the end of the tunnel as far as the FBI is concerned? Because there is a lot of confidence that's been lost in the FBI in recent weeks.

Though the results of the earlier peace talks were not encouraging, there seems to be some light at the end of the tunnel this time.

This cliché is an extremely popular one that expresses a fairly simple idea in many syllables, but not as many syllables as its full-blown literal expansion. Often words or phrases like *improvement* or *a better prospect* adequately cover the same territory but the cliché is apt when both the struggle and the reward are clear from the context.

a _____ litany of _____ 2

It's a whole litany of complaints that went on and on.

Long litanies of problems may preclude any solution, for people become too overwhelmed to take action.

You've got the usual litany of hurdles that have to be attacked at the same time.

For twenty minutes my hostess listed the now familiar litany of complaints.

In clichéspeak, *litany* means "list." It's never a happy list: the items most likely to appear in a litany, in descending order, are *complaints*, *problems*, *failures*, *lies*, and *woes*. To make the cliché look professional it's also best to qualify it with an adjective, and here the favored choices are *long*, *familiar*, *usual*, *whole*, and *endless*. This phrase is essentially a mix-and-match cliché but there are unfortunately so many extant examples of each possible combination that it is difficult to do anything original with it.

manicured lawns 2

The property rests on Millionaire's Row, where palm trees, manicured lawns, and multicolored million-dollar mansions are the norm.

They live in colonial-style farmhouses which are usually surrounded by manicured lawns and hedges.

This cliché also appears in the singular *manicured lawn*, though the plural outnumbers it by more than two to one. It was a striking image for the writer who coined it around a hundred years ago and its popularity is still increasing, propelled mainly by lifestyle journalists, for whom it is stock-in-trade. It is the most frequent cliché in a nest of them often found together to characterize the real estate of rich.

all manner of things 2

Eddie rightly copped plenty of heat for all manner of things, but there were a couple of juicy details that David Marr missed out on.

People google for all manner of things and there is no reason to think they wouldn't google for information on the Tory's health policy or any other issue.

The guys entertained a full audience in the Stage Area with a nostalgic look back at their on set antics and answered questions about all manner of things.

All manner of _____ is a frequent formulation to characterize wide variety and it does that job effectively. *All manner of things* is occasionally put to good use to spare the reader further details: *We've had human excrement, sanitary towels, and all manner of things flowing on to our driveway.* Often, however, it suggests a failure of imagination or a fit of laziness in the writer that an editor, if one were present, might suggest a remedy for. It is more frequent in blogs than any other genre.

meteoric rise   4

Tomlin's coaching career and meteoric rise began in 1995 when he became wide receiver coach at Virginia Military Institute, right after he graduated from college.
Ryanair's meteoric rise to the top ran into turbulence last month when it gave its first-ever profits warning.
Shaun Cassidy's music rise was meteoric that year as he added two more Top 10 tunes to his number one hit "Da Do Ron Ron."

When it is not modifying *rise* (a job that takes up well over half of its active life), *meteoric* is at loose ends, rarely having anything to do with meteors. Unexplained by any of the many users of this cliché is that the human experience of meteors is to see them fall, not rise. Perhaps it is the brilliant streak of light produced by a passing meteor that writers wish to evoke with this cliché, but that streak has long since dimmed through overuse. Sports and entertainment celebrities, closely followed by entrepreneurs and politicians, are the most likely to be characterized by this chestnut.

missing link   5

To hail him as a missing link in the formation of modern sculpture would be to misunderstand his art and even do him a disservice.
There is a difference between just playing an instrument and becoming a musician. The missing link is the discipline in the music.

The most frequent genres for this cliché are religion and science writing where it has a lexicalized meaning that refers to the hypothesized evolutionary missing link between higher primates and humans. It is a useful term to characterize an apparent gap in a temporal or logical sequence, but is not necessary when no sequence is actually involved, as in the second example above.

the mists of time 2

The army has changed quite a bit since I did my National Service way back in the mist of time.

The recipe we used is long lost in the mists of time, but there's a recipe on the excellent BBC Food website.

This simple tale of a sword lost in the mists of time and rediscovered by a couple of unwitting innocents in the twenty-first century is as spectacular as they come.

Writers evoke *the mists of time* in a number of contexts where a more straightforward expression would be less obtrusive and it's not clear what advantage they imagine by use of the cliché. Journalists are the chief perpetrators, followed by bloggers.

movers and shakers 5

Made up of the movers and shakers from large transnational corporations, these groups shape policy to serve their own interests in ways which go far beyond legitimate political input.

The movers and shakers in this whole criminal enterprise, in my mind, were the realtors and the loan officers.

Give yourself time to assess the political structure of the workplace before joining a clique. Then seek out movers and shakers and those who can help guide your career.

The choice of this cliché over the more straightforward *leaders* is sometimes simply a choice for informality, and other times an implication of slight or considerable contempt; the first two examples above illustrate this. About 10 percent of instances are singular to designate a prominent individual, nearly always in a complimentary or merely informal way.

a needle in a haystack 3

☛ *a rare and hard-to-find thing*

Finding a home in Marin is like trying to find a needle in the haystack.

It's impossible to track genes once they have been set free, it's like a very small needle in a very big haystack.

A VC's biggest problem is filtering the incoming heap to find what they consider to be that needle in the haystack that's worth funding.

There's no better or more vivid way of describing something that's rare and hard to find than this cliché, and it only falls flat when used as mere hyperbole, as in the first example. Many writers use it productively to good effect, as the other two examples show.

beginning/dawn of a new era   3
This report in many ways marked the beginning of a new era in Irish politics.
The 2005 Australian Grand Prix marks the dawn of a new era because drivers are now obliged to use a single set of tyres for a full grand prix distance.
Since their first hit in 1961, which hailed the dawn of a new era in music, the Beach Boys have evolved to become part of rock 'n' roll music folklore.

The somewhat flowery *dawn* teams up with the hyperbolic use of *era* in this cliché to deliver a picture that the underlying reality does not often live up to. The phrase would be considerably less frequent but more effective if confined to events and periods in the past that time has proven to be worthy of this kind of designation. See also *herald a new era* and *enter a new era* in the predicate clichés, and *end of an era*, above.

a new initiative   5
The president announced new research initiatives and reiterated his complaint that Kyoto's mandatory cuts don't cover the developing world.
Tyree Scott, a retired crane electrician, works with a new initiative to challenge the corporate giveaways at the Port of Seattle.
A number of new initiatives are being planned to implement the study's recommendations.

When used as a count noun, *initiative* is rarely—only 3 percent of the time—unmodified by an adjective. Those seeking an adjective to intervene between the article and the noun do not usually seek far; they go for *new*, which far outnumbers any other adjective in this position and gives rise to this cliché. Surrounding context, and the word itself, usually suffice to convey that the initiative in question is new, and it is rarely necessary to contrast with old initiatives, which are not often talked about.

nooks and crannies   4
☞ *secluded, sheltered, or hidden places*
He was besotted by Sydney and its harbour, and spent a lifetime capturing its nooks and crannies, boats at work and play, and the dance of light across the water.

The birds are having trouble nesting thanks to all the flash new houses that
don't have the nooks and crannies that older buildings might have had.
The Toho Universe still has its share of unexplored nooks and crannies, some
of which may be home to things best left undisturbed.

This cliché is slightly more frequent than the form *every nook and cranny* but is used in a different way. Of the two, *nooks and crannies* is the more hackneyed because of its more general meaning and its being more loosely applied, though it is not unwelcome in informal writing and conversation. The notion of "bucolic" is often not far from this plural form, which can suggest the pleasant and unexpected features of an area or notional space.

numerous occasions   5

I have tried on numerous occasions to obtain the date and information
necessary from her, but she did not respond to my many requests.
There were numerous occasions in which we had these meetings with the
Sudanese government.
On numerous occasions she has been totally beyond control both of herself
and others.

Lawyers may have been the inspiration for this somewhat formal alternative to *many times*; the cliché is frequent in legal writing. Its vagueness saves the user from having to specify a number and in many contexts it seems suspiciously to mean simply "more than once." Ninety percent of instances are *on numerous occasions*, effectively making this an adverbial cliché.

a palpable sense of _____   3

There's a palpable sense of fear in General Augusto Pinochet these days.
There is a palpable sense of shock and we are waiting to find out what
happened.
There is a palpable sense of raw bravado underpinning the contemporary arts
scene—a healthy sense of optimism.

Since you can't be there, news reporters and arts journalists want to make sure you really feel what they're feeling, and they attempt this, often feebly, by documenting various palpable senses. *Relief, fear,* and *excitement* are the big three. The canonical context of the cliché is to set a scene beginning with a *There is* statement, as in the examples above. In most cases, the impression is adequately conveyed without the cliché.

a perfect storm 4

Lightning struck twice when the US border was closed to Canadian beef due to a case of BSE, creating a perfect storm of hardship for farmers.

The economy is going into the toilet here, Mr. President. We've got, actually, kind of a perfect economic storm going on.

Berlin is the perfect storm of urban planning gone wrong: too much government money, too much top-down planning, and too great a desire to build a tourist attraction masked as a symbol.

Sebastian Junger's 1997 book lodged this eighteenth-century phrase firmly in the public imagination and it is now the go-to cliché for situations in which a seemingly coincidental confluence of events aggravates a situation. Today, many storms far less than perfect earn the buzzword epithet. Those drawn to the phrase will help their audience by at least listing the storm's constituent influences. It would be an additional service to be sure that the constituents of perfect storms number at least three.

the _____-pound gorilla 2

☞ *a large and powerful organization, especially one having excessive influence*

The company's dream acquisition began to unravel and the prospect of a competitive new product sold by an 800-pound gorilla became more real.

Alfie Kohn keenly examines the role that corporations, the "500-pound gorilla," play in educational curriculum and testing.

Companies ranging from the smallest start-ups to the 800-pound gorillas are lining up to get in on the action.

Most gorillas that participate in this late twentieth-century cliché weigh in at 800 pounds. All of them are overworked by the writers, mainly in business and tech journalism, who find the characterization apt for the biggest players in their fields. The cliché is currently still rising sharply in usage; it is occasionally conflated or confused with *the elephant in the room* (q.v.): *Throughout his discussion of religious conflict, in fact, the 800-pound gorilla in the room is political power.*

the power behind the throne 1

The Ba'athists pulled off a coup and Saddam remained the power behind the throne until he deposed his fellow Tikriti, Ahmad Hassan al-Bakr, in 1979.

There's a feeling that runs deep in twentieth-century American literature and films that women are the power behind the throne.

*Mr. Raymond Arteaga Zuniga, a very quiet soul according to all who knew
him, was the power behind the throne of Key West charity society.*

This cliché does not require an actual "throne" to succeed, but it does require
an institution or figurehead represented by "throne" and a party identifiable
as the "power" as in the first example. When either of these is absent or
weakly represented (other two examples) the epithet misses its mark.

a proven track record   4

*Mike Enzi brings a proven track record of standing firm on conservative
principle.*
Grant has a proven track record of successful rom-coms, as does Bullock.
*Lakes signed up two firms with proven track records in building ethanol
facilities.*

The prevalence of this cliché over other varieties of track record (good,
strong, long, successful, etc.) would suggest that spurious track records are
being continuously put forward that must be established as genuine. But
this is not the case: a track record either exists or doesn't and speaks for
itself, and it's superfluous to emphasize this with *proven*. The cliché is most
prevalent in sports and business writing. *Track record* without the *proven*
modifier is well lexicalized as a concise way of expressing the idea of measured past performance.

a race against time   4
a race against the clock   1

*Experts are facing a race against time to bring an ancient Egyptian statuette
of Tutankhamen's step-sister to Bolton Museum.*
*A frantic race against the clock by cabin crew to refreshments, as well as
carry out security checks on a one-hour flight left passengers bemused.
Shocked detectives were last night facing a race against time to catch the
killer before he strikes again.*

This cliché is primarily a trope for journalists who wish to dramatize the
pressing or dire nature of some eventuality: it is four times more frequent in
news reports than in any other genre. *Face a race against time* is frequent
enough to merit status as a cliché unto itself and seems particularly inapt,
facing being a posture not favored to succeed in a race. Those wishing to
extend the analogy may wish to consider adding *work around the clock* or
race/work against the clock (in the predicate clichés) to their narrative.

raging hormones 1

For a group prone to bouts of raging hormones, text messages offer an
*   alternative and safer way to communicate.*
Celebrities such as Leah, Debra, and Natalie, like all expectant moms, must
*   deal with their raging hormones.*
We need to ignore our raging hormones and leave a few car lengths ahead of us.

Three groups can expect to have this cliché flung at them regularly and with abandon: teenagers, and pregnant and menstruating women. If there is a genuine metabolic condition underlying those so afflicted, a less disparaging name for it would suit everyone better. In the third example above the writer apparently wants to stretch the meaning of the cliché to include simple anger or frustration.

a raging torrent (of _____) 1

Asda, first supermarket to dip its toe into the raging torrents of the clothing
*   market, is not exactly resting on its laurels either.*
We splashed our way through the raging torrent of a broken water main,
*   burst by bulldozers digging up the streets.*
When society's thin moral veneer is punctured, a raging torrent of passion
*   and terror sends life spinning over the edge.*

Most raging torrents are quasiliteral ones—great rushing flows of water— and the raging part of them is perhaps acceptable if rather weary flowery license: writers do not seek far in characterizing such flows, reaching instead for this ready-made cliché. Other things that flow in raging torrents (abuse, emotion) are less convincing, mainly because of the frequency with which they are encountered.

the real truth 3

It is possible that the real truth about reality will eventually be given by a
*   different physics, one that is deterministic.*
We could debate on the rights and wrongs for years to come, and you can
*   never know the real truth until you can reproduce the effects.*
The Fur Council of Canada, they will continue to do their best to cover up the
*   real truth behind fur.*

The tautology in this cliché is excusable when contrast is intended with some "false" or mistaken truths (first example) but it is not effective as a mere intensifier of truth (second example). In the third example, some adjective other than *real* would probably convey the idea more effectively.

a recipe for disaster   4

You have the local police and then you have special forces in there and then
you have local citizens who have weaponry. It's almost a recipe for
disaster in some ways.

Now, instead of athletic ability serving as a means to a valuable end, it has
become the goal itself. This is a recipe for disaster, especially for young
African American males.

In a country where over 70 percent of the population makes a living from
agriculture and related industries, stealing the water and poisoning the
water and soil is a recipe for disaster.

Recipes for disaster outnumber recipes for success by about two to one in usage; recipes for any particular thing you would actually eat (soup or cake, for example) represent only a small fraction of recipe mentions in text. In sympathy for the journalists who trot out this cliché with stunning regularity, it is surely their duty to report imminent dangers or misfortunes when they exist and before they become *perfect storms*. The repertoire of phrases to do this is not large. *A recipe for disaster* is the most frequent, but *a ticking time bomb* is also popular, as well as *an accident waiting to happen*, which is treated above.

a resounding success   5

Moving the sale from its traditional position at the end of the autumn horses
in training sale has been a resounding success.

The return to school or rather, the start at brand new schools for both of them
was a resounding success.

The opening weekend was a resounding success with a turnout of 3,000 at
the outdoor lifestyle expo and concert at the Marina on Sunday.

A minor quibble with this cliché is that *resounding* is used merely as an intensive, without any consideration of its meaning. For whom do these successes actually resound? A major quibble is that writers lasso *resounding* to characterize *success* far more often than they give it any other job to do, diminishing the effectiveness of *resounding* in other contexts. There are many particular ways to characterize success, all of which can be put to good use by a writer who pauses for a moment to survey the inexhaustible field of English adjectives.

a rich tapestry   3

The New Yorker gushed, "A night at the theater that leaves the viewer with
a rich tapestry of experiences."

Once a bird like the gallinule wanders into a region, however briefly, it
    becomes a part of its natural history, its rich tapestry of life.
Quirky beats support rich tapestries of sound, working a tension between
    repetition and variation expertly and effortlessly.

Too many writers seem unwilling to characterize figurative tapestries with any qualities other than *rich*, and that's where the cliché begins; *rich* outnumbers every other adjective preceding *tapestry* by ten to one. Those wishing to ensure that they've knocked down the most conventional target may write about *life's rich tapestry* or *the rich tapestry of life*. There is also the option to credit those who *weave a (rich) tapestry* (in the predicate clichés).

rubber stamp   5

The board was little more than a rubber stamp for management's high-risk
    ventures, the lawsuit says.
Blagojevich's attorneys call US District Judge James Zagel a "rubber stamp"
    for prosecutors, and seek a new trial.
Fears that the House will become a rubber stamp or footstool of the Executive
    are unfounded, Majority Leader Neptali Gonzales II said.

The derogatory idea behind this cliché is not expressible with a simpler formula so any alarm about its high frequency should probably be more concerned that there are so many occasions to use it, than that it is overused. Governments and corporations are usually the subjects of disapproval. An abuse of power consisting of approval without due consideration is at the heart of this term. Study of context is required to determine whether the stamping authority itself wields power or whether it acts on behalf of another. The latter is usually the case and *rubber stamp of/for* _____ makes up a significant fraction of instances.

the ultimate/supreme sacrifice   5

Firefighters arrive at every duty shift with the unspoken understanding that
    they may be called upon to make the ultimate sacrifice.
It should be remembered that a number of men from this region paid the
    supreme sacrifice in service for their country.
They say they are willing to defend what they call their god-given right, and
    endure the ultimate sacrifice.

Both versions of this cliché are used prominently in writing about the military and in news as pompous euphemisms for death in the line of duty or while exercising defiance. The cliché is unavoidable in prayers, ceremonial speeches, and other solemn occasions, but it does not provide any valuable service to readers or listeners in other contexts.

salad days   2

☞ *a period of youthful inexperience or indiscretion*
The mid-1960s were, of course, the salad days of Pop art and Minimalism.
The CBS of Walter Cronkite's salad days is gone.
I spent my salad days on the west coast of southern Florida, easily one of the most gorgeous places on the planet.

Writers now seem to use this cliché, which is from Shakespeare, interchangeably with *Halcyon days*, perhaps because *salad* is so much easier to spell and pronounce. The phrase is an unfortunate sitting duck for food writers: *Our expert Jamie Goode picks seven wines for a week of salad days.*

seamless integration   2

Vierra notes that the schools that did not score well in design lacked a seamless integration between design aesthetics and technology.
The representation of a metaphysical, transcendent self can be achieved only through a seemingly seamless integration of exactly that which autobiography claims to oppose: fiction.
The seamless integration of US and Kuwaiti Patriot firepower that proved so effective during OIF epitomized effective coalition operations.

This cliché began a sharp ascent in usage starting in the late twentieth century that continues today. It has the ring of business jargon but it is most common now, perhaps surprisingly, in writing about computers and the military. Its vague suggestion of painless transition or change makes it seem like a desirable thing in most contexts and that is perhaps a small compensation for the degree to which the term irritates people.

seismic shift   3

This type of attitude represents a seismic shift in business school admissions.
The bottom line is that many men want to look better, and that alone underscores a seismic shift in the attitudes of men toward their own appearance.
That kind of seismic shift would destabilize some of California's most successful companies.

Seismic shift is contemporary journalese for "big change." Candidates for seismic shifts (apart from completely legitimate tectonic plates) are attitudes, policies, and the political landscape (see *change the political landscape* in the predicate clichés). The cliché is used hyperbolically to dramatize change that looms larger in the writer's mind than elsewhere.

serried ranks   1

Eventually, we filed into Selfridges' Accessories Department and sat in serried ranks on the floor.

What man is so busy that he will not pause and look upward at the serried ranks of our grandest waterfowl?

I was there, along with serried ranks of Indians taking in the sunset on Mumtaz's marble magnificence.

The participle *serried* is largely unemployed in English when it is not modifying *ranks*, and many things often described with the combination of these words are neither *serried* nor in *ranks*, thus plunging the unfortunate phrase into clichédom. Of the examples above, the first one is a felicitous use of the phrase and presents an alternative to "crowded rows." The other two are imagined and failed elegant variation.

a shift in/shifting dynamics   1

Cole uses the shifting dynamics of oriental dance in his knee drops and slides, in floor work alternated with jumps and extended poses.

This shift in the dynamics of the industry has helped Indian companies carve a niche for themselves in the global market.

Connelly's achievement is to embed the Algerian conflict and the challenge of Third World nationalism within the shifting dynamics of the cold war.

If you were to deduce the meaning of this cliché from the instances of its usage you would probably come up with something like "changing changes" or "different way." Perhaps it has advantages over both of these, but often it is just wool to polish over a kind of movement or change that the writer is not equal to capturing more creatively or precisely.

a silver bullet   5

We haven't seen this amazing rush to cottage cheese as the new silver bullet for low-carb dining.

Information technology and open source in particular is not a silver bullet for long-standing development issues.

While NASA did not come up with the silver bullet this time, scientists at JPL toasted to future Mars missions in which they are already involved.

About a third of the clichéd instances of *silver bullet*—that is, those in which it is not actually being used to talk about killing werewolves—are accompanied by a negation, making *no silver bullet*, *not a silver bullet*, and so forth, clichés in their own right. From its original fanciful meaning as the only weapon effective against werewolves, the silver bullet has evolved to mean a simple solution to a difficult problem. Such solutions being often sought, much talked about, and rarely found, journalists perhaps imagine that they have found the silver bullet for characterizing them. But alas.

a slippery slope   5

The importance of the case transcends its immediate facts as it should be considered to represent a significant step down the slippery slope towards professionally assisted euthanasia or mercy killing.

By taking this approach it will be possible to deflect claims that we are on a slippery slope to designer babies and keep a lot available for people in practice.

The "even bolder steps" towards population reduction that Mr. Kaufman speaks of in his letter can be a very slippery slope.

This cliché is the preferred trope to warn people of dystopic or apocalyptic results that should be feared from a proposed action; in that respect it is a very specialized and sometimes alarmist version of *ultimately lead to sth* (q.v. in the predicate clichés). *Slippery slope* has the appeal of alliteration but like *ultimately lead to*, it is not convincing or effective without discussion of how the frightening process would unfold.

stamp of approval   4

They're supposed to give their stamp of approval before it goes on to the president for his signature.

Fish and Wildlife has no problem with the expanded boat launch, having put their stamp of approval on it months ago.

Another cloud vendor will receive the institute's stamp of approval this spring.

It doesn't matter that few *stamps of approval* are actual stamps but it's not clear why writers so often prefer a construction using a verb + *stamp of approval* when all they mean is *approve*.

sweeping (new) powers   3

The Patriot Act gave tremendous and sweeping new powers to the government.

The government imposed a state of emergency last June with sweeping
powers of arrest.

The image, evoked by the participle *sweeping*, of a broom that collects everything in its path is popular to characterize a number of nouns: *change,*
reform, statement, generalization, victory, overhaul. Sweeping new powers is
the modern journalistic code to characterize a government or leader that
has curtailed liberties. There are innumerable ways to convey the same idea
and this cliché might benefit from being given some time off.

a double-/two-edged sword　5
　☛ *something bringing both advantage and disadvantage*
Celebrities need to understand that fame is a double-edged sword, and they
cannot expect to reap all of the benefits without paying the costs.
Because freedom of the press is a double-edged sword, Iraqi newspapers had
begun to exercise their newly gained freedom by denouncing the
occupation.
Using more and more of our financial aid to offset higher tuition was a
double-edged sword: Increasing financial aid led to higher tuition—which
in turn created the need for more financial aid.

Phenomena that carry simultaneous advantage and disadvantage are richly
described by idioms and clichés: *double-edged* (sometimes *two-edged sword*),
mixed blessing, and things that *cut both ways. Double-edged sword* loses some
effectiveness simply by being so frequent. Those intent on wielding it can
help their readers by always being clear about what the contrasting results
are (as in the first example, but not the second). When one phenomenon
causes the other (as in the third example), it's actually a vicious circle, not a
double-edged sword.

an undisclosed location　4
He will be whisked away to an undisclosed location, held as an enemy
combatant, and interrogated as quickly as possible.
A Chinese source tells CNN the twenty-four crew members are now being
held separately in an undisclosed location.
With a $75,000 annual budget, this facility which can house up to sixteen
women is providing aid and comfort at an undisclosed location in the
capital.

In most cases this cliché is semantically equivalent to simpler expressions
using words or phrases like *secret* or *hiding place*. Users of the cliché (mainly

journalists) may feel that the simpler formulations lack gravitas, this giving this phrase its impressive usage statistics.

a very real possibility   3

I think there's a very real possibility that if this race stays close, it could well go into overtime, just like it did in 2000.

As I pass as a man on a regular basis currently without any bodily modification, were I to pursue surgery or hormones there's a very real possibility that I would just disappear into maleness.

There is a very real possibility of various plagues breaking out, cholera being the chief suspect.

This cliché is at the service of speakers and writers who wish to be taken seriously but have insufficient grounds or are not willing to commit themselves to "likelihood." It rarely says anything more than "possibility" says without modification. It is a species of *very real* modifier fatigue (q.v.) but I have singled out *very real possibility* here as being the most frequent phrase in which *very real* acts as a modifier of a noun. Journalism, hard and soft, accounts for the greatest proportion of instances.

a virtual certainty   1

Your Honour, in the Metals matter, the finding of the trial judge was that there was a virtual certainty that the taxpayer would reacquire the plant.

It now appears a virtual certainty that in addition to the nation's 800 hotels a further 8,500 B & B bedrooms will now not be included in next year's ban.

League sources say it is a virtual certainty Tim Tebow will land a job back home with the Jacksonville Jaguars in 2013.

This noun phrase has origins in logic and technical uses in law (see first example), where it is a formula, not a cliché, and not inaptly used: *virtual certainty* is a state of conviction concerning a truth so thoroughly supported that a denial would be absurd. In contexts other than law and logic—as when talking about quarterbacks—there is always a way to convey the idea without sounding so grandiose.

a walk in the park   4

☞ *something easily or enjoyably accomplished*

I think on Tuesday when Mr. Lay comes before our committee we will be respectful but tough. It should not be considered a walk in the park when you have this kind of scandal to come before a congressional committee.

Compared to Aversion Therapy, Reparative Therapy may seem like a walk in the park, but there are still hidden dangers.

"You grew up in a different household, did you not? I mean, Sir Michael Redgrave was not a walk in the park, was he?" "Well, I guess it was—no, he really wasn't except when he did walk in the park and then he was fun."

This phrase is often used with a negation to characterize something unpleasant, or ironically to contrast with something unpleasant. In its favor are monosyllables that evoke a vivid and specific image. It is not particularly apt when used of people, though the third example illustrates an interviewee cleverly turning such an infelicitous use to good effect.

the weight of the world on your shoulders   1

He doesn't mention that sometimes he carries the weight of the world on his shoulders.

In the second half they played like a side with the weight of the world on their shoulders.

Rossiter's shoulders sagged as if the weight of the world were upon him.

The stark image evoked by this cliché is compromised only by its frequency of use and by the glut of syllables required to spell it out. It is perhaps inspired by Atlas, though he supported the heavens rather than the earth. It is most effective when used to depict some unshiftable burden, least effective to characterize mundane human suffering or passing moods.

where the rubber meets the road   1
☞ *a critical test of truth or viability*

Where does the rubber meet the road with respect to the president's budget?

At retail, where the rubber meets the road, Bandai's toy sales quintupled in each featured market.

Domestic issues are where the rubber will meet the road in the Democratic primaries.

This late-twentieth-century cliché sprang to life from business jargon and is still mainly found there, though it gets some traction in politics and other domains as well. It may be vivid to those unfamiliar with it but it is widely derided for overuse by consumers of business writing.

the whole point (of sth)   5

The whole point of a baby is to be the creation of two people, mother and father.

There had been earlier scripts written that he was very unhappy with and felt had kind of really missed the whole point of the book.

The whole point of computerization of anything is to allow a whole bunch of things to happen automatically, with no human attention or involvement.

The dizzying frequency of this cliché stems from its implementation when the point so designated is in fact not the whole point, but rather a central or salient point (in the mind of the speaker or writer) among others. It is often a marker of polemic and of arguments containing more bluster than fact.

---

the whole nine yards   2

In Ohio, the GOP is pulling out all the stops, frankly, to steal it in the courts, trying to get courts to stop voting for people who were already in line when the polls closed, ruling against provisional ballots, the whole nine yards.

The album I'm doing now is very introspective, on me and my life, and what I've been through. Drugs and the whole nine yards.

Not to be satisfied with a mere "pull the story or we sue your ass off," Adobe has gone the whole nine yards and filed a lawsuit alleging MacNN "willfully and maliciously misappropriated ... confidential and proprietary information."

This cliché evokes a maximum limit of possibility, often after a list, to suggest that other things of the same kind might be added to include everything imaginable. If the imaginable list is actually long, perhaps the listener is well served by not hearing it recited. When the speaker leaves the burden of imagination entirely on the listener (second example) the expression is not effective. *Go the whole nine yards* suggests undertaking something to the fullest possible extent and expresses that idea efficiently in informal contexts.

---

the/this whole process   5

This leads me nicely onto the ethics of the whole process, as well as the ethics of cloning in general.

This whole process has been railroaded through and we are seeking a fair and reasonable industrial solution in the interests of the public and firefighters.

There are some who believe that he's philosophically opposed to any kind of deal-making that comes before this whole process of looking at all the candidates.

This vague cliché can easily be made more specific by inserting a noun between *whole* and *process* and thereby making clear what the boundaries of the process are: *Allowing them to renegotiate would bring the whole franchising process into disrepute.* Without specifics the phrase is often a lazy way of designating something for which a specific noun exists. Sometimes the phrase can be eliminated altogether, as in the third example above.

whole wide world   2

So there is no doubt in the whole wide world the prosecution must tell you
   about all eyewitnesses, and they did not.
As it happens it is next door to one of my favourite pubs in the whole wide
   world, ever: The Windmill.
This student of Chinmaya Vidyalaya, Vaduthala, has opened up for herself a
   whole wide world of colours.

This cliché is most frequent in blogs and other unedited text, suggesting that copyeditors recognize its lack of credentials and find alternatives to it. It is often used after "favorite" or a superlative (as in the second example) and it reinforces a tone of informality that is usually already well established.

a woman's right to choose   3

We see attacks on a woman's right to choose, attacks on the right to marry
   whom ever you wish, and we see attacks on our civil rights.
The immediate political result was the Abortion Act, which eventually
   appeared in 1978, but which was judged to be not wholly satisfactory by
   feminists because of the limitations on the women's right to choose.
"A woman's right to choose is not affected by the denial of taxpayer funding,"
   one Los Angeles Times *reader wrote.*

Most formulaic language in the debate about abortion is disagreeable to one side or the other. This phrase has passed from euphemism into cliché by being used without the word *abortion* nearby in nearly 90 percent of instances, effectively unmooring it from its meaning and implications.

a world of difference   4

The easing of restrictions will make a world of difference to livestock farmers.
There is a world of difference between eating well and eating properly.
The small contribution made by each participant will make a world of
   difference to the Foundation's work.

The most frequent nouns appearing after *world of* are domains (*politics, work, music, business,* and the like) that identify nominal institutions or fields of endeavor in which people are engaged in the same activity. Unique among these high-frequency collocations in not constituting such a domain is *world of difference*, which writers use when they mean "big difference" or sometimes, merely "significant difference." What would actually constitute *a world of difference?* Perhaps the same situations that merit description as *a whole new world of* _____ (q.v., in the chapter "Modifier Fatigue"). The phrase is not effective when it is used to characterize simple and easily understood differences, as in all of the examples above.

The following noun clichés are treated in later chapters in this book. Please consult the index for their location.

abject failure
abject poverty
close proximity
consummate professional
consummate skill
dirty/dastardly deed
distinct advantage
distinct possibility
far-reaching consequences
far-reaching implications
forward/positive momentum
general consensus
general overview
general pattern
general trend
heated argument
heated debate
heated discussion
invaluable resource
invaluable tool
legendary coach/singer/producer/player/director (etc.)
quite the _____
staunch conservative/Republican
a veritable feast/cornucopia/smorgasbord/treasure trove
a whole new _____
a whole new level
a whole new look
a whole new world

3
Adjectival and
Quantifying
Clichés

Clichés that modify nouns and noun phrases are not typically found in the standard adjective position—before a noun—since they are likely to consist of two or more words. Therefore, English syntax is inclined to send them to follow the noun or to take up a slot in a predicate after a linking verb. They usually characterize or categorize a person, place, or abstraction in a stereotypical way: The administration is now *at a crossroads*. In this respect their function is not very different from noun clichés, which also often have a characterizing function. Adjectival clichés are so classified for their ability to modify (and thus characterize) a wide range of nouns, either attributively or by supplying their copular predicates.

The motive of writers and speakers who opt for a modifier that is clearly a cliché or that borders on cliché is not often discernible after the fact. Surely in many cases it can be put down simply to thoughtlessness: the tendency to let a well-worn form of words fill a compatible syntactic slot without pausing to reflect on what exactly the words mean or are meant to accomplish. In other cases there may be a subtle distinction the author wishes to impart by choosing a somewhat figurative over a literal expression. What does *hardly surprising* say that is missing in *not surprising?* Apparently something valued by language users because it is by far the most common *hardly + adjective* collocation in English. After examining many instances of *hardly surprising* I did not feel that it met the qualifications I have set out for clichés: though extremely frequent, *hardly surprising* seems to communicate an attitude on the part of the writer or speaker that is not available in the more literal near-equivalent.

Many clichés that serve as adjectives can be called "joined by and" phrases: they consist of two adjectives (often synonyms) joined by *and* that usage has settled a long-term relationship upon. A sensible explanation for people using two adjectives where one would do is that some emphasis is desired, and this is sometimes the case. However, "joined by and" clichés fall flat where they are inserted randomly, merely to informalize text or because they seem to occur to the writer or speaker as an atomic unit.

Also included in a separate section in this chapter are clichés that characterize a quantity. They are grammatically adjectival, always modifying a noun phrase, but usually have the form of a noun phrase themselves that is followed by a prepositional phrase: for example, *a whole host of software vulnerabilities.*

absolutely fantastic   4

Helen Lindsay has done an absolutely fantastic job in creating a retro folk theme so this session is simply not to be missed.

It was an absolutely fantastic show, and I was even more pleased to see a competitor from my local gym win not only his class, but also the overall championship.

We're doing a job that's going to be absolutely fantastic, a sixty-four-story condominium tower.

This cliché is a ready-made mark of high approval for occasions that don't quite merit originality in praise, or for the use of appraisers not given to originality. It has enjoyed increasing usage since the late nineteenth century, though it may eventually be eclipsed by *totally awesome* as users of the older phrase retire from speech and writing. *Absolutely fantastic* seems set to live on in sports journalism for some time to come because of its popularity among sportswriters and the athletes that they quote.

after sb own heart   1

☞ *sharing one's tastes, views, or preferences*

A man after my own heart, Kaplan did his elective year in the Seychelles.

Redknapp has found a club after his own heart where he continues to perfect the art of reviving players' careers.

Rachel is a girl after my own heart—she chooses to take lunch at the organic Elderberry Pond Farm where the burgers look amazing.

This cliché is used to signal some similarity to the speaker's views or tastes with those of the person referred to—an idea for which most associations of "heart" are much richer and wider-ranging than is required.

---

alive and kicking   3
alive and well   4
👉 *active; thriving*

African Americans were no longer slaves, although the pseudo-science that legitimated their inferior status was alive and kicking.

We were most surprised with our gate attendance of 5,000, which shows that community spirit is still alive and kicking.

After demolishing Arsenal's eight-point lead, the rivalry is alive and kicking.

A surprising number of abstractions (racism, spirits, genres) are characterized as *alive and kicking* in informal contexts or as a way of establishing an informal note in a more formal context. The *kicking* aspect occasionally attempts to capture a troublesome aspect. Does the expression achieve anything not present in a single adjective? Usually not, and many sentences would benefit from the placement of a single, more thoughtfully arrived at word in place of this standard pairing. The phrase *alive and well* is twice as frequent as *alive and kicking*. It usually stays clear of perception as cliché when applied with literal meaning to people but falls into a border area in gushing sentences like *At the time he was not divorced from his first wife and she remained very much alive and well.*

---

all systems (are) go   3
👉 *everything is ready or in working order; everything can proceed*

It was all systems go for the Zambians who looked set to play against Madagascar and the Moroccan referee who evidently made questionable decisions.

The new committee brings with it a wealth of experience, and it is now all systems go towards the start of the new season on Sunday, March 28.

With the annual holidays over and the good weather still lasting, it was all systems go for three Northern Ireland fleets this month.

The appeal of this cliché, which is particularly popular in sports writing, is its ability to dismiss or minimalize anything that could be considered an obstacle to progress. It expresses a complete sentential idea but is always used to characterize some other sentence element, thus its classification here. In informal contexts it is an acceptable alternative to more plodding phrases like "There is nothing to stop…" or "Everything is on track for…"

armed to the teeth   3

The entire family had taken to answering the door armed to the teeth,
  waving crosses and garlic at the swarms of salesmen.
The delirious Pentecostal of postmodernism, Fredric Jameson, approached
  things armed to the teeth with inverted commas.
Hunt armed himself to the teeth as leader of a desert expedition.

When used of weaponry, as it usually is, this cliché presents an agreeable stand-in for "heavily armed." It has mixed success when used for equipment other than arms or abstractions. As a predicate cliché (third example above) it is not an obvious improvement on *arm oneself heavily.*

sick/fed up to the back teeth   1

I am absolutely sick to my back teeth with the attitude I encounter every time
  I have a planning idea.
People are fed up to the back teeth with their annual insurance bills.

This hyperbolic cliché is not terribly frequent, owing perhaps to the fact that the image it contains is inapt in nearly every context. Speakers—and they are often politicians expressing the imagined outrage of their constituents—have the option of letting the teeth rest and saying *fed up to here* while indicating a level of their anatomy at the neck or higher. But in any case, does the cliché accomplish anything more than *fed up* on its own, which is now thoroughly lexicalized? A related and far more frequent cliché is *sick and tired* (see below).

beneath contempt   1

For years, Apple Computer has regarded Windows as beneath its contempt.
I think of my deceased parents, who closed out their lives in the decade that
  now is being recast as beneath contempt.
The idea that women could not be priests, for instance, she treated as
  beneath contempt, not even worth discussing.

When used of people, behavior, or speech, this cliché can be regarded as compositional and literal; many dictionaries do not identify it as a phrase that needs unpacking. A sentence like *Stealing from a dying woman is beneath contempt* illustrates this use. Contempt is not a lightweight attitude or emotion, and using the cliché with abstractions of various kinds, as in the examples above, weakens its force because such matters don't often merit contempt.

bright-eyed and bushy-tailed   1

The past six months, though, have seen Kristian emerge from hibernation in typical Canadian fashion—bright-eyed, bushy-tailed, and ready to rock Montrealers again.

I've been staggering in around 9 am lately, half knackered and not terribly impressed with the world in general, but I was all bright-eyed and bushy-tailed this morning.

Before long, bright and bushy-tailed PowerPoint users at countless meetings started to make me look like an antique piece.

This cliché operates adjectivally and adverbially to characterize alacrity. It's common and not out of place in conversation; in writing, bloggers and lifestyle journalists use it with mixed success for the same reason. It is most effective when something sharply contrasting is presented along with it. Without that, it's a lot of syllables for a small idea.

cannot be overstated/overemphasized/underestimated   3

The role of private landowners in this success story cannot be overstated.

For a study of meaning-making in cultural psychology, the primacy of the process underlying the research relationship cannot be overemphasized.

The job that Alan Reynolds and his team have done this year cannot be underestimated, especially when one considers the numerous injuries that they have suffered throughout the season.

In its canonical use this variable predicate with adjectival function has a word like *importance* or *significance* as its subject and is a hyperbolic way of stressing the importance of something. Of course one always could, but certainly wishes not to, imagine how various phenomena could be overemphasized. Problems arise from the widespread, elliptical, and imprecise usage of this emphasis-by-negation construction, many cases of which may leave the reader head-scratching as to what is meant, but also partly in wonderment that the writer did not simply choose a positive way of stating the matter. *Cannot be underestimated* is unusually common in sports journalism, perhaps a result of copycatism.

(stand) at a crossroads 5

Are cooperatives at a crossroads? In many ways, yes, given the challenging
    environment and instances of demise.
Today, Africa stands at a crossroads, a decisive time when its future hangs in
    the balance.
It is a country in turmoil, Iraq. Is the leadership in question, too? The country
    may be at a crossroads.

Users of this cliché (journalists predominate) seem to have the intention of
dramatizing an imminent critical decision, or the opportunity for one. The
cliché misses the point that the default action at a crossroads is to whiz
through it, without pausing, when the destination lies straight ahead.
Countries and careers are both favorites for crossroad placement and both
are nearly frequent enough to be considered clichés unto themselves. It is
often adequate to simply say of a person or organization that they "need to
decide."

cut and dried 3

☞ **completely settled; straightforward and well understood**
The origin of the name isn't cut and dried.
There are no cut and dried solutions to life's problems.
It turns out that the case for global warming isn't cut and dried by any means.

This cliché originally applied literally to herbs sold by apothecaries and in
that meaning it gave a mixed message: convenience and readiness at the ex-
pense of freshness. Its message today is more neutral. *Cut and dried* is nearly
always accompanied by negation, the message being that the subject is not
a simple, easily solvable, or understood one, contrary to what people may
think or desire. *Cut and dried* doesn't offer any advantage over more literal
ways of expressing the idea but it has the advantage of brevity and it introduces a note of informality.

dead and buried 3
dead and gone 2

If Sublime is dead and gone, this just might be the next band in line to
    emulate their sound.
Exciting plans for a modern hospital in Devizes looked dead and buried this
    week.
We now need the Fire Brigade and the government to honour their
    commitment because this is an issue that will never be dead and buried.

I can't argue with him when he dismisses my idea that spear-fishing is dead and gone.

The time when we could have voted ourselves out of this mess is dead and gone.

These two clichés are often used to characterize things that are finished, no longer viable, no longer current, and, in a minority of cases, literally dead. Like some other "joined by and" clichés, it may provide what seems like the right emphatic sound pattern, but whatever stark finality may be intended by the use of *buried* and *gone* is mitigated by the clichés' frequency.

dead in the water   3

The moratorium is now dead in the water and new GM products can be approved.

All Google has to do is pull the plug on Wikipedia hits and Jimmy Wales is dead in the water.

If you underestimate the role of the Chinese government in creating demand and fostering enterprise growth, you are dead in the water.

Users of this somewhat modern cliché have imparted to it a notion that the figurative death it reports is dramatic, sudden, unexpected, or undesirable from someone's point of view. Because of its frequency, just which of these nuances is intended is not always clear. The cliché can be animated in combination with other dead or water clichés, as in *Mr. Cameron went from dead in the water to walking on water.*

down and dirty   2

Where are the down and dirty, no-holds-barred investigations that will jail these criminals?

I have heard a lot of good about this down and dirty western series.

The past six months of his normally pampered existence have been more than a little down and dirty, shall we say.

Few dictionaries define this cliché and among the ones that do there is not much agreement as to what it means. Earthy, funky, unscrupulous, nasty, explicit, and highly competitive are among the synonyms offered for it. This alone should give pause to a writer who wishes to impart a particular meaning with the phrase. See also *get down and dirty* in predicate clichés.

due in large part/in large part due to _____   4

Where there are shortages and starvation, this is in large part due to other factors such as war, poverty, political systems, or poor distribution.

In a stunning turnaround due in large part to a misunderstanding over
procedural maneuvers, the International Whaling Commission voted 19
to 18 this month to readmit Iceland.
The present good health of buildings in South Beach is due in large part to the
influential Miami Design Preservation League.

This cliché, a variant of the frequent and perhaps overused collocation *largely due to*, can often be given respite by rephrasing a sentence that includes a verb such as *follow*, *result*, or *arise*, or a participle construction using one of these.

dyed-in-the-wool   2

☛ *thorough; complete; inveterate; unchanging in belief*
Even the most dyed-in-the-wool liberal on our staff will acknowledge that
80–85 percent of our cases involve suppression of speech by the Left.
The pomp and circumstance does nobody any harm, other than raising the
bile of dyed-in-the-wool Republicans.
The Harvard student had become a dyed-in-the-wool entrepreneur.

The typical instance of this modifier has a word after it denoting political affiliation, and so it should perhaps be considered a cliché only in such contexts. It is true to its origins in denoting something that, while not present in original form, is now so thoroughly absorbed as to be inseparable. The phrase misses the mark when applied to things rather than people—*a lifetime of dyed-in-the-wool service*—because it is not clear what aspect of the noun the meaning is attached to.

each and every   3

Each and every one of us is different, but the idea is to give men insight on
what is considered overdressing and underdressing on first dates.
He was a tangible threat each and every time he touched the ball.
It is up to each and every individual to make a choice about what he/she
wants to believe in.

The long-expired coiner of this alliterative compound was perhaps mindful of inattentive listeners, since either part of it does the whole job. *Each and every* emphasizes by compounding but is never actually required for meaning. The example sentences illustrate the things most often designated with *each and every*: people and occasions.

emblazoned with _____   2

Mr. Clark strode through the civil rights era wearing a lapel button
emblazoned with a single word: "Never."

Somebody told him the player already had a tattoo emblazoned with his
   number.

Emblazon is infrequent as a finite verb but the participle *emblazoned* is now
the preferred way to express "marked with" or "that reads _____." For
things clearly and distinctly marked, *emblazoned* is a suitable descriptor. Its
effectiveness is somewhat compromised by frequent use to describe incon-
spicuous marking or writing.

(sitting) on the fence   4

Come Monday or even Tuesday, many people still on the fence or soft in their
   support for one candidate or the other will break, mostly in one direction.
So, given that most fund managers are sitting on the fence and refuse to
   attempt to time the market, what chance do we ordinary investors have?
Though my son almost certainly received a vaccination containing thimerosal,
   I admit I'm still on the fence as to whether thimerosal can be blamed for
   some cases of autism.

It's extremely common for writers to use this expression to mean "undecided." The *sitting* element is often used as an imputation of inaction on the
part of someone who should decide and act. The cliché is most effective in a
case where a clear alternative has not emerged for want of information or
developments. Where this is not present, "undecided" and "unsure" work as
well.

few and far between   5

He used to spend $500 a month on vet bills but vet visits are few and far
   between now.
The other girl was intelligent, loyal, and determined; such people were few
   and far between.
The crop itself, though, seems to be few and far between, with more than 77
   percent of US hop production coming from Washington state.

This popular cliché qualifies as a "joined by and" phrase, despite the second
element, "far between," having little independent attestation and uncertain
grammatical credentials. Its high frequency notwithstanding, it can be effective in emphasizing the idea of "infrequent" for events that can be placed
on a timeline, as in the first example. It usually falls flat as a synonym for
"rare," as in the second example, and does not work with nouns in the singular, as in the third example.

fine and dandy   3

Michael Moore is a fine and dandy Everyman, gunslinging with a movie camera.

Democracy is fine and dandy, but it has to be looked at in a mature manner.

Trademe winning the Site of the Year award is all fine and dandy, but it's not really going to make a splash beyond the IT pages.

All instances of this cliché suggest that its meaning cannot be construed additively from its constituents—but what exactly does it mean? The first example above, and in others where the phrase is used attributively, suggest a characterization that is not wholly complimentary. A quarter of the usages of *fine and dandy* are followed by *but* and a clause that detracts from the first, as in the other examples. The cliché is most frequent in blogs and soft journalism, where fuzzy meanings are frequent and perhaps expected. In other genres, readers would probably benefit from a clearer expression of the writer's meaning.

on the front line/lines   5

He solicited information and case reports from parents, who are on the front lines of the battle against autism.

McBride was on the front lines of the fight against consolidation in 1992, when the archdiocese first broached the idea of merging Neumann and Goretti.

But what about those who have lived on the front lines of the struggle to build better relations between Israel's Jewish and Arab citizens?

The most hackneyed use of this phrase characterizes people or groups as dealing with a volatile, contentious, or strife-ridden situation—whether or not they actually are. Literal military use is frequent but is closely followed by use where the conflict (if there even is one) is dramatized to give the flavor of combat. Are readers well served by such characterizations?

fully human   3

We are hungry for these tales—they remind us of what it means to be fully human. We always want to hear more.

What becomes available to us when we greet one another as fully human? This is an important question as we struggle through this dark time.

A true vision of the human cannot exclude the divine; we are only fully human when we manifest our inner potential, a potential that cannot be reproduced by machines, however sophisticated.

This characterization is perhaps only a cliché in religious writing, where it is more frequent than in any other genre. Some decades from now, when cyborgs roam the earth, *fully human* may have a more specific and helpful meaning than the current one, which is somewhat sentimental, polemical, and cloying.

hale and hearty   1
Young Frank Mace grew up hale and hearty on the Wairau farm, a strapping Taranaki lad.
He had been a hale and hearty man, and she watched him as he lost a tremendous amount of weight.

The components of this "joined by and" cliché are infrequent in independent use so perhaps they should be seen as supporting each others' meanings, though they are synonyms. *Hale and hearty* is used several times more often of males than of females, and it is there that it finds its most clichéd use, rarely accomplishing more than "healthy" would do on its own.

half the battle   3
Deciphering government regulations and ensuring conformity to policy may be only half the battle.
Brand recognition is half the battle, and if they can bring themselves into the present century then they stand a good chance.
This was one occasion when the old saying that a good start is half the battle was truly wide of the mark.

This common phrase has two uses: when preceded by *only* the idea is to emphasize the difficulty that remains in a complicated or arduous struggle. Without *only*, *half the battle* is more optimistic in suggesting that a difficult prospect is simplified by conquering a manageable aspect of it. That's pretty good mileage out of a four-syllable cliché and it may explain its popularity and effectiveness. The third example above illustrates how a potentially effective phrase may be completely anesthetized, by burying it among other clichés.

hard-pressed to do sth   4
The United States would be hard-pressed to maintain the current level of 130,000 troops in Iraq indefinitely.
I think you would be hard-pressed to find anyone charging more than 5 percent to 10 percent of the fee you mention.

Somehow this seemed a fitting end to her present journey, although I am
    hard-pressed to explain why I feel that way.

This cliché is aptly used when the difficulty described actually involves some
kind of pressure, distress, or urgency—as in the first example. It is been
cheapened almost to the point of worthlessness by being used to characterize mundane difficulties and obstacles. *Hard-pressed to find* accounts for
almost a quarter of instances of the cliché, giving it status as a cliché unto
itself.

has seen better days   3

Halfway down its long, jagged Pacific coast, Chile's second city has seen
    better days.
Ninian Park Road is two long rows of terraced homes, which have clearly
    seen better days.
The 8,000 capacity stadium has certainly seen better days and lacks the
    facilities needed by a modern club to develop further.

Though in the form of a full predicate, this clause always serves as modifier
of the clause's subject, most typically a building or a town in disrepair because of neglect and age. Writers half-heartedly dress up the cliché by inserting *certainly*, *clearly*, or *obviously*, a ploy that does not elevate it above its
rather tired condition.

(the) high and mighty   2

Has he become too cozy with the Bush White House, has he become too much
    of an insider, is he retelling the accounts of the high and mighty?
I don't know why everybody was getting all high and mighty, and giving me
    attitude. Because, as I explained to the teacher, they started it.
The high and mighty attitude of the French now is a good excuse to stop
    drinking an over-priced, inconsistent product, but what are the
    alternatives?

This phrase began life more than six hundred years ago as an epithet of dig-
nity. By the nineteenth century it had lost that distinction, and a cliché was
born. Today *high and mighty* has a dual life as noun "the high and mighty,"
most popular in journalism (first example), and simply as a modifier, more
common in other genres (other examples). Journalists like the noun form
as a slightly disparaging term for powerful people. As an adjective it is
always derogatory to characterize conceit, arrogance, or haughtiness.

if ever there was one 4

Alejandro decides to drown his sorrows in beer, a temporary solution if ever there was one.

The future of individual directors could hang in the balance in every decision they make—a recipe for accountability if ever there was one.

Everyone wants this Mortal Cup thingy (a Hitchcockian Macguffin if ever there was one), and there's also this watery portal that allows for time travel (and apparently, magic tricks and practical jokes).

It's not always easy to discern what value writers imagine this cliché adds to a sentence. The intention may be to emphasize the exemplary status of a thing they have characterized, but the phrase often seems only to be an attempt to prop up a weak observation. *If ever there was one* is regularly found in text that is repletely larded out with dozens of other clichés and colloquialisms; it may just be part of the stock-in-trade of the imitative writer.

in and of itself 5

Milk, in and of itself, is an unmodified whole food that has functional properties.

Serigraphs were a new medium, and we were promoting that medium as a form of art in and of itself.

Film has an identity in and of itself that travels and changes through space and time.

He's also the most visible part of their marketing strategy, which becomes a plot point in and of itself.

As the examples show, this phrase occupies a syntactic slot that in many cases causes no harm by being unfilled. In nearly all cases, the speaker or writer who uses *in and of itself* is at pains to clarify the treatment of the noun preceding the phrase as being considered apart from other things that may influence or interfere with it—things that have been or will be mentioned shortly. Is the phrase actually necessary? If so, there are alternatives that may do the job more succinctly, such as *by itself, unto itself, per se,* or in philosophical or academic language, *qua.*

not altogether surprising 1

It is lowering, but not altogether surprising, that the home secretary's response to animal rights terrorism has been yet further restriction of freedom of speech.

They gave no guidance on what might be thought reasonable or
  unreasonable, and it is not altogether surprising that juries lacked an
  instinctive sense of where to pitch their awards.
If, as I suspect, my home is typical of other British households, then it is not
  altogether surprising to discover home shopping is one of the fastest-
  growing retailing sectors.

This cliché, which lawyers have considerable fondness for, is a slightly grand and not usually necessary expression of "not surprising." It is a syntactic cousin of the even more common predicate for sentences with a personal subject, *not be at all surprised.*

nothing short of _____ 3

With manager Joe Torre back for a fifth season, nothing short of a three-peat
  will satisfy owner George Steinbrenner.
This huge two-volume work was published in 2009 and was nothing short of
  a breakthrough in the historical study of English.
It is nothing short of criminal to spend in this way thousands of dollars which
  could be better used for needed community projects.

The first example shows a legitimate example of this cliché, in which a literal construal is possible. In the other two examples, *nothing short of* acts merely as a threadbare intensive for characterizations (*breakthrough* and *criminal*) that do not need or benefit from modification. *Nothing short of* is most popular with sportswriters, though journalists of all stripes find occasions to use it.

not immediately clear/apparent/obvious 4

It was not immediately clear who might be called from the defence list.
How a figure of £25,000 articulated with the personal injury tariff is not
  immediately apparent and is not explained in the judgment of the court.
Although blood vessels are known to lie within the area of the scan, their
  location is not immediately obvious from the amplitude scan.

These phrases are all ways of saying "unclear" or "unknown" using more syllables. Despite their superficial similarity there is considerable variety in their usage. *Not immediately clear* is most common in news reportage and in the past tense, where it may introduce something that was in fact later clarified but is often reporter's code for "I couldn't find out." *Not immediately apparent* abounds in legal writing, where there is sometimes a subtext suggesting "no rational person could make sense of this." *Not immediately obvious*, the least frequent of the three, is more evenly distributed across genres and is similar in force to *not immediately apparent*, but in scientific writing (as in the third example above) it can serve legitimately as an element in a narrative about scientific observation.

not rocket science   4

Organic weed control is not rocket science, but it does take understanding the anatomy and physiology of the crop plants, the weeds and the soil, as well as a cultivated anticipation of how each will respond to the implement used.

This is not a hard problem to fix. Tort reform is not rocket science. A reasonable bill passed the House of Representatives just last year but died in the Senate, where the trial-lawyer lobby rules.

Setting a SCSI ID, connecting a cable, and attaching a terminator aren't rocket science. Installation was easy.

This cliché, which is typically the predicate of a copular sentence, emerged in the late twentieth century to characterize something as being simpler than people are inclined to think it is. Its usage is still rising sharply, due partly to the many sentences in which it appears without any good reason, as in the second and third examples above.

null and void   3

They sound good doing this kind of music, and even if it's artistically null and void.

Are you saying that all the work that's been done so far is null and void and should not be viewed as having made some progress?

What the library associations are trying to do is make the voice of the people null and void.

The frequency of this cliché was arrived at by discounting its use in legal texts and reporting, where it is formulaic (if redundant) and not a cliché. Writers who use *null and void* outside of a legal context seem to be at pains to emphasize the idea of ineffectiveness or futility.

overcome by/with emotion   2

During a tragic scene toward the end, she is overcome with emotion, but we haven't witnessed her emotional investment in the plight of the pygmies before.

Overcome with emotion, McGahee realized in that moment that all of his
hard work had paid off.
Baghdad's mayor was overcome with emotion by the turnout of voters at City
Hall, where he said thousands were celebrating.

This cliché is most typically journalistic shorthand to prevent the writer from having to unearth more specific adjectives and verbs from the lexicon. Sportswriters in particular use it, perhaps out of a sense that any more specific description detracts from the manliness of their subject. The vagueness of the cliché is often unsatisfying and readers would nearly always benefit from learning exactly what behavior expresses the strong emotion.

par for the course 4

☛ *what is normal or expected*

Belle has a distinctly businesslike tone, and has demonstrated considerable
savviness at marketing, although this may be par for the course for those
who sell themselves for a living.
Instability, violent clashes, and increasing sectarianism have been par for the
course since the peace process got under way nearly 10 years ago.
Your ignorance in these matters is amusing and sad and unfortunately
appears par for the course with your company.

Though a noun phrase in isolation this cliché functions invariably as a copular predicate to characterize something, often with a hint of disparagement, as expected in the circumstances. Bloggers and journalists are equally fond of it. The generality of its application undesirably conflates the status quo with expectations, and for that reason it would be helpful for writers to consider which of the two they mean before trotting out the phrase.

of particular concern 4

An underactive thyroid can affect and be affected by oestrogen, which is of
particular concern to women planning to conceive.
Of particular concern to policy makers has been the absence, in many
households headed by lone mothers, of a role model in paid employment.
As an ecological problem of particular concern to the north, but largely
beyond the control of northerners, biomagnification is gaining increasing
recognition.

This cliché shares some of the motivations of the framing device *There is real concern that . . .* It predominates in formal and technical contexts and is often a marker of a sentence that could have been written more directly and simply but was not—sometimes out of a legitimate desire to place emphasis on the subject at the end of a clause. When placed at the beginning of a sentence (second example), it also acts as a kind of framing device.

on the same page   5

☞ *sharing the same information, approach, or point of view*

You get a bunch of guys on the same page, you can win in this game.

Bernie and I are on the same page regarding salvation by grace through a faith that works.

Obviously the Supreme Court is not on the same page with the Ninth Circuit in this matter.

This cliché developed as a figurative extension of its literal meaning in the twentieth century and is still increasing in usage, despite often meaning nothing more than "agree." It has vaguer connotations than the similar but much less frequent "sing from the same hymn sheet" and may be preferred by writers wishing to avoid the religious association.

over and above   1

They would have made an offer to him over and above that which they made on a pari passu basis to the other part-owners.

Every penny we raise over and above that will be a further boost for a truly deserving cause.

This symbolic value was over and above, but nevertheless inextricably linked with, the estimated research value of the collections.

This double-barreled cliché is syllabically as long as its most usual equivalent—"in addition to." It came into use in the fifteenth century and soon became popular with lawyers to give emphasis; it is still proportionally more frequent in legal writing than elsewhere. In usage today it acts either as a preposition that together with its object forms a predicate of a copular sentence or as the introduction to an adverbial. In both cases, "above" alone usually conveys the same idea.

passionate about sth   5

They're very passionate about their art because they're writers first.

I'm really passionate about my work and I want to be competitive and take my club forward to compete against the big, national clubs.

To everyone reading this who is passionate about any issue—if you're going to educate people, educate them right.

Mere enthusiasm does not suffice for many today: they apparently experience grander feelings, and being passionate is the way that they express this heightened state. The objects of these passions are most typically *music, issues, work,* and *sports,* each of which is frequent enough to be considered a cliché in its own right. This unfortunate cliché is the more frequent counterpart of the verbal cliché *feel passionate about sth.* See also *believe passionately* in chapter 7, "Modifier Fatigue."

quick to point out   5

Artisan gelato makers are quick to point out that it's not the product's lower fat profile that attracts consumers. "People like gelato primarily because it's an intense pleasure."

The Pentagon is quick to point out that the number of insurgents involved is small, estimating the number at about 1,000 people in a country of 25 million.

The three-point line, the shot clock, and the defensive three seconds circle under the basket are all additions that have made the game better. Even so, many fans and critics are quick to point out the numerous shortcomings of today's NBA.

The virtue of this cliché—its capacity to telescope a fairly specific type of contrast in four syllables—should be measured against its high frequency, which mitigates its effectiveness. What is more, there is never any context supplied in which quickness might be assessed. When the actual pointing-out is supplied (first example), the cliché is more convincing than when the pointing-out is merely reported (second and third examples).

ready, willing, and able   2

I mentioned that while it was great to have Buffy *on the shelf ready, willing, and able to be viewed whenever the moment was right, the set was somewhat of a letdown.*

There is now a group of knowledgeable, outspoken journalists around the world who are ready, willing, and able to raise the issue.

But even without dramatic natural disasters, the news media are ready, willing, and able to downplay news about war and the antiwar movement for any number of reasons.

The three adjectives that compose this phrase are not a cliché in the small minority of instances when it is used literally in sentences where a check-in from each of them actually makes sense. In its more common use, *ready, willing, and able* squats in sentences where usually only one of these adjectives is required for the meaning; thus it merely slows the progress of communication.

sick and tired   5

I am sick and tired of a season that starts with four comfortable wins at home
and ends with a consolation home Tri-Nations win against Australia.
They are sick and tired of hearing about race because it never seems to go
anywhere.
I am sick and tired of Bible-thumping frauds and myopic morons that puff
their chests in pride and wrap themselves in the flag as if they are The
Only True American Patriots.

This frequent cliché is a mark of petulance, or simply a failure of imagination, in the speakers and writers who use it. Its highest frequency is in journalism, usually in direct quotations, and bloggers also use it to vent their frustrations. While the far more frequent idiom *fed up* has a suggestion that a limit has been reached and that something might be done to rectify the situation, *sick and tired* achieves its tiresome status partly by communicating impotent negativity on the part of its users.

sick to death (of something)   3

The people of this country are sick to death of the prime minister telling them
they are very well off.
Every time I go to Australia I am sick to death of the paranoia about refugees.
I am sick to death of purchased, ready-made items that are soooo expensive.

If this condition, taken literally, were as frequent as it is reported, usage would drop off abruptly when the sufferers, in due course, quietly succumbed. But in fact, usage of this tired cliché has been increasing since the mid-1970s. Though only about half as frequent as *scared/frightened to death*, those expressions are effectively lexicalized as intensives of "scared." *Sick to death*, on the other hand, is always embedded within a long-suffering narrative and is an unimaginative and dull way of expressing exasperation. It completes a trio of similar clichés, the others being *sick to the back teeth* and *sick and tired*.

on steroids   4

The Firefly family, who seem to be the Texas Chainsaw Massacre family on
steroids, wake up one morning to find their carnage-strewn house
surrounded by the police.

I think all of a sudden, Hillary Clinton has become Jimmy Carter on steroids in foreign policy.

Costing the thick end of $1,000 Apple's stylish new iPad—a smooth 10-inch screen with no keyboard, like an iPhone on steroids.

This modern cliché characterizes extremity in some respect by comparison with a standard. It has a good comic effect when the basis of comparison is already itself extreme (first example), but it is used too often in situations where the basis of reference is not completely obvious (second example) or when the contrast between the items compared is not very great (third example).

too clever by half   1

It appears to be a case of the mayor and his colleagues and city government being too clever by half.

But to sound tough on bankers and then enact a spending freeze is too clever by half.

But strengthening our hand by withdrawing our troops is one of those gambits that is too clever by half.

This characterization is not frequent enough in American English to be considered a cliché there but it abounds in British English to disparage a person or abstraction that is annoyingly, ostentatiously, or self-consciously clever. Its descent into cliché is purely through overuse: mindless application of it to single acts, utterances, or developments that would probably be better portrayed with greater specificity or by simply being called "ineffective."

totally awesome   2

I have this totally awesome job in the media, and I get to watch TV shows before they go on TV, and movies before they're at the movies.

I have been a big fan of the Backstreet Boys for at least two or three years and attended their concert in Greensboro in February. It was totally awesome.

There was a cool quote that led me to the site of a tattoo shop in Manhattan called Last Rites Tattoo, run by somebody named Paul Booth, who sounds totally awesome.

This relatively new and lifeless cliché is the *absolutely fantastic* (q.v.) of a younger generation. If it were sampled in a corpus of only contemporary, spoken English it would undoubtedly be as frequent proportionally as its older synonym. *Totally awesome* is most common in unedited text—blogs, for example—but is also alarmingly frequent in writing about the arts. It is still a mark of youth slang and uses by older writers are perhaps facetious.

touch and go   2

☞ *uncertain or unpredictable; precarious*

For the first four or five hours, even just keeping adequate oxygenation in his blood was very touch and go.

Bottom line: this is a touch and go situation fraught with significant problems, on multiple levels.

The Greek organisers were so slow off the mark that it was touch and go whether the various stadia would be ready in time.

The most typical placement for this cliché is at the end of a copular sentence, where it can only be inelegantly modified by an adverb (first example). The *touch and go whether* construction (third example) is also common and not clearly preferable to "uncertain whether."

various and sundry   1

Adrian Monk (Shalhoub) suffers from an acute case of obsessive/compulsive disorder along with a plethora of other various and sundry phobias and neuroses.

An education should be first and foremost about learning the various and sundry time-honored subjects.

There's nothing specifically wrong with doubling up adjectives that mean the same thing for emphasis, but there's nothing particularly virtuous about it either, and in the case of *various and sundry*, both rarely accomplish more than either would do on its own. See also *all and sundry* in the noun clichés.

worth its weight in gold   2

Put in basic terms, compatibility becomes the most important ingredient, and players with a team-oriented attitude are worth their weight in gold.

Our return budget flight was delayed by more than an hour and we reached home early the next morning yet these few days had been worth their weight in gold.

Critical components that are reliable and that require minimal attention from the press operators are worth their weight in gold.

An expression with roughly opposite meaning, *not worth the paper it's printed on*, at least has the virtue of limited application to things that are actually on paper. *Worth its weight in gold* is a long-winded way of saying "valuable" and is applied indiscriminately to all things, whether their weight, if they are even capable of having weight, is of interest or not. The cliché is nearly always terminal in a sentence, which may be part of its appeal, giving writers and speakers a rhythmic five-syllable emphasizer with which to rest their case. Using it means a missed opportunity to characterize worth in any number of more original or striking ways.

QUANTIFYING CLICHÉS

A small group of clichés are noun phrases joined to other nouns by *of* where the first noun phrase specifies the quantity of the second. I treat them in this chapter of adjectival clichés since they effectively modify the noun or noun phrase that follows them. Conventionalized ways of describing quantities exist in all languages and are a convenience when making generalizations. These expressions veer into cliché when they are used hyperbolically, or without consideration of whether a more precise or less shopworn way of characterizing the quantity might serve the purpose better. It is often the case that the quantity presented with one of these clichés is surprisingly large, and also sometimes undesirably so.

A feature common to a few of these clichés is that they begin with *a whole*, "whole" having become in these expressions an intensifier of a quantity word: *a whole range of issues, a whole host of problems*. Writers who wish to avoid this gaping cliché pothole would do well to stop and think for a moment as soon as *a whole* has escaped their fingertips and consider whether the quantity really benefits from being emphasized in this way.

a bewildering/dizzying array   4
The inclusion of twenty-one selections over the course of not quite sixty-eight minutes creates a pleasantly bewildering array of impressions.

Faced with a sometimes bewildering array of choices, buyers seek to simplify their choice process, for example by sticking with brand names with which they are familiar.

Another English manufacturer, Original Style in Devon, also creates reproductions of Victorian tiles in a dizzying array of patterns.

These two clichés are not exact synonyms though some writers may use them in identical contexts, where there is a need to characterize a quantity as both large and surprisingly diverse. They both fall flat as substitutes for "wide selection" but may be effective where genuine bewilderment is present (second example above).

a considerable amount/number   5

A considerable amount of labor, including irrigation and weed control, is
*   required to establish the plants.*

The results are a considerable amount of confusion paired with a
*   discriminatory disregard for local practices that do not comply to the*
*   dominant model.*

The parties' valuers had helpfully agreed to a considerable number of points
*   before the hearing.*

The use of *considerable* to characterize quantity is literal and compositional; it merits designation as a cliché on the basis of its great frequency and the tendency of writers to use it when it is not required, or where some other word might give a clearer idea. This is the case in all of the examples above. What is *inconsiderable* rarely merits mentioning; what is *considerable* is manifestly worth mentioning and can often be characterized with a simpler quantity word like *some* or *many*, or with no adjective at all. The items most likely to come in considerable amounts are time and money: each of these is frequent enough to merit designation as a cliché by itself.

a great deal   2

That is a result you get to only by giving the word "unacceptable" a very great
*   deal of work to do.*

One of the difficulties in state procurement is the great deal of time that
*   passes between the initial design and the signing of the contract.*

Stibbard generates a great deal of sympathy among audience members who
*   have experienced his kind of restlessness.*

Great deal comes to the rescue of any writer or speaker who feels that *lot* or *large amount* would make them sound unconvincing or too informal. The things most likely to come in *great deal* quantities are time, work, and money. It is a harmless but unnecessary way of characterizing a large quantity.

an iota of _____ 1

None of the events hold the slightest iota of interest.

If there was one iota of a chance I'd get off, I'd go for the day in court.

Without creating an iota of additional wealth, directors can increase earnings
*   per share, their bonuses, and share options.*

When his hand dropped to her breast, she summoned every iota of force in
*   her being and pushed him away.*

Iota is the Latin ancestor of *jot*, an informal word, but the original retains an air of formality that people use to emphasize, often vehemently, the minuscule nature of something, typically something abstract. The things most frequently so belittled are *difference*, *evidence*, and *doubt* and there is usually a negating word in the sentence: *None of this will make one iota of difference to those who are continuing the struggle for a free and independent Iraq.* The fourth example above, from romantic fiction, suggests perhaps that the heroine was imparting locomotion at the molecular level to save her virtue; here *iota* is an unfortunate word choice and was probably not understood by the writer.

the vast/overwhelming majority   5

The vast majority of Scots are reasonable, tolerant, and educated people who accept that discrimination should not be enshrined in statue.

The overwhelming majority of experts consulted warned of the dangers for personal privacy arising from new supervisory powers.

The vast overwhelming majority of Islamic people are utterly horrified by what has happened.

Each variant of this cliché taken separately is frequent enough to be designated in the "5" category. Taken together, they are a juggernaut of hyperbole for writers who find something wanting in a humble word like *most*. *Vast majority* is many times more frequent than *overwhelming majority* and is in fact one of the most frequent clichés noted in this book. Its intention is usually to diminish or marginalize a minority. The same is true for *overwhelming majority*, which is used even when nothing is obviously overwhelmed. Both clichés can usually be replaced with *most* with no damage to meaning.

a whole host   5
a whole (new) set   5

It is easy to be critical of the NPS regarding fire policy, wolf reintroduction, grizzly management, elk controls, and a whole host of related issues.

Stress wreaks havoc on the immune system, opening us up to a whole host of health problems.

They had the choice of speeding up equity retirement programs—which would result in a whole new set of problems—or liquidating the cooperative's assets in whole or in part.

In the Shadowlands there will not be mission terminals as of such, but there will be many quests that take you into a whole new set of dungeons.

These two clichés are used in nearly identical contexts, most typically for grouping *issues*, *reasons*, and *problems*, along with general purpose *things*. *Challenges*, surprisingly, come in *sets* but not often in *hosts*, and they are usually *new* sets. Both *hosts* and *sets* are used simply to characterize a large number of things but *host* hasn't completely abandoned its roots—it's from a Latin word that meant "enemy" and is related to *hostile*. Perhaps because of this, the cliché is most effective in characterizing a large quantity of unwelcome things appearing all at once. *A whole host of other things* is a sure sign to listeners and readers that you are running to the nearest exit from the theater of engaged thought.

a whole range 5

There is a whole range of issues facing the sector at the moment, from social housing to stamp duty, and I'd like to see the leadership taking a proactive role on them.

Large amounts of information can be brought out and put on to Maori television, so that we can be educated about a whole range of things.

Unions nowadays operate a whole range of activities that are not necessarily confined to union members in their operation.

A range is properly the area of variation between two limits, though the word now enjoys extended use to include any notional area with notional boundaries. From there it is only a short step before *range* is used in the same way as *bunch* with only a patina of formality to distinguish it. This cliché is most effective when followed by *from* and *to* constructions that in fact specify a particular range, or when accompanied by a list that suggests what the limits of the range might be. It's least effective when used merely to suggest a large number of things. *Emotions*, *issues*, *subjects*, *reasons*, *factors*, and *things* are among the most typical fillers of the slot after *range of.*

The following adjectival clichés are treated in later chapters in this book. Please consult the index for their location.

abundantly clear
as it were
deeply concerned
deeply rooted
dramatically different
eminently readable

eminently reasonable
eminently sensible
entirely likely
entirely possible
hotly contested
hotly debated
justly/deservedly famous
largely due to _____
largely ignored
massively popular/successful/important
perfectly entitled/justified
perfectly normal/capable/possible
the proverbial _____
quite right
rather different/large/good
thoroughly modern
truly great/amazing/remarkable
very real
virtually identical
virtually impossible
virtually nonexistent

4
Adverbial Clichés

Words and phrases that do the job of an adverb—that is, to modify a verb, an adjective, or another adverb—can be called *adverbials*. Adverbs are the least numerous among the four main parts of speech in English, but adverbials are among the most numerous, diverse, and versatile of expressions because they add many different kinds of information about the way things happen. Some adverbials can be called expressions of manner (such as *horrifically* or *like a bolt of lightning*). Others characterize accompanying circumstances, like *on a whim*, while others characterize some aspect of an action, like *to an unconscionable degree*. Still others play a more straightforward role in indicating where or when something happens: *in Memphis, on Thursday*.

Perhaps more than other categories of cliché, adverbials are the easiest to excuse in informal speech because many of them are expressions associated with a particular dialect or style of humor and are thus taken as an integral part of the speaker's charm. Even a swayback workhorse like *between the devil and the deep blue sea* might be excusable from a speaker who uses it in the context of other diverting entertainments. It is likely that many of the adverbial clichés in this chapter began as original and clever phrases by authors largely unknown. They slipped into the fetid stew of clichédom as their popularity increased and they started finding employment in sentences that don't require them or that actually need a different form of words to better express their author's meaning.

This chapter focuses on a relatively small number of adverbials in relation to the vast number of them in English. I have examined and rejected a number of frequently encountered adverbial phrases that others have labeled as clichés because examination of their usage shows that, however frequently they find their way into sentences, they are used aptly or they efficiently communicate a sometimes complex idea. Adverbials in the cliché reject pile include *by default*, *down the track*, *fair and square*, *in light of the circumstances*, *to a fault*, and many others. The adverbials below that I deem clichés are several times more frequent than adjectival clichés as a class.

in actual fact 5

In actual fact, there's an undercurrent of black humor in the portrayal of Helmut's manipulations and Martha's reactions.

I fear the United States Government is now trying to give some semblance of legitimacy, whereas in actual fact it's only a review panel that makes recommendations to the president.

One can only assume, looking at the rather sad picture of an empty wheelchair with birthday balloons on, that Princess Margaret was, in actual fact, delighted to be a grandmother.

In fact is an indispensable formula in English for introducing a statement that refutes or contradicts what precedes it. *In actual fact* is never required, though frequently used by many who wish to bolster, however needlessly, the presentation of facts.

in the affirmative 2

After proceeding with the plea inquiry, the court asked Mr. Cherniak if he was prepared to proceed to which Mr. Cherniak replied in the affirmative.

Does it sound good? Judging by the fact that this record sounds so similar to Vrioon, it's hard not to answer in the affirmative.

Robert didn't wait for Red to respond in the affirmative.

This phrase has crept into general usage from legal writing, a sample of which is seen in the first example above. English is blessed with a simple and straightforward affirmative particle—yes—and *say yes* will nearly always do the job better than *respond in the affirmative*. The phrase might have seemed like elegant variation when first borrowed from legal writing; now it just seems pompous.

after what seemed like _____ 1

I felt my eyes close, and after what seemed like minutes, I heard the slapping of a stick on my desk.

We were cleared directly to runway 36, and, after what seemed like an eternity, began our descent.

He reappeared after what seemed like hours and informed me that I would have to come back again.

Though not frequent as a cliché overall, this construction is found so often in blogs and online fiction as to make it a hallmark of unedited, poorly considered writing. The favorite way of completing the phrase is with *an eternity*—by writers who cannot be bothered to consult their imaginations about what such a wait might entail.

in all conscience 1

Pity he couldn't, in all conscience, leave her to her own devices and get on with his own troubles.

If the combined boards and CEOs don't know what they're doing, then can one, in all conscience, expect anything more than a mess?

Britain's fishing ministers should, in all conscience, have accepted the total closure of the North Sea for the protection of threatened fish stocks.

This cliché is relatively infrequent and would not merit the label at all if always used appropriately—that is, as a shorthand way of saying "as a matter of conscience," as it is in the third example above. The first two examples don't have any obvious connection with conscience; they use the phrase merely as a digression to emphasize the clause that follows them.

for/to all intents and purposes 4

The fuel is, to all intents and purposes, useless and has to be disposed of at special disposal centres.

The hypersensitive Spector closed his label and, for all intents and purposes, stopped producing.

To all intents and purposes, the 1/3 million who vote Sinn Fein on the island may well continue to do so.

This cliché is extremely frequent in legal writing, where it should probably be considered a formula rather than a cliché. It is in fact first attested in Shakespeare but lawyers get the credit for bestowing upon it an officious ring. Most speakers would find it challenging to separate *intents* from *purposes* semantically and in any case, the cliché is usually only a wordy way of saying "practically" or "virtually."

at any given time   4

The vast majority of users are not interested in drug treatment; only 10
*   to 15 percent are enrolled at any given time.*
Those of you who are easily confused can rest assured that only one door is
*   ever accessible at any given time.*
This means that at any given time young people learn how to drink by
*   following the rituals of drinking pertaining at the time.*

The meaningless component in this frequent cliché is usually "given." In the first example above it performs a useful function by standing in place of "particular." In the second example, "given" is not needed, and in the third, the entire cliché can be eliminated without damage to meaning.

by any means   5

People would like to see on the statute book a law allowing homeowners to
*   defend their property by any means.*
I am not by any means the first to suggest the relationship between the
*   frustrated altarpiece program and these over-door images.*
This has not been by any means a vintage year for fiction.

This phrase is not a cliché in the tiny minority of cases in which it's used literally (first example). Most of the time it is an intensifier for a negated predicate. It has an air of bluster and wordiness and many sentences in which it occurs read better without it.

in any way, shape, or form 4

Opponents of cloning fall into two basic categories—those who are against it
*   altogether, in any way, shape, or form, and those who only disagree with*
*   cloning of human cells.*
I can't complain in any way, shape, or form about the way we played.
I don't see in any way, shape, or form that this impinges our ability to
*   negotiate with each individual union.*

The very general meaning of *way* in nearly every context makes it unnecessary to cover more bases with *shape* and *form*, and furthermore, abstract things don't generally admit of shape and form anyway. The presence of this cliché is usually a mark of a speaker's wish to emphasize whatever negation is being stated and also a mark of a want of originality in doing so. The first example above is perhaps the only admissible use of this cliché, to refer to a multifaceted and complex process like cloning. The other two examples are from speakers who simply reached indiscriminately into their rather small bag of intensives.

behind closed doors   5
The dark, smelly laboratories where scientists worked in isolation behind
   closed doors will soon be relegated to horror movies.
Whatever might have been said behind closed doors, the public truth is that
   the US is Beijing's second-largest trading partner.
He's going to be going over and meeting privately behind closed doors with
   some of the family members.

This cliché's great frequency is evidence of its popularity to emphasize—occasionally to dramatize—the fact of secrecy or privacy. At the end of a clause its sound pattern seems to be more satisfying than any of the single-word adverbs that could replace it, but it needn't be used in combination with these adverbs, as in the last example.

between a rock and a hard place   1
   ☞ *in a difficult situation; facing a dilemma*
We find ourselves between a rock and a hard place and we have to decide
   which is the greater good for the town.
One of the most dangerous starfighter squadrons in the galaxy was closing in
   from their port-side and a Battle Cruiser closing in on their starboard.
   Indeed, Pride of Pegasus was between a rock and a hard place.

This cliché is intended to enliven the notion of "dilemma" with an image and is used routinely in journalism and informal contexts to convey that idea. The second example, from unedited fiction, detracts from the narrative by bludgeoning the reader with a point that has already been made.

beyond the pale   1
   ☞ *transgressive of a commonly accepted boundary*
Many entrepreneurs become part of the establishment while others remain
   well beyond the pale.

El Greco, whose extravagant distortions made him seem beyond the pale before Modernism, appeared to Modernists as one of their own.

To my mind, these supremely physically fit and highly trained folks have achieved a level of excellence that goes beyond the pale.

The infelicitous use of this common cliché (third example) results from a failure to understand that being *beyond the pale* is not, in principle, a desirable or intentional position. When applied aptly, the cliché is convenient shorthand for expressing the idea of unfavorable separation from the mainstream.

---

to a certain degree 4
to a certain extent 5

However, to a certain degree, almost all buildings are prefabricated in that they are made from components manufactured off site.

The baroque classicism had been to a certain degree motivated in an arguably heroic age.

I was very shy and very uncomfortable being in the spotlight, and to a certain extent I still am now.

This pair of synonymous clichés tease the reader with the suggestion that there is something certain being said; there is not. English's one-word ways of designating intermediacy on a scale (*somewhat, fairly, rather, quite, a bit,* and many others) do an unobtrusive job but writers who wish to backpedal even from the general nature of these must resort to cliché, and then it's a matter of choosing your weapons. There are these two, as well as minor variations on them, such as *to some extent* and *to some degree. In regard to reverse engineering, your best luck would be with the Chinese—and the Russians, to some extent.* Other choices include *more or less* (see below) and the informal *kind of, sort of,* and generally disfavored *like.* These last three function more often as fillers than as genuine clichés and are not treated here.

---

at certain points 2

At certain points this approach was very helpful, encouraging people to help win the war. But then it became counterproductive and artificial.

Liman is a bright guy, perceptive and admirably candid about the ways his personal political philosophy informs the story choices at certain points.

But, as Meyerson pointed out, the demand for identity which we impose upon nature is met with resistance at certain points. An example is Carnot's Principle, the Second Law of Thermodynamics.

This phrase is a cliché when no particular points in time, place, or narrative are identifiable or pertinent, and it serves merely to make a formality out of the idea expressed by "sometimes," as in the first two examples. It may have arisen naturally as a pluralization of the more common and less-abused "at a certain point," which normally identifies a moment of change with reference to cause rather than exact time.

up a/the creek (without a paddle)   1

☞ *in difficulties; in a desperate situation*

I would rather walk away from a dodgy deal than to be caught up a creek without a paddle.

Really up the creek for a post today so maybe I will bore you with my breakfast.

But then where are you if your readers feel no imperative to send their ideas and commentary? Up a creek, that's where.

This cliché is uncharacteristically much longer than its more literal near equivalents and rarely survives editor's marks; it is more frequent in blogs than elsewhere. Vulgar variants, not illustrated here, don't generally improve the effect.

on a daily basis   5

The program draws upon the experts who watch our business on a daily basis.

They withdrew hundreds of dollars on a daily basis and bought the children new bikes for Christmas.

This reality, which workers have been experiencing on a daily basis for years, has obviously not yet penetrated into the study chambers of the professors.

There are other temporal adjectives that can fill the slot of *daily* in this cliché, such as *on a weekly/monthly/yearly basis*, and all have frequencies sufficient to merit examination as clichés. *On a daily basis* is nearly five times more frequent than its next competitor (weekly), and its meaning in nearly all cases is precisely conveyed by *every day*. Why then do speakers and writers lay out the entire phrase? Examination of usage suggests that authors hope to impart gravitas to their writing with the phrase but its frequency surely makes this impossible. It is legitimately employed where some other temporal basis might be in consideration (for example, *Are the rides/attractions inspected on a daily basis for any hazards?*). *On a daily basis* is often terminal in a sentence and so may partly serve to inform listeners that a pause in discourse has begun.

day in, (and) day out   3

I know she has kidnap risks and the paparazzi follow her around, day in day out.

I was there every day, day in and day out, and it was tough, but he never lost his cool.

Day in day out there were problems with people not being paid, in some cases for weeks.

This cliché attempts to represent via repetition the idea of monotony or relentlessness and it is a suitable expression where one of these is present, as in the first example. In many cases, and in the other two examples, it is difficult to perceive what advantage the phrase has over *every day*, already present in the second example, or *ongoing*.

in this day and age   4

In this day and age, most of the artists are adding hand embellishment to their works.

There is no excuse for not having disabled access any more—this shouldn't happen in this day and age.

I am very thankful to have grown up with both of my parents in this day and age of divorce.

Though speakers can probably never be broken of the habit, *in this day and age* is never necessary when all you mean to say is *today*. The first example illustrates this. The more usual use of this cliché is to suggest some failure of modernity, with "age" evoking a hazy time in the past when it would have been more understandable that some desirable thing wouldn't have happened or been attainable. Even here though, it is hard to see what the cliché accomplishes that the word *today* doesn't do as well. Writers who follow the cliché with *of* and some specification, as in the third example, redeem it from its most vapid use.

down the pike   2

☞ *in the course of events; in the future*

Our own philharmonic has begun to think about a successor to Kurt Masur a few years down the pike.

Completely integrated lifecycle management applications are a year-and-a-half to two years down the pike.

The stock market has been looking for its canary in the coalmine, that perfectly reliable indicator for what's coming down the pike.

He just came right down the pike with his personal beliefs and sort of wore that as a badge.

Users of this phrase introduce a note of informality, and perhaps of vagueness, into the idea of reasonable expectations. The *pike*, if it represents anything in the expression, is perhaps an allusion to the notion that activities in a particular sphere will proceed on an established or expected course. *Come down the pike* (examples three and four) is a predicate or adjectival cliché and often carries a slightly different idea of "appear on the scene, come to notice, be imminent." It is used conventionally in the third example, rather opaquely in the fourth.

at the drop of a hat 2

☛ *without delay; as soon as there is the slightest provocation*
Working in America would be hell. They sue at the drop of a hat.
Because of lower tax rates, a warmer climate, and more opportunities, many
*   young Canadians tend to flow south at the drop of a hat.*
Although I could discuss Baudelaire at the drop of a hat, how many situations
*   were going to crop up where I could use that?*

A wide variety of contexts call forth this cliché, which is popularly placed at the end of a clause or phrase because of its agreeable meter of successive anapests. It occupies this place so naturally that it may sound jarring elsewhere, as if it were to be taken literally: *At the drop of a hat he'd jump into the car and head for Tubbercurry, Ballymote, Sligo to watch a match.* The second example above shows what is perhaps the least effective use, where it seems only to express the idea of "readily," which is at odds with the eventive notion of the "drop of a hat."

in effect 5

By looking at how it's gone wrong, we can figure out what the genome means
*   to the body in the first place. We can in effect find out the meaning of*
*   every one of our 30,000 genes.*
The president will make the final decision and, in effect, we'll let you know
*   something.*
Help us understand where you're coming from, where you want to bring the
*   word of God, in effect, into the Constitution.*

The frequency of this cliché was determined by looking at its usage in speech only, where it is several times more frequent than in edited text. While it is not entirely meaningless, it seems to serve more as a filler than as an intentional utterance for many speakers. Some speakers use it as a hedge against full commitment to what they are saying, which may be the case in the second and third examples above. Others may imagine that it imparts a subtle nuance to their statement, though this is often lost on the hearer. It is best avoided except in cases where it represents one of its agreed-upon meanings, such as "virtually" or "for practical purposes."

in the extreme 4

Expecting that price to hold indefinitely is naive in the extreme.

Simple and restrained in the extreme, the beautiful horizontal house is an expression of his principle that "less is more."

In my view it was negligence in the extreme for Mitchell to be driving about in the vicinity of the tigers with a tiger cub in her vehicle.

The most typical use of this cliché is shown in the first example; that is, following an adjective that represents a negative or undesirable condition. Frequent fillers of this adjective slot include *naïve, unlikely, foolish, disingenuous, foolhardy, reckless*. In all cases the intention seems to be an intensification of the quality expressed. The more natural order would be to leave the content word at the end of a clause: *extremely naïve* as opposed to *naïve in the extreme*. Does this startling reversal achieve the effect intended by propagators of the cliché? Probably not, because the trick is extremely frequent and attention-grabbing only for its shopworn feel.

at first glance 5

Although at the first glance this article and Bhuyan may seem to address the same issue, these two articles are different in terms of their respective objectives, theoretical principles that led to the empirical models, and their estimated results.

At first glance, North Campus appears to contain nothing but parking lots and empty fields. Upon closer inspection, it becomes clear that North Campus is more than just a barren wasteland.

At first glance I thought Brian Sabean was nuts for giving up so much young talent, but my views have cooled.

The almost invariable function of this cliché is to signal an upcoming contrastive observation, usually preceded by *but*. When volumes of detail separate the initial observation and the contrastive one, you may wonder how so much could be gathered in a glance and this is probably a good opportunity not to use the cliché. It works best to contrast appearances—the literal, visual kind, as in the second example—rather than cognitive phenomena, as in the other two examples.

as a general rule (of thumb) 3

As a general rule, I am not often a big supporter of causes and entertainment mixed together.

As a general rule of thumb, a potential overseas buyer should never consider doing anything they would not do at home.

The adverbial *as a rule* is concise and indispensable in English. Rules are themselves generalizations, applying to many instances, so it's rarely necessary to talk about general rules unless there is contrast with particular rules. A *rule of thumb* is a rule based on experience and common sense, or a general principle that is accurate in practical circumstances and hardly ever needs qualification as "general." *As a general rule of thumb*, a phrase accounting for 5 percent of this cliché's instances, is merely a syllable slurry. *As a general rule* doesn't often mean anything more than "generally" or "as a rule."

at the grand old age of _____ 1

Arthur C. Clarke passed away at the grand old age of ninety in his beloved Sri Lanka, where he lived for the last fifty-two years of his life.

The singer-songwriter went public in 1995 at the grand old age of fifteen.

By 1950, after years of pills and psychoanalysis, and at the grand old age of twenty-eight, she was fired from MGM.

The low-end cut-off for grandness seems to be about five for users of this cliché and it is more often completed with double digits in the twenties than in the nineties. The well-intentioned humor or irony that writers hope to bring off surely succeeds with only a minority of readers. Despite that, the cliché is on an upward frequency curve today. It is a darling of lifestyle journalists.

(come) hell or high water 2
☛ *(despite) many obstacles*

That was the time I decided to learn Russian and to—come hell or high water—visit Moscow and Leningrad, about which my new friends told me so much.

We just invaded come hell or high water and then sent in a bunch of college Republicans with planeloads of cash.

He has always been insistent that his career will progress, come hell or high water, on his terms and no one else's.

This wordy colloquialism, most popular today in written form with sportswriters, is meant to evoke a context of severe hardship, firm determination, or both. It has continuously lost luster since its nineteenth-century introduction. It is not out of place in conversation and chatty blogs today but is excess to requirements in most written contexts.

at this juncture   2

He vowed that the people of Azad Jammu and Kashmir and Pakistan would not let their Kashmiri alone at this critical juncture.

It is an annual thing at this juncture in the season that pressure begins to mount on football managers.

For reasons that don't need exploring at this juncture, I had left a plastic shopping bag halfway up the stairs.

The clichéd use of *juncture* results mainly from writers thinking that "time" needs an elegant variant—very often the same writers who thought that "now" needed an elegant variant in the form of "at this time." *At this juncture* is appropriately used in narratives that identify the coming together of two things temporally or the occurrence of a significant event in a timeline, as in the first example above. The other examples, one from journalism and one from a blog, are less convincing.

by and large   1

☛ *on the whole; largely*

By and large within the women's movement today, white women focus upon their oppression as women.

By and large the traffic plan at Royal Ascot was successful.

By and large Bahrain is cosmopolitan enough that most of its inhabitants have been exposed to Western ways.

This awkward cliché nearly always appears at the beginning of a sentence but is not a framing device; it usually modifies the verb or whatever follows a copula. The nautical origins of the phrase are lost to most modern users, who like it mainly as a hedging device against full commitment to the predicate. An adverbial placed closer to the words affected, and perhaps with more detail, is usually more effective.

far and away   3

Knees are far and away my least favourite body part on a female.

Ryanair and easyJet—still far and away the two largest operators—have both been increasing their own capacity.

I realized that this was far and away the best hymn I had ever sung.

This cliché is typically used with a following superlative to emphasize the distance between it and its next competitor. *By far* has the same meaning and is syntactically more versatile. Those who use *far and away* may do so to introduce informality.

going forward 5

Owners Henry and Susan Samueli have made a major commitment to this organization going forward.

These are the areas we think have the greatest potential for price increases and earnings growth going forward.

But I think, going forward, people need to diversify across markets as well.

China will be a key element in our strategy going forward.

This short phrase has seen rapid increase in usage in this century and is now irresistible to politicians, business spokespersons, and even sports journalists, all of whom use it in preference to a number of plainer expressions such as *now, in the future*, and *from now on*. Part of its appeal may be the slippery way that it avoids full commitment in the way that *in the future* and *from now on* suggest. The initial appeal of *going forward* may have been a suggestion of progress that comes with the word *forward* and of bridging a gap between the future and now. This has surely been eclipsed by the frequency of the cliché, which makes it nearly impossible to live a day without hearing it. The phrase is merely ornamental when other sentence elements point to the future. It is occasionally ambiguous as well, as in the first example above, where it could be construed as either modifying the whole predicate or only predicating "this organization."

on a grand scale 3

Lightning is formed by static electricity on a grand scale.

The "Porn" Squad was riddled with graft on a grand scale.

This whole mess is remarkably dull and uninteresting on a grand scale, narrowly edging out most Gamespy sites.

Scalability is a chief means by which we transfer meanings, so expressions with scalar reference are frequent and necessary. All the more reason then that reference to grand scale be truly grand and not merely aggrandized. The first example is an apt use of this cliché but it is unnecessary in the other two examples and adds nothing to the sentences but syllables.

head and shoulders above _____   2

Mr. Bayley showed himself to be head and shoulders above his
    Conservative opponent, and I think he deserves our ringing endorsement
    on June 7.
While his last few novels paled, his main body of work stands head and
    shoulders above that of every other SF writer, living or dead.
This game is head and shoulders above the original in terms of polish and
    level design.

This cliché straddles an adjective/adverb divide, being frequent both after *be* and after verbs such as *stand, rise, tower*, and the like. While certainly livelier than *much better than* it is somewhat overworked in contexts where people and their achievements are not involved. *Head and shoulders above* also seems to have a hidden agenda of manliness, as it is used nearly ten times more frequently of men than of women.

---

in high dudgeon   1

☛ *showing strong resentment or indignation*

Joyce left Ireland in high dudgeon and then spent the next decade or two re-
    creating the city he left.
When the chap was sentenced he was in high dudgeon and he threatened to
    kill the jury for finding him guilty.

This cliché is a darling of writers on social and society topics. It may be lost on less educated readers, who would prefer something along the lines of *in a huff.*

---

in an ideal world   3

In an ideal world, marriage vows are sacred and everyone lives happily ever
    after. We do not live in an ideal world, and to make moral judgments
    about the behaviour of others is demeaning.
In an ideal world we would have freedom to do whatever we wanted; but in a
    socially responsible society, this cannot happen.
In an ideal world there should have been an opportunity for the Appellant to
    appeal but we find that the absence of an appeal is not a defect which
    renders this dismissal unfair.

As a longwinded way of saying "ideally," this cliché has nothing to recommend it. Often it is used to starken the contrast between a present reality and what would be desirable, which may be a useful exercise if the contrast is not already apparent and if the desired state might be attainable. If the ideal world posited is merely fanciful, as in the first two examples, the cliché is a pointless rhetorical exercise.

if you like   5

Brown is a dictator by default, if you like, undemocratically staying in power not because he wants to force through some terrifying new measures, but simply because he can.

Our client was, if you like, unreasonable in that she took the view that she would object to the judge hearing the case because of the fact.

And in a sense, quite rightly, the McCanns have attempted to, if you like, use the media and control it so that they don't end up as victims of the media.

The purpose of this awkward cliché seems to be to warn an audience of a self-conscious or nonstandard use of the word or phrase that precedes or follows. The phrase offers no recourse if you don't like what you hear or any clear indication of what is suspect about the marked usage. In many instances, and in all of those above, it is simply the mark of a writer or speaker who has not taken time to express an idea more clearly.

if you will   5

Call it delusion if you will, but I like to think that I have a full working life ahead of me.

We've already seen the ripple effect, if you will, of democracy in Afghanistan and Iraq.

Some firms here on Wall Street are asking their employees to pay to attend the parties. Pay to play, if you will.

Imagine, if you will, three kinds of desserts united into one unforgettable bowl.

As the examples show, this form of words is used for a number of functions, with varying intentions on the part of the writer or speaker. The first example above, *Call it . . . if you will, but . . .* counts as a cliché unto itself for writers who wish to qualify or backpedal from the way that they have characterized or are about to characterize something. Sentences of the type illustrated by the second and third examples are also extremely frequent, in which writers issue a sort of apology for a term they have just used—often without need or reason. This usage is not distinguishable from *if you like.* An imperative immediately preceding *if you will,* as seen in the fourth example, is usually filled by *imagine, picture,* or *consider.* This expression, with a variable verb slot, is also a cliché unto itself and adds nothing meaningful but may be intended simply to slow down or decorate the narrative.

lock, stock, and barrel   2

☞ *wholly; completely; thoroughly*

You want that consultant to take your business and move it lock, stock, and barrel to the Web.

They may have rights, but their lifeline is cut by throwing them out lock, stock, and barrel, sometimes permanently.

So you sell everything, lock, stock, and barrel. OK, you keep the barrel, that will come in handy on your journey.

This cliché serves to introduce or continue a tone of informality but does not add any element of meaning beyond its single-word synonyms in the gloss above. In the third example, the writer injects some life into the phrase by suggesting a literal interpretation of it.

by a (country) mile   3

☞ *by a wide margin; by far*

Cathy Moriarty is the best performance by a long mile, balancing dry humor with wisdom and unexpected steel.

MLB Zach Thomas (Dolphins) leads the NFL in tackles by a mile.

The ideal ticket for next September is Chris Windsor for mayor, and Nick Dyer, the most intelligent of the Libs by a country mile, as deputy.

It's questionable whether the use of *mile* or *country mile* adds a note of interest to the examples above that would be missing if the writers had simply said *by far*. The cliché is largely unobjectionable where actual distances are involved but overworked in other contexts.

more often than not   5

The interested student will more often than not turn to see what the most contemporary artwork in the book is.

First impressions are more often than not correct, especially in politics, and nowhere was this better proved than with Denis Thatcher.

A decision to marry someone is more often than not a decision for life, at least for women.

More often than not is indispensable shorthand for the much more complicated but literal syntax that it replaces and its high frequency alone should not be taken as evidence that it is alarmingly overused. It is abused only in cases where there is no clear indication that it means anything more than *often*, as in all three examples above. Speakers and writers who do the math, at least mentally, will often find that a single word accurately conveys the frequency of the phenomenon they describe.

more or less   5

The essential idea in all of these sculptures is more or less the same.

Firms run by degreed managers were more or less likely than other firms to complete diversifying acquisitions.

Fifty-five percent of Americans believe God created humans, more or less complete, sometime in the last 10,000 years.

The popularity of this extremely frequent cliché may be that it covers all possibilities but one, that one being characterizable as "exactly" or "precisely." Speakers and writers use it as a hedge to avoid precision in comparisons, and indeed, *more or less the same*, as a complete predicate or followed by a noun, accounts for more than 20 percent of the cliché's use. *More or less* is also used to avoid precise characterizations of states, qualities, quantities, and the like, where even "almost" or "nearly" would seem too much of a commitment.

The cliché can be confusing or meaningless when followed by *than* without an earlier negation, as in the second example above. Writers who use the phrase simply as a way of being vague might profitably consider whether their readers would be better served by a more original characterization. The phrase is helpfully literal and not a cliché in sentences like *Would you be more or less likely to shop there if you knew it was a cooperative?*

in no small part/measure   4

Buffy realizes that she does not need the council and that its directors have tried to control her in no small part because they fear her.

For liberal thinkers, the First World War was in no small measure attributable to the egoistic and short-sighted calculations and miscalculations of autocratic leaders.

Of all Marvel's titles, Spider-Man probably has the most name recognition, due in no small part to the late '60s animated TV series that became a staple in syndication.

Users of this cliché might be excused for choosing it over many others that express the same idea and exhibit an equal measure of fatigue: *to a considerable degree, to a certain degree*, and perhaps *in large part*. The motive seems to be a wish to emphasize the importance of some factor while also stopping short of the implications of *largely, mainly*, or *primarily*. It is often adequate and less obtrusive to use the one-word adverbs *partly* or *significantly*.

in no uncertain terms 3

*We condemn in no uncertain terms the violent behaviour exhibited by the
remandees.*

*The Sunfood Diet describes in no uncertain terms why the author believes
eating raw will renew and revolutionize your health.*

*He had told her in no uncertain terms that he was the only person allowed to
drive his car.*

While uncertain terms are a regular feature of discourse, they are not so frequent as to require notification of their absence. But that is not the purpose
of this verbose cliché anyway; it is an intensifier for whatever statement is
being made or reported, usually one that is adequately showcased with "def-
initely," "fully," or a few other simpler adverbs.

in a nutshell 4

*The story in a nutshell is that Lt. Cmdr. Hunter is assigned as the
replacement executive officer of the U.S.S.* Alabama, *a nuclear missile
submarine.*

The longer you look, the more you'll see, is his philosophy in a nutshell.

*Our argument in a nutshell is that is what happened under the nonfeasance
rule and because of the interpretation over time that has been placed on
this decision, what is happening now is that those responsible for roads
are maintaining that if a danger is . . .*

This cliché is an agreeable and popular way of packaging a summary and it
works best when what is presented is short and sweet. Either of the first
two examples are typical and unproblematic usages. The third, clipped example is one that fails the purpose of the phrase because it presents far
more material than can be fitted in any imaginable nutshell.

once again 3

*Once again, we're waiting now, about an hour and twenty minutes away
when we should hear from the Scott Peterson jury, having reached a
decision on the life or death decision, which they faced after deliberating.*

*But once again, if the Internet Well of Speculation and Obnoxious Fanboys is
right, both will be released before the end of the year.*

*Once again, many shops in the States have a casting area where you can
make some casts with the rod of your choice.*

When used to introduce a narrative with parallels to one just before it, *once
again* is a helpful contextualizer and not a cliché. When there is no such

continuity of narrative, *once again* is often little more than a pointless filler and probably should not be strictly regarded as a cliché because of the many speakers who use it without traceable meaning. Newscasters and flight attendants, for example, seem to regard it as a general introduction to any utterance, without particular reference and perhaps only to signal their supposition that their audience was paying attention to something they may have said before. But it's annoying for any listener to seek, and not find, the referent of the phrase in memory, and it is much better to eliminate it when there is no need for an audience to know of something coming around, in the speaker's mind, as a reintroduction.

onward(s) and upward(s)   2

Holding her torch aloft, liberty is pointing the way onward and upward and saying to America, "Come."

While some of the Conway residents remain in this crime-infested hole, those who encouraged them have moved onwards and upwards.

Frankly, if Paul Holmes is upsetting the usual clump of jealous lefties and media Pharisees, then his show is sure to go onwards and upwards.

As a standalone exhortation, this cliché is meant to be encouraging rather than irritating to its hearers. As an adverbial modifier—or an adjectival one, after a copula—it usually encapsulates the idea of progress, either achieved or hoped for, but doesn't have any obvious advantage over single words that suggest this, such as *forward*.

at this/that/any particular point in time   2

It may well be that we are actually looking at different species of rock wallabies, but we just don't know enough at this particular point in time.

I'd often wake up, and not even remember what town I was in at that particular point in time.

The study concluded that the NAIRU is essentially a moving target and that no one can be certain where it is at any particular point in time.

Used with *this*, this cliché usually means *now*. Used with *that*, it means *then*. It can often be eliminated altogether since context makes clear what time period is in focus, but writers and especially speakers are fond of tacking this mouthful onto the end of a clause, perhaps in the belief that it adds authority or gravitas to their pronouncements. Used with *any*, the expression is a slightly drawn-out version of another cliché, *at any given time*. Like *on a daily basis*, at ____ *particular point in time* is nearly always at the end of a clause and may help signal the beginning of a pause in spoken use.

at the present time 4

It is important to remember that many diseases, such as viruses and orange rust, cannot be controlled with fungicides at the present time.

At the present time there are no plans to practice diverting asteroids.

At the present time we have a very serious problem, because it appears that there was a predetermination not to hear his case.

It is nearly always preferable to insert a strategically placed *now* in place of this cliché. Like *at this particular point in time*, it simply formalizes and lengthens a straightforward expression of time. Some speakers may use it to suggest that whatever is stated to be the case is subject to later change; this seems to be the motive in the second example above.

---

quote unquote 1

I was setting out to get some idea of what capitalism is and what, quote unquote, communism was.

That was another problem. I didn't want to be one of those quote unquote chicks.

So, at the stroke of midnight, or whatever it was, I was told that it was time, quote unquote.This cliché is frequent in first-person narratives, after or before the word that the speaker wishes to flag for special attention. But why quotes, and what kind of quotes? Is another speaker being quoted? Are they scare quotes? The intention seems to be to signal some distance from the word on the part of the speaker but the nature of the distance is not usually clear and listeners might be better served by an explanation of the problematic use of the word.

---

to a T/tee 2

☞ *exactly; properly; to perfection*

Each team's introduction, entrance, stadium, cheerleaders, mascots, etc. are represented to a tee.

And to a T, every person has been involved in either local politics or their own community, trying to change things.

There are, of course, hate-mongers who are quick to condemn any biblical scholarship that doesn't agree to a T with their ultra-conservative views.

The obscure origins and polysemous nature of this cliché make it a poor substitute for its more literal synonyms but it is popular in conversation to favorably characterize something done well. The second example above is an infelicitous use, where the idea might be better expressed by *everyone* or *every single person*; the writer may have confused the expression with *to a man*.

at this/that moment in time   3
at this/that point in/of time   2

At this moment in time the population is really sensitive about the whole GM issue and they don't trust these companies.

At this point of time I sincerely apologise for any mistakes I made while writing this chapter.

At this point in time, the European Union troop lacks prerequisites to act internationally without NATO support.

This cliché invites the reader or listener to step back and place an event against the eternal backdrop of time. Because English has the word *now* to focus our attention on the present, and because of the cliché's frequency, few of us bother with the eternal backdrop, having learned from experience that it is not rewarding. The cliché is not out of place when it refers to an event already mentioned (as the first example does in fuller context) and it may be used to express the idea of "right now" more formally, as in the third example. The cliché needn't be invoked when formality is not required or when it is not necessary to point to the time, as the second example does.

in the true/truest sense of the word   2

With a latitude of 85 degrees north and 12 degrees east, we traveled to a part of the world that can only be described as awesome, in the truest sense of the word.

What happens next is tragic in the true sense of the word, as the boys find the horizons that had so recently broadened beyond belief, come crashing back in on them, with wildly differing results.

John Lennon was a special guy, a special genius in the truest sense of the word.

Some writers bring this phrase to life by using it to direct readers away from a more usual interpretation of a word's meaning, as here:

This is an adult film in the truest sense of the word. The more one has experienced of life, I expect, the more one will read into the subtle clues as to Marie's relationship with Jean, and the more one might comprehend her pain.

This usage is helpful to the reader and not a cliché. In other uses the phrase would seem to place an unfair burden on the listener by suggesting that a moment of semantic analysis is required for proper comprehension. But the phrase is usually a worn-down intensive, perhaps coming to the rescue of writers who feel they need to go a little further than merely using *true* or *truly* but refraining from further effort.

with bated breath 2

The decision to elevate him from the position of chief operating officer was taken a while ago. Did he spend the intervening period with bated breath?

I await with baited breath the howls of anger directed at the self-proclaimed Maori Government, who have the temerity to engage in the same behaviour as our elected government.

The coalition cannot speak for anybody but themselves, however we wait with bated breath to see what obligations and commitments we are being called upon to fulfill.

Most people *wait* with bated breath, but a small number anticipate and look forward, as well as engage in other activities. The idiom captures the idea of eager anticipation or apprehension succinctly (first example) and is tiresome only in sneering, ironic use—which is frequent. The misspelled *with baited breath*, most frequent in blogs, accounts for more than a quarter of instances of this cliché.

The following adverbial clichés are treated in later chapters in this book. Please consult the index for their location.

after/when all is said and done
all things considered
as a matter of fact
as it were
at the end of the day
broadly speaking
by no means/not by any means/not by any manner of means
by the same token
for what it's worth
generally speaking
in my humble opinion
in point of fact

literally _____
lo and behold
needless to say
quite frankly
quite possibly
quite simply
relatively speaking
to be perfectly honest (with you)
to say the least
very much _____
with all due respect

5
Predicate Clichés

Predicate clichés are those that begin with a verb (usually transitive) other than a linking verb. They are a way of characterizing an activity: one being carried out by a person or a group, or one that can proceed without an agent directing it (for example, a situation that *spins out of control*). The clichés I have included here meet the criteria set out earlier: they are frequent, often used without regard to their appropriateness, and they may give a general or inaccurate impression of an idea that could often benefit by being stated more succinctly, clearly, or specifically—or in some cases, by not being stated at all.

When a predicate cliché is followed immediately by "and" it is often a sign that the writer or speaker means for the cliché to classify or stereotype the action that follows in the next phrase:

I'll throw caution to the wind and try to spell out just what is at issue.
At some point you are going to have to face the music and respond to the comments you made.

In such cases it is worth considering: does the presence of the cliché really add some meaning to the sentence that cannot be taken away from what follows it?

Most dictionaries of clichés include many predicate phrases that you won't find in this chapter. There is, for example, *back the wrong horse*. Frequent? Yes. Ineffective? It would be a challenge to express the same idea in four syllables or less, and any expression that has a horse in it is probably more effective than one without a horse; it is especially better than an expression that contains only abstract terms. So, in this book, *back the wrong horse* is no cliché. While we're on horses, you might just check whether yours is a roughshod horse (one wearing shoes with projecting spikes). It's probably not, and it's probably the case that you don't think about horseshoes when you hear *roughshod*; so *ride roughshod (over sb/sth)* has effectively lost its literal meaning and become lexicalized as a way of saying "act with arrogant disregard of others." *Ride roughshod* then is, by my reckoning, no cliché, despite its high frequency, because it does its job better than any of its literal competitors. Likewise, *blow someone's cover, give someone carte blanche, drive home a point/idea*, or *look/stare daggers at someone*, while compilers of cliché dictionaries often include these, they all have very limited and specific meanings, which they express concisely. When they're used properly, it's hard to think of a context in which they would not be preferable to their longer, literal alternatives, such as *divulge someone's secret identity, give someone unlimited discretionary powers, make something clearly understood*, or *glare angrily at someone*.

Many sources identify as clichés a class of short idioms that serve mainly as variants for standalone verbs and that are employed mainly to provide variation. Thus, *tie the knot* is frequently found in proximity to *marry, marriage, nuptials, couple*, and other associated words. Despite frequency I do not consider this kind of usage to be a cliché, since repetition of a verb previously used is often deemed to be a worse stylistic choice than introducing a variant.

Of all types of cliché classified in this book, predicate clichés are perhaps the most pernicious because they are often the chief means by which we are given an understanding of things that happen. If you read or listen regularly to news media it becomes clear that predicate clichés constitute a nearly complete ontology for reporting and interpreting events deemed worthy of reportage and that it is possible to abridge nearly everything that happens in the world using a filter of predicate clichés. This gives rise to the disturbing idea that our worldview may be strongly influenced by clichés and the stereotyped ways of understanding events that they represent.

race/work against the clock   1

Rescuers have told how they found the baby screaming in her mother's arms,
and how they felt her slipping away as they raced against the clock to get
her medical attention.

Firefighters are racing against the clock in the West, where more than thirty
large wildfires are burning.

Archeologists have been working against the clock for two years at the site in
south County Dublin to try to record details of the medieval fortress and
surrounding settlement before contractors build the motorway.

This predicate cliché is a counterpart to the noun cliché *a race against the clock* and is related to several others that depict time as an adversary. All of these clichés are journalistic staples, providing the most readily available and effortless news hook for any story that does not present another obvious one. Use in past tenses is relatively infrequent, since the dramatic element is provided by the clock that the writer would have you imagine is ticking now.

aid and abet   4

One of APW's goals is to create a collection of sample ceremonies to aid and
abet you in the creation of your own wedding ceremony.

This potpourri of unsubstantiated rumours of drug use by Armstrong is the
creation of Pierre Ballester, aided and abetted by London Times
sportswriter, David Walsh.

Deans, provosts, chancellors, presidents, and other high academic
administrators silently aid and abet the faculty in not committing to the
project, because most of them have bailed out.

In legal writing (where this phrase is most frequent) and in reporting about crime, *aid and abet* is more properly considered not a cliché but a formula, derived from the criminal code provision called *aiding and abetting*. In other writing the phrase is often used to connote a connection, sometimes humorous, with criminality. When this is not present, *aid and abet* doesn't have an obvious advantage over *help* and falls flat (as in the first example) where a connection with criminality is fanciful or gratuitous.

avoid sth like the plague   2

Learn to recognize the difference between financing and borrowing, then
avoid borrowing like the plague.

Does he still return her phone calls, or avoid her like the plague?

Although the mum-to-be avoids nostalgia like the plague, there are moments
worth rescuing from her past.

This cliché has achieved remarkable staying power, given that it did not emerge until the nineteenth century, several centuries after the plague was topical. It serves mainly to intensify *avoid* but adds nothing to the force of the verb other than an informal tone and is a clear sign that the writer or speaker has a ready supply of stock phrases. Today it is used mainly of situations and other abstractions that have no connection with the possibility of contagion or infection—a fact that further contributes to its cliché status. When used of a person it may suggest the undesirability or a risk of being in their company, which is not necessarily intended.

get/go back to (the) basics   3
☞ *return to an earlier, simpler condition or approach*
Kickboxer 4 *makes an attempt to get back to the basics, by reinstating the*
good ol' villain from the original kickboxing movie.
It is extremely important for all of us to get back to basics and find the things
that are really important and are readily available to us.
The fifth-year linebacker went back to the basics, returning to his old
stomping grounds at Clemson to go through hell this summer.

This cliché is usually used to classify an experience or circumstance that is spelled out in more detail in context—and because of that, it doesn't often add significantly to meaning but it sometimes puts a positive spin on the idea of "revert" or "return" that might not be inferred without it. The "basics" vary with the context, and use of the cliché without some expansion of what they are is not always helpful.

bang the drum (for sth)   3
☞ *promote or lobby for loudly, enthusiastically, or conspicuously*
He continued to bang the drum for shareholder value within an industry
riven with conflicts between the need for spending on infrastructure
renewal and the need to reward investors.
On the one hand they bang the drum of cultural projects, while on the other
hand they don't provide the necessary funding.

This cliché may be used effectively when the intention is to diminish the subject of it because it presents a somewhat crude image; it is now widely used in contexts where it means no more than "promote" and doesn't usually add anything useful to that idea aside from an informal tone.

beat a (hasty) retreat 3

As darkness fell we beat a retreat to the Pousada Chez Les Rois in a quiet
neighbourhood of the city and a tasty dinner nearby.
Their daughter, granddaughter, and the taxi driver had beaten a hasty
retreat to the back of the house and were not harmed, the police reported.

The idea of *retreat* may have been enhanced by the addition of a rhyme (*beat*) the first dozen or so times it was used, but that was all finished by about 1860. Now this cliché is used in contexts where it doesn't even mean "retreat"; it just means "go." It might still be used successfully in a situation where a hasty retreat is not expected.

----

beg, borrow, or steal 1

☛ *obtain by whatever means possible*

The possibilities really are limitless, as long as you can beg, borrow, or steal
the means of transporting your chosen item.
Many of today's producers, screenwriters, and filmmakers beg, borrow, and
steal from plotlines, characters, and situations of the past.

Little is added to the idea of "obtain" by this colloquial cliché, other than a folksy informality that does not enhance the quality of most writing and lies dead on the page wherever found. The phrase is widely distributed and most frequent in soft journalism.

----

beg the question 5

☛ *assume the truth of a point raised in a question*

The report begs the question "what kind of capital city do we want?"

When used accurately this phrase is not a cliché but a very specific speech act, the need for which does not frequently arise in casual conversation. It has become the most dire kind of cliché when it is used to mean "raise the question," as in the example above. This is nearly always the case when the phrase is followed by a question. Some writers also use the phrase in other ways in which the meaning isn't at all clear:

> *Noting that "the French Revolution licensed a frenzy of anger and cruelty*
> *that the American Revolution generally avoided," he explains that*
> *Americans simply wanted a new government, while the French wanted*
> *"a new culture and a new emotional stance toward life." This is true as*
> *far as it goes, but it begs the question of Jean-Jacques Rousseau and his*
> *influence on Western civilization's attitude toward emotion.*

Except when writing for a narrow legal or academic audience that uses the phrase regularly, use of the phrase simply dilutes and further confuses its original meaning. Modern journalistic use of the cliché seems largely unaware that a meaning exists aside from "raise the question."

bite the bullet   5

☞ *decide to do something difficult or unpleasant that one has been putting off or hesitating over*

Blade 2 finds Wesley Snipes's mixed-up anti-hero in Prague, pursuing his quest to slay all vampires and to track down his father figure, Whistler (Kris Kristofferson), who looked to have bitten the bullet last time around.

And the Times *has yet to bite the bullet on its correspondent Herbert J. Matthews, the clueless Castro groupie who wrote that the comandante was winning his guerrilla war in Cuba at a time when he actually commanded fewer than twenty men.*

Dictionaries differ about exactly what this cliché means, perhaps because writers use it to mean a number of things. The definition above, from Oxford dictionaries, is more specific than the one in Merriam-Webster ("enter with resignation upon a difficult or distressing course of action") or in Random House ("force oneself to perform a painful, difficult task or to endure an unpleasant situation"). In the first example above, the writer seems to confuse the cliché with "bite the dust." In the second, it's not clear what action the *Times* would need to take to qualify for biting this particular bullet. Writers who feel they need the expression, said to be from the Old West, could reflect whether their readers might be better served by plainer language. It was recently reported that a certain bellicose Asian government would "literally have to bite the bullet" in not carrying out aggressions on minorities in its country, with the meaning "refrain from using military force." The reporter seems to have married two clichés in an attempt to create a novel meaning.

bite the dust   3

☞ *be killed; suffer defeat; come to an end*

The first bandstand bit the dust after four years and was replaced by the present one.

Greeting card shops are forced to bite the dust as most of the e-greeting services are free, barring a few major gift shops online.

This year's event looked as if it would bite the dust before it started.

The point of this cliché is nearly always to introduce a note of informality or to perpetuate such a tone that is already established. Its extreme frequency has robbed it of the colorful or poignant image it must have evoked when first used, of men falling in the battlefield.

be/get bitten by the _____ bug   2
☞ *develop an irresistible enthusiasm for something*

David Ferry was bitten by the acting bug at fifteen years of age when a theatre festival came to St. John's.

Like Peter Mandelson and myself, if you have been bitten by the political bug, it doesn't leave you.

Mr. Overington, who enjoyed hunting with the Middleton Hunt for many years, was then bitten by the golf bug, joining both Fulford Golf Club and Allerthorpe Golf Club.

When accompanied by mention of a particular "infecting" incident this cliché does not seem to lose its force; it completes an analogy in which an experience is viewed as having had a profound effect that resulted in a persistent condition, as in the first example above. It finds no purchase, however, when simply used as an informal way of saying "developed an enthusiasm for." The most frequently biting bugs, based on corpus evidence, are the "acting" and "travel" ones.

blow hot and cold   1
☞ *waver, vacillate, equivocate*

The Pirates have blown hot and cold in their three league games, winning and drawing twice and will be looking for a much better show this afternoon.

They've been blowing hot and cold and in fact the initiative has come entirely from Sistani, and he has averted what could have become a blood bath.

The Respondent who previously had been blowing hot and cold about the termination of services, had become resolute and from thenceforth tenaciously maintained the position that the services would be terminated.

Speakers often prefer this four-syllable cliché to the two-, three-, or four-syllable verbs that can substitute for it in most contexts. It is particularly common in sports writing where *hot* often takes on the specific meaning of "lucky, favorable, on a roll" (first example). In other contexts it may have a slightly disparaging edge, suggesting that someone is unable to be consistent or make a decision.

boast (a quantity or feature)   4

The movie boasts a 2.35:1 widescreen transfer, which, considering the barren wasteland that is the bonus material, Paramount probably didn't have to go and do.

Philadelphia later became the first free city north of the Mason-Dixon Line and boasted a number of stops on the Underground Railroad.

Boasting an 11 percent LCV voting record, Murkowski has been an equally vigorous advocate of drilling in ANWR, as well as a big backer of the Alaska pipeline project.

Precisely quantified entities are extremely common after the verb *boast* when it simply means "contains," "features," or "has." In many cases, it is the writer who is boasting, not the reported subject (which is typically inanimate). There is not any clear reason for diluting the meaning of *boast* to predicate things with no agentive capacity. Movies and films are both great boasters among critics, who seem to imagine them as doing the boasting that their promoters are already quite successful at: *The film also boasts an excellent performance by Stewart Rome who totally convinces in the dual roles of Benedik and Marsh.*

bring the house down/bring down the house   3
☞ *evoke vigorous applause*

At a dramatic Board of Estimate hearing the mayor brought down the house when, in consideration of the objections, he canceled his plans to travel to Albany.

The adults and children in the two orchestras joined forces and virtually brought the house down with a performance of Carnival de Paris.

They are all strong singers and their gritty four-part treatment of "I'm a Woman" brought down the house.

If houses fell as easily as users of this cliché report we would be surrounded by ruins. Today *bring down the house* is used vaguely to represent a range of meanings from "was warmly received" to "received a standing ovation." Its high frequency makes it a not very effective way of expressing ideas at either end of this spectrum, or in the middle. Writers about the arts are mainly responsible for propagating the phrase.

burn the midnight oil   2
☞ *read or work late into the night*

An average of 37 percent of respondents around the world aren't usually tucked up in bed until after midnight, with 40 percent of people in Asia Pacific burning the midnight oil.

Fortunately I have never yet missed a deadline for a new piece, but I do
   usually have to burn the midnight oil to get pieces done in time.
Every employee we hire says, "I'll work my butt off and burn the midnight oil
   for this job."

This cliché shares a quality common to many in which mention of a supplanted technology is perhaps intended to foster a sense of informality. In the first two examples the cliché gives the reader nothing of value not present in "stay up late" or "work late." The third example creates an amusing illusion that work is being offered in a cliché factory.

bury your head in the sand   3
☛ *willfully ignore unpleasant realities*
Serby defended himself by saying that anyone blind to this potential reality is
   burying their head in the sand.
The worst thing they can do is bury their heads in the sand and pretend that
   the problems will be solved with a win.
This Federal Reserve has had its head buried in doomed policy sand for two
   decades.

The popularity of this cliché is perhaps explained by the graphic image it communicates and the fact that it has no possibility of literal realization, at least for humans. It often accompanies a description of the very act it represents metaphorically and so is effectively redundant, having only a classifying function. Inventive uses, such as in the third example, show a better use of the cliché.

change the calculus   1
☛ *change the strategy or approach*
If US forces can effect targets at will, they can change the battlespace
   calculus for warfare.
China has reportedly changed its security calculus and been forced to
   reevaluate its geopolitical position vis-à-vis its relations with the United
   States.
Obviously the probability that terrorists and rogue states can lay their hands
   on weapons of mass destruction has changed the calculus of war.

Usage of this late-twentieth-century cliché that does not come from military writing often has some reference to military matters, suggesting that it may be military jargon that has crept into the mainstream. The cachet of the cliché is surely the word *calculus*, which for most people conjures the rarefied branch of mathematics that ordinary mortals never venture into. This provides users of the cliché a license to convey a suggestion of complexity or importance without the responsibility of supplying the details of it.

change the political landscape   1

An unexpectedly nasty recession or other terrorist strikes in the United
    States could change the political landscape once again.
Demographic shifts also have changed the political landscape in Florida.
Brown's argument is that Labour has failed to change the political landscape
    in any real sense.

Journalists keep this cliché alive since its very presence suggests that there is something newsworthy to write about. It is probably natural for the political landscape to change constantly without the aid of various agents and agencies; this cliché is typically used to nominate a cause for some momentous change. Part of its popularity may also stem from the vague denotation of *political landscape*. The phrase is regularly combined with the noun cliché *seismic shift*: *The divisive vote on the proposed new abortion legislation has resulted in a seismic shift in the political landscape in Galway.* An online query returns nearly 900,000 hits on this rather dire pairing.

come down the pike   2

See *down the pike* in the adverbial clichés.

come out of the woodwork   3

   ☛ ***appear suddenly and unexpectedly, especially in abundance***
Scum like this always seem to come out of the woodwork when big matches
    come along. They have nothing to do with football and will crawl back into
    the ground until the next occasion.
Why aren't people coming out of the woodwork to say "I want this job, I have
    a chance to shape the future face of US intelligence?"
In previous years people have come out of the woodwork to take part. It is the
    fourth year and we are hoping for a party event.

This cliché, with its image of infestation, works best to characterize something abundant and unwelcome, as in the first example. It's less effective when it simply means "appear unexpectedly" or "appear in large numbers" of something that may actually be welcome.

cost an arm and a leg   1

☞ *be very expensive*

Banter is banal, or embarrassing, and the club a filthy basement where drinks cost an arm and a leg.

We wanted to make a sturdy commercial mower that can take the abuse, but that bridges the gap and doesn't cost an arm and a leg.

A complete Pro Tools system costs one arm, one leg, and some of the more tender bits of your anatomy.

The import of this cliché is immediately graspable by its vivid image, which perhaps accounts for the popularity it achieved in the early twentieth century. Today it is nearly impossible to bring to life, even when writers resort to invented variations, as in the third example above. It adds nothing to the idea of "be very expensive" other than an air of informality.

count on (the fingers of) one hand   3

In almost twelve years in business, I can count on one hand the number of times we had to fix something.

The band has only performed live enough times to count on the fingers of one hand.

And I can count on the fingers of one hand the number of days in my career when I didn't want to come to work.

This long-winded cliché attempts to dramatize the unexpected or undesirable smallness of a number. Could you count on the fingers of one hand the instances you have found where it is actually preferable to, for example, "three"? It is highly variable in form and writers who play with the wording may or may not succeed in bringing the cliché to life: *You could count them on one hand with fingers to spare.*

cross the finish line   4

The reasons some students do not cross the degree finish line before they turn twenty-two are many, not the least of which are financial.

As you progress through the cups you'll notice that the CPU pulls less and less punches when it's doing its best to keep you from crossing that finish line.

I do think that if George Bush makes no stumbles he's going to cross the finish line.

The majority of instances of this frequent phrase are literal and serve as an alternative to the more prosaic *finish the race.* It occasionally dips into cliché when there is an attempt to falsely characterize something as a competition or when there is no obvious advantage over a simple verb like *win*.

cross swords (with sb)   2
☞ *have an argument or dispute*

There is no sign so far that the ECB is ready to relent as Frankfurt and Madrid cross swords in an escalating test of will.

An Internet company devoted to aiding the artificial insemination of lesbian and single mothers has crossed swords with one of the country's leading maternity hospitals.

Japanese side Urawa Red Diamonds and Sepahan of Iran advanced to the final of the AFC Champions League, with the two sides set to cross swords in November.

The image on which this cliché is based—that of a duel between individuals—makes it usually unobjectionable in reference to disputes between individuals who are rivals. It is now stretched to many other uses, such as disputes between countries or institutions, where it is unwieldy. In sports writing it has taken on a new and unnecessary meaning, "play," as in the third example above.

cry over spilled/spilt milk   1
☞ *lament what cannot be undone*

There's no use crying over spilt milk, but the fact is that President Roh Moo-hyun's prolonged vacillation over the matter did serious damage to the country's relationship with its most important friend.

As we live in a rapidly changing world, there are times when we feel like crying over spilt milk and catching a straw as though we were drowning.

This is like saying that, since there is no point in crying over spilt milk, there is no point in taking steps to avoid spilling milk.

The canonical form of this cliché is shown in the first example above, which also illustrates a good reason for not using it: when you proceed to do the very thing the cliché figuratively warns against. The third example recasts the cliché helpfully by using it, in fuller context not shown, to criticize a failure of government to implement measures that would almost surely prevent future casualties.

cut both ways   3

Like all the best jokes this one cuts both ways, and Shonibare manages to make it continually productive.

Aid dependence, he argues, cuts both ways: Africa depends on the aid
  agencies and the agencies substantially depend on Africa.
If lawmakers in Congress decide to cut back on funding for affordable housing
  the District could lose as many as 6,000 Section 8 affordable housing
  vouchers by 2014. If this scenario were to unfold, the District's strategy
  for ending homelessness in ten years would be a wash. The double-edged
  sword of coordination cuts both ways.

This cliché can be used as a succinct way of conveying the idea of inseparable advantage and disadvantage, as in the first two examples, where two distinct parties or outcomes are either stated or obvious from context. The cliché gets lost in more complex situations involving multiple players (third example) and in any case, it need never be associated with the similar *double-edged sword*.

cut a _____ figure   4

The rest of the band cut equally stylish figures, with everyone lit up by eerie
  red floodlights.
Tall, blond, and muscular, he cut a dashing figure and was nicknamed "Doc"
  because of his striking resemblance to the pulp magazine hero Doc Savage.
A Commons committee has been forced to cut a pathetic figure, asking
  permission of Scotland Yard as to whom it can interview and when.

Many different adjectives fit into the variable slot in this cliché, all of which are probably inspired by the original and still most frequent (and groan-inducing) *cut a dashing figure*, a phrase that takes up considerable bandwidth for communicating little more than "look attractive."

damn sb/sth with faint praise   3

At the risk of damning with faint praise, his acting is the best thing about this film.
If I can say "plain good" without insinuating damnation by faint praise, I'll
  do that.
She may look luscious, but Liz Hurley's devil in a red dress is damned with
  faint praise by Wendy Ide, who takes a dim view of dodgy remakes.

This cliché gets good marks far communicating a complex idea in few sylla-bles and it might not have fallen over the cliché cliff at all if writers used it only when it is appropriate: for example, when some muted form of praise is actually present, and when there is an implication that the limited amount of praise conceals or stands in place of criticism that would be forthcoming otherwise. Many examples of usage reveal this not to be the case.

darken sb's door   1

☞ *appear when unwelcome*

The contract manufacturer is enforcing a series of rigid procedures to ensure the epidemic doesn't darken the door of its 150-acre factory complex in Zhuhai.

Some of the best and most loyal supporters of county teams never darken the door of a clubhouse.

I was convinced that Christianity was just a bunch of simplistic rules and empty rituals, and left the Catholic Church planning on never darkening its door again.

The purest form of this cliché is an imperative *"Never darken my door again!"* with the meaning "stay away permanently." Writers are apparently so taken with the image that the meaning has been stretched to uses without a negative. The worst abuses are cases where no meaning stronger than "visit," "go to," or "enter" is required by the context.

---

deal a _____ blow   5

Investors, hoping for a share in future profits, have been dealt a serious blow.

The economic security, which we had come to take for granted, was dealt a major blow with the outbreak of foot-and-mouth disease and the demise of the IT sector.

Microsoft has dealt a fatal blow to an ambitious effort by Internet engineers to create a technical standard for curbing junk e-mail.

The stupefying frequency of this cliché in journalism can give the impression that reporters start their day by surveying the world for parties whose setbacks can be characterized as being of the blow type. The standard for inclusion is clearly very low, because any sudden disadvantage for anyone is reported in news today as the dealing of a blow. Such blows, except in writing about boxing, are never literal ones. The cliché may once have had some force but is now simply a lifeless form of words. The standard varieties of dealt blows are *severe, serious, major, mortal*, and *devastating*. The cliché is far more frequent in news and soft journalism than in other genres.

---

defy description   2

Flying ninjas, building-shattering punches, gender-swapping super-villains—they're all here, and they utterly defy description.

She has a bosom that defies description.

The music most recalls James Turrell's explorations of light that, in their experiential nature, ultimately defy description and need to be witnessed to understand their bewitching substance.

It's a hard choice to decide which is the more unfortunate experience: coming across this cliché, or being subjected to the attempt at description that the user of it might put in its place. Often *defy description* is merely a signal that the writer has run out of original words; at other times it's a preface to or summation of a description that perhaps should have been forgone. It is always possible to make the cliché worse by preceding it with a submodifier such as *literally, utterly, nearly, almost*, or *really*.

deliver the goods   5

Miner's band Art Rock Circus delivers the goods with newcomers Nolan Stolz on drums and Ken Jaquess on bass.

Both Howard and Reith, well aware of what is at stake, have been at pains to demonstrate that they can deliver the goods.

I think that the union movement's future is in its own hands and I'm talking as a trade unionist. We have to deliver the goods and we have to turn things around.

Deliver the goods is a frequent cliché with very general meaning. When it is used appropriately it's an efficient way of expressing the idea "provide what is promised or expected." Its abuse arises from application in cases where it has no reference to rightful expectation and simply means "do a good thing" or "create a favorable impression," which is the case in the examples above.

do everything (with)in your power   5

If we give you a task, you will do everything within your power to do it.

We will do everything within our power to co-operate with the expedition and efficient hearing of that.

I do everything in my power to warn people against faith itself, not just against so-called extremist faith.

It's hard to account for the popularity of this expression, which is used mainly to intensify the idea of "do everything possible." Since no one is equipped to do things beyond their powers the cliché is blustery from the moment it is released. It may occasionally be used as a kind of hedge, suggesting that the writer or speaker is already aware that his actions will be ineffectual, but its extreme frequency makes it nearly impossible for audiences to accurately gauge any intended nuances of meaning.

don the mantle/role   2

When television's most popular science teacher, Bill Nye, puts on his white lab coat, he is donning the mantle of science, not just protecting his clothes.

*General Musharraf, donning the American mantle and pursuing a policy of
military aggrandizement as America's vassal, is not endearing himself
with his own irate people.*

*Donning the role of the traditional match-makers were people from
TeluguMatrimony.com, assisting them with minute details.*

Both forms of this cliché are unusually prevalent in Indian English and are
also used widely elsewhere. The meaning has become somewhat generalized
and the cliché now serves mainly as a faux-elegant variation on a number of
other more literal phrases such as *act as, assume the role*, and *take responsibility*.

double down (on sth)   3

☛ **engage in risky behavior when there is already danger present**

*You could sit around and focus on how your job feels like it has hit a dead end
or you could look at this as an amazing time to double down at your
company.*

*Mr. McCain, a member of the Senate Armed Services Committee, is
effectively doubling down his bet on the war, figuring that embracing a
strong resolution in Iraq will give him an effective campaign cudgel.*

*In July, AstraZeneca doubles down on its earlier layoff announcement and
says that 7,600 jobs will disappear.*

*As scary as the statistics might be at face value, the more important
takeaway from this for me is that as my wife moves out, I need to double
down on building a solid and meaningful social network.*

This phrasal verb gets a lot of its cliché cachet by being relatively new and
unsettled in meaning. There was a surge in usage beginning in 2012 and
instances of the verb in context do not clearly reveal that people who use it
share an understanding of what it means. The gloss given above is the meaning known to be a figurative extension of the verb's original literal meaning,
in the game of blackjack. Other meanings may emerge as a result of the zeal
with which speakers embrace novelty.

get/have one's ducks in a row   1

*As long as you get your ducks in a row, offering employees the chance to
telework is usually a great idea.*

*We wanted to have our ducks in a row before we started publicizing the
project so we only started calling attention to it recently.*

*"This is the time to get your ducks in a row in Iowa," said John Feehery,
a Republican strategist.*

This cliché, American in origin, is now distributed internationally in English and found relatively evenly across various genres of text but most commonly in speech, where it is a harmless marker of informality. It calls undue attention to itself in writing, especially where its reference is vague, as in the first example above.

echo the sentiment   4

☞ *express the same feeling or opinion*

The professor also echoed the sentiments of congressional critics and others, who say the US military is too small.

The editorial echoes the sentiments of many Americans and speaks volumes about our battered democratic system of government.

Darling-Hammond echoes this sentiment when she advises teachers to "make sure the emphasis is on powerful learning, not rote memorization."

The extreme frequency, and attendant tiredness, of *echo the sentiment* arises from its work in sentences when there is actually no genuine sentiment involved—just a view or an opinion. It probably gets across the idea of "express the same opinion" in fewer syllables than some alternative expressions but isn't a very good choice to express this idea, since so many tens of thousands of writers have already tried that.

explore/pursue/exhaust every avenue   1

☞ *try all possible means*

We're exploring every avenue and seeking advice at the highest level.

Some of the villagers however were determined to exhaust every possible avenue and make a concerted effort to save the baby.

Things are looking a little less hopeful, but we are still pursuing every single avenue, and will continue to do so.

The most frequent form of this expression is *explore every avenue*. It has the virtue of making sense compositionally: avenues can in fact be explored. They can't, however, be pursued or exhausted in a way that will bring desirable results. The use of the expression in any form is mainly a way for writers to characterize zeal or determination. In the first and second examples above the cliché is curiously juxtaposed with another, leading the reader to hope that more effort is put into the activity being reported on than in the reporting of it.

exhibit a tendency (to do something)   1

He exhibits a tendency to personify the culture in his lyrics, usually as beaten, exploited, and exhausted.

We exhibit a tendency to view members of outgroups as being more similar to
   one another than members of ingroups.

This cliché has been parachuted into mainstream usage from scientific literature but it need not ever have been provided with the transport, especially when it serves no purpose, as in the examples above. Both sentences would be more concise and direct without the cliché: the first by elimination altogether, making *personify* the main verb, and the second by using *tend* as the verb. In ordinary writing this phrase is rarely needed if tendencies of various kinds are not the main subject.

face the music   3
☛ *accept or deal with inevitable consequences*
Someone must face the music for such a brazen misuse of scarce public resources.
Eventually, the company had to face the music and today the FTC announced
   that it had settled with DirectRevenue.
This morning, the world's biggest military computer hacker Gary McKinnon
   is facing the music in court.

Face the music has the benefit of concisely telescoping the more literal versions of its meaning, such as "take responsibility for" or "deal with the consequences." When it characterizes a situation that is expanded in surrounding text, as in the second and third examples above, it doesn't fully merit its appearance.

face a race against time   1
☛ See *a race against time* in the noun clichés.

feel passionate about sth   2
Display tenacity even if the going gets tough. Feel positively passionate about
   change. Remember—it is okay to have fun whilst you are working.
My friends and I felt passionate about trying to open up football to Asian
   and ethnic minority kids.
I wanted to do this job because I feel passionate about patient safety and
   I feel passionate about improving patient care.

The first example above, taken from a list of things you can do in order not to be miserable in your work, illustrates the most likely point of entry of this expression into clichédom—namely, the kind of self-help pep talk that litters American English. For many writers and speakers, *feel passionate* now comes to mind in place of the somewhat reduced meaning that it carries—"be enthusiastic." This cliché is effectively a variant of the adjectival cliché *passionate about*, which normally follows the verb *be*.

fight tooth and nail   4

German unions fight tooth and nail to win wage concessions that hurt
  German competitiveness.
Are they prepared to fight tooth and nail to keep off the bottom of the league
  table or will they wilt under the pressure?

The usual way to informally intensify "fight" or "struggle" is with this cliché, which contributes to its frequency and its diminishing efficacy. The expression is nearly five hundred years old in English, giving it excellent credentials for retirement.

forge a bond   2

Some of the songs don't work, but the ones that do forge a bond between
  filmmaker and audience.
The backups have forged a bond with the rest of the team that should be kept
  intact.
So many of the neighbors were toughened by the experience and forged tight
  bonds.

Writers are fond of using *forge* when the context doesn't suggest that anything stronger than *form* is required, perhaps because *forge*, by virtue of its connection with metallurgy, suggests something more effortful and enduring. Need so many things be forged in a world where we know that not much endures? Other goals of forging that can take on a somewhat hackneyed feel are *links*, *alliances*, and *relationships*.

fuel speculation   3

Rising health costs and an aging population across the globe have fueled
  speculation that many more people will be looking for an early way out in
  the years ahead.
One of the things that has fueled speculation in the press, by finding this
  much water, is it makes Mars a potential habitat for life in the future.
The move is fueling speculation that a year-and-a-half rate-rise campaign
  could be winding down.

Journalists use this cliché to accomplish the very thing that the cliché describes: to increase or incite speculation, which they then often go on to engage in. The cliché is in effect a self-generating news hook and is nearly five times more frequent in news journalism than in any other genre. A related noun cliché is *fevered speculation*, q.v.

fully intend   3

Sandusky said, "We fully intend to put together the best defense we can. We're going to stay the course and fight for four quarters."

If the White Sox fully intend to make him their shortstop next season, I will begin a countdown until Willie Harris moves Valentin back to short.

When confronted about the trips, a confident Martin flatly stated, "I fully intend to take holidays with my friends."

Fully collocates more frequently with many verbs than *intend* but they are all verbs that easily admit of degrees of achievement short of "full"—such as *understand, support*, and *develop. Fully intend* achieves its irritating cliché status by typically being part of a blustery utterance in which the speaker is trying to give an assurance that is subject to doubt.

gain traction   4

Hammered by the media and snubbed by hardcore gamers, the device struggled to gain traction.

His product has gained national traction for one reason, he says. "We look at our market as mainstream but very niche specific."

If we continue to support Karimov, Islamist hatred of the United States will gain traction with some of the liberals.

This cliché is most frequent in business and technology writing; it has the ring of jargon there and elsewhere. It's more efficient than *attain influence* or *win acceptance*, which are its nearest more literal equivalents. When the meaning is simply "increase" (third example), *gain traction* offers no enhancement.

get down and dirty   2

They plan to get down and dirty and Harry's dosed up on Viagra in anticipation.

It's a US election year, and things are getting down and dirty.

Clint Eastwood put on his poncho and got down and dirty with director Sergio Leone in several Westerns.

Like its relative in the adjectival clichés (*down and dirty*), *get down and dirty* is more than the sum of its parts but not precise in meaning, leaving open the possibility that readers of it may be confused. The first example above illustrates a common and unambiguous meaning; the other two examples leave the reader wondering what exactly the cliché means.

gild the lily   1

From the beginning of his career, Karajan liked to conduct this music, but sometimes he interfered with its natural flow too much, gilding the lily, as it were.

Tucked right in the middle of the State of the Union Address in an attempt to gild the lily of his case for war to the American public and the rest of the world.

Yes, the producers gild the lily when they claim to be "now, for the first time" revealing things about the five leaders being examined.

This cliché is derived from a misquotation of Shakespeare but it has gained considerable currency nonetheless because it can efficiently convey the idea of a needless attempt to improve something that is already fine or perfect (first example). Lately it is detached from its moorings to mean "go a step too far," where it is not effective.

give sb/sth a wide berth   3

Unless you want to eat tepid, bland food, and be treated like an inconvenience by some of the worst staff in London, give this place a wide berth.

It was only a matter of time before pitchers started giving Giambi a wider berth.

If writers use this cliché out of a sense that they should avoid *avoid sb/sth like the plague* perhaps they should not be discouraged. This phrase, however, is likely to arrive almost as stillborn. It can still strike home when applied to something large, mobile, and unstoppable, like the ships that it refers to literally, but it is incongruously applied to places and to people, who do not generally require berths.

go the extra mile   4

But Frist went that extra mile, repeatedly lying through his teeth not to cover up a crime—but to make himself look better.

We went the extra mile knowing our clientele and knowing what we wanted to achieve in the long run.

It was Ross who first realised that there were plenty of courier, transport, and haulage firms around, but few were willing to go the extra mile.

This twentieth-century cliché is an athletic metaphor used far more often of ordinary people and companies than of athletes. It is now used with increasing vagueness to indicate an unusual or unexpected effort to excel, with occasional ironic use (see the first example). About 10 percent of instances are *willing/willingness to go the extra mile*, giving that phrase standalone cliché credentials.

go from strength to strength   4
☞ *develop with increasing success*
I am looking forward to helping the group go from strength to strength.
*I think it is fair to say that any lesser man would have been broken by what
    happened in 1998 but David Beckham has gone from strength to strength.*
*Since outgrowing their first tea room last year, Sue and Peter Chilvers'
    business has gone from strength to strength.*

Sportswriters alone might be credited with robbing this phrase of any possible impact by the frequency with which they employ it; but *go from strength to strength* is also surprisingly common in news stories, rarely meaning anything more than "improve" or "grow."

go through the motions   5
☞ *do something insincerely, halfheartedly, or routinely*
*Maybe the FBI, grappling with more pressing law-enforcement concerns,
    merely went through the motions in trying to check out this seemingly
    outlandish conspiracy.*
*It's hard to tell where my teammates are. Sometimes I feel some of them are
    going through the motions, but it's not the whole team.*
*We are shown that Karen and Harry are still together, but things are now
    cool between them, as if they were going through the motions.*

The broad nuances of meaning in this cliché make its application problematic since it is not always clear in what sense the depicted activity is perceived to deviate from what is expected or desirable. It works economically when all possible meanings seem to apply (first example) but is perhaps least effective where it is quite frequent, in writing about sports and the arts, where *the motions* is vague and not often supported by surrounding context.

go (the) whole hog   3
☞ *do something completely, thoroughly, or expensively*
*Money would help because the things I really want are expensive and if
    I can't go the whole hog I don't want to do it at all.*

*If the BBC is engaging in market economics, then they should go the whole
    hog and live by the market alone.*

This cliché is rarely out of place in informal conversation because it characterizes succinctly a thorough way of doing something. In writing, and particularly when it is followed by *and*, it is used for the same kind of characterization
that is often not necessary because a succeeding clause expands on whatever idea has been introduced. It is approximately equivalent to the more
frequent *pull out all the stops*.

go the whole nine yards   1
☛ See *the whole nine yards* in the noun clichés.

grind to a halt   5
*If the Defense Department must seek court approval every time it wants to
    search its own files electronically, national security protection will grind
    to a halt.*
*As the coach was grinding to a halt, Adam opened the coach door and jumped
    the short distance to the ground.*

Despite its extreme frequency, this cliché can be effective in supplying an
image for a large, unwieldy, and multifaceted enterprise ceasing to operate,
as in the first example. It is pointless in the second example, from online
fiction, describing a simple stopping operation.

grip the country/nation   3
The administration deliberately fostered the fear that has gripped the country.
*The sense of a national crisis that gripped the nation at the time was
    reflected in a period of unprecedented political instability.*
*The natural surroundings of the airfield, draped in early morning mist, look
    too lush and fecund for a country gripped by a grim war.*

This cliché is a journalistic special that is so closely associated with news
reporting that it can pass as parody when used in any other genre. What
grips a country most? *Crisis, violence,* and *fear* are major contenders. About
10 percent of usage is with a participial phrase, like the third example.

hang in the balance   4
☛ *be in a precarious state*
*It is not merely a question of deterring other abusive dictators; the viability
    of a future democratic Iraq also hangs in the balance.*

What hangs in the balance is the future of the human race, and US voters
have a choice about what that future will be.
So with the future of the franchise (as well as the prime years of Bryant's
career) hanging in the balance, the Lakers turned to Phil Jackson.

This idiomatic cliché dramatizes the possibility of a perilous outcome and so is perhaps an understandable staple of journalism. *Future, lives,* and *fate* most typically supply the subject. A shorter and more straightforward way of expressing the same idea is the predicate *be at stake. Hang in the balance* often supplies the elegant variation when that one has already been used as a lead-in.

have another think/thing coming   1

But any member of the proletariat who thinks that, in the natural course of
events he will become a capitalist, has another think coming.
If Cllr Kirby and his group think they can hijack the memories of those who
died, he has another think coming.
If you're expecting to get a round of applause the next time you appear at The
Valley, you've got another thing coming.
Deputy O'Shea said the minister has another thing coming if she believes
that he is going to be fobbed off with that type of reply.

The original British form of this cliché is *have another think coming.* In American English it is usually *have another thing coming,* which liberates the phrase from being bound to another sentence containing *think,* but not from the clutches of clichédom. The phrase is often a vehement way of pointing out that someone is mistaken in his or her perception or interpretation of something.

have the bandwidth (to do sth)   1

As head of the country's largest cable operator, he certainly has the
bandwidth to strike terror in the L.A. establishment.
With Sarbox nobody has any bandwidth to think about innovative ideas or
new models.
I think you can expect some improvement here with the Bank of America
coming in. They're much better capitalized. They really have the
bandwidth to help people out.

This twenty-first-century phrase is at present perhaps not so much a cliché as a possible cliché in the making. The first example is a clever double entendre that takes advantage of a relatively new idiom while not abandoning the literal sense. The jargony tendency of the other examples suggests that *bandwidth* may simply be on its way to becoming a buzzword variation of "capacity."

bang/beat/hit your head against a/the (brick) wall　4
☞ *engage continuously in an activity that brings no reward or result*

It's hard to keep banging your head against the wall, trying to bring violence down in the community, when a real driver for the violence is economic deprivation and a lack of hope.

Aren't we really just banging our head against the wall here, trying to impose our sensibility and our institutions on Iran?

The intention behind this cliché is usually to show that effort is being wasted, resulting in frustration. Its widespread use detracts from the force of the image, and in many contexts the audience would benefit more from a clearer exposition of what effort is being expended and why it is ineffective.

hear a pin drop　2
Talk about hearing a pin drop—and not from the kind of interest one hopes for. The film was a bomb. Not a single question followed. The moderator just had to up and leave.

While a speaker laid out research evidence of the link between heart disease, stress, and long hours, you could have heard a pin drop.

One could hear a pin drop at the end of Terry Fellon's rendition of Michel Schonberg's "Bring Him Home" and the evening's penultimate item was sung superbly well by the chorus.

This nineteenth-century cliché doesn't seem to lose popularity by never being literally true. It is used to characterize silence that results from rapt attention or engagement. In many contexts, it would benefit readers to learn more about the nature of the attraction that produced such attention rather than simply being told that it left everyone speechless.

hit a/the wall　5
☞ *encounter an (insurmountable) obstacle*

If his body does hit the wall, it likely will be for good at his age.

Nobody's hit a wall like the Nuggets. Denver had just 25 points in the first half last night.

Early in the interview, Russert asks Mehlman whether the president has hit a wall with his domestic agenda.

This cliché is much more compact than its literal expansion but its high frequency mitigates against effectiveness. Sportswriters are particularly fond of it and seem to find walls standing wherever athletes, teams, and enterprises are in motion.

let/allow your imagination (to) run riot   1

He loved to strike poses, to attitudinize, and in these last years allowed his imagination to run riot.

For the primary classes, there was no fixed theme; the children were asked to let their imaginations run riot.

Director Gary Burns lets his imagination run riot, creating a visually striking piece that uses stylistic tricks like jump cuts, split screens, speeded-up film, and colour manipulation.

While perhaps preferable to its literal equivalent, *be very creative*, this cliché is an unfortunate fixture and an unimaginative, lengthy depiction of something that people do all the time. The communication of an imaginative or creative process or achievement is surely more effective when expressed in a way that is itself imaginative and creative.

impact negatively (on sb/sth)   2

Mr. Cansdell said the dangerous conditions were impacting negatively on local businesses and had already cost jobs.

The country's land reform policy also impacted negatively on the group's businesses.

Market manipulation through the distorting of prices clearly impacts negatively on the efficient functioning of capital markets.

Leaving aside the unfortunate substitution of *impact* for *affect*— it's too late to do anything about that—this grating cliché firmly establishes its user as a master of jargon in preference to clear communication. Most sentences with *impact negatively* can be written more clearly with *hurt*. The cliché sprang to life fully formed in the mid-1970s and has been ascendant since then. It is most frequent in news journalism and business writing. The earliest citations are spread across sociology, business, and finance writing.

look/gaze into the crystal ball   1

☞   *make or attempt a prediction*

Several expeditions are gazing into the crystal ball and trying to decide which is the magic date to try for the summit.

After looking into their crystal balls, executives from companies including
   Intel, IBM, Compaq, and EMC could only point to a murky future.

Crystal ball without either of the above-noted verbs preceding it is a convenient token for characterizing a way of predicting future events. It is widely understood and the plodding addition of a verb merely clips the wings of the metaphor.

---

jump the shark   2
☞ *act in a way that signals an imminent decline in quality, popularity, or success*

Accusing Paul Krugman of condoning anti-Semitism is still quite enough for
   me to think that Luskin has jumped the shark and needs to be put out to
   pasture.
The Red Sox jumped the shark when they sold Babe Ruth.
He jumped the shark last month, suggesting he might defy the State
   Supreme Court.

The complex idea behind this late-twentieth-century cliché arose from the popular TV sitcom *Happy Days*, in which a character jumps over a shark while waterskiing. This is thought to have marked the beginning of the show's creative decline. The cliché is used today in much broader and occasionally unclear contexts; the general idea, which the gloss above tries to capture, is to characterize a creative or strategic failure.

---

keep your head above water   3
☞ *avoid bankruptcy or financial ruin*

Graziers are making loan payments and fighting tax problems, while other
   farmers are trying to keep their heads above water.
Businesses were struggling to keep their heads above water due to a
   30 percent drop off in trade.
I'm seventy years of age, unable to live on Social Security, and still have to
   work to keep my head above water.

This cliché is perhaps the most frequent representative of a set of watery expressions that represent a metaphor of debt and financial obligations: *a sea of debt, drowning in debt, about to go under,* and the like. The images are apt but centuries old and the situations that evoke these expressions, while suitable targets for sympathy, are not likely to get much of it when they are described with such worn-down phrases.

---

know for a fact   5

I know for a fact that most blokes don't check themselves—they think "it's
never going to happen to me."
Deep in his heart he knew for a fact that fighting them all was out of the
question.
I know for a fact that pretty much no one in Cambridge reads my weblog, due
to my Wondrous Computer Powers.

The popularity of this cliché clearly does not rely on its economy of expression. It is used overwhelmingly in the present tense, nearly ten times more frequently than in other tenses, suggesting that its main purpose is to bolster an argument in progress. It has an element of redeeming value only when accompanied by evidence supporting the assertion of fact, as in the third example.

know full well   5

We will attempt here to develop a franchise-ready model for an organic grain
farm, knowing full well that some vital elements may be quite difficult to
transplant.
Why do you insist on drinking lattes and eating ice cream when you know full
well that this is going to cause headaches and mild nausea?

Know full well adds no additional meaning to *know* but is often used to add emphasis, in the form of two extra accented syllables, to the verb. It often imparts a scolding tone, as in the second example. It differs from *know for a fact* in being used more often of subjective knowledge.

lay down the law   3
   ☞ *strictly enforce a rule or law*

He is not a writer who lays down the law; he only seeks to convey the
sensations that have given him pleasure.
According to Juliet Price, it is much easier to lay down the law if you have a
carefully worded policy.
If I started laying down the law with my wife, I'd be in big trouble.

The alliteration in this cliché makes it a popular, and not necessarily undesirable, choice in contexts where the meaning is essentially "enforce a rule." It misses its mark mainly when it is not clear from the context what rule, law, or norm may be referred to, as in the first example.

leave sth/much/a lot to be desired   3
☞ *be inadequate*

When it comes to switchgrass production, a natural means of soil conservation, current law leaves much to be desired.
She claimed that manpower levels in suburbs left a lot to be desired.
Aristotle's criteria of causal relatedness leave much to be desired.

The popularity of this cliché is anomalous since it is longer and more awkward than any more literal alternative and it adds no value to a sentence that is not contained in the word *inadequate*. Like many very old clichés, it rests on dusty laurels that it acquired in its earliest usages, when it must have sounded strikingly original.

leave no stone unturned   3
☞ *search or seek diligently and thoroughly*

In their search for new and more environmentally friendly herbicides, scientists are leaving no proverbial stone unturned.
They left no stone unturned in their efforts to care and protect their environment.

Like other clichés that use a particular metonymic image to convey the idea of an activity, this one is long-enduring and popular. It fails when it is pushed beyond the idea of searching and seeking and is only meant to convey the idea of "being thorough," as in the second example.

leave an aching/empty/huge void   1

Her leaving has left a huge aching void in the lives of her family, friends, neighbors, and former colleagues.
Now we know he's not coming back and it leaves an empty void.
Clearly, Frank will be missed. His passing leaves a huge void.

Words rarely suffice to adequately express the experience of bereavement, but of all words, those strung together into clichés express it worst of all. Such expressions from the bereaved may be excused as those in mourning should not be called upon to be articulate in their grief, but those reporting or summarizing the feelings of others would do better to give some thought to making their expressions more meaningful.

lull sb/be lulled into a false sense of security   2

Breaches of clear disciplinary rules are waived with such regularity that an employee is lulled into a false sense of security.

The music almost lulls you into a false sense of security over the first
  eight tracks of the CD because the final will really catch you off
  guard.

This cliché, frequent in all genres of writing, including law, is not out of place when it describes the common experience of believing something to be true that is not, through self-deception or deception by others, as in the first example above. In the second example, it seems a stretch to think that one's security could be seriously influenced by music and the reader would be served better by a clearer description of the music's effects.

make political capital   1

The Tories manifestly failed to make political capital out of the war, choosing
  instead to play cheerleader. Now that it's all over, they are back to simply
  being unelectable.
This is an idiotic charge by a communist newspaper that is obviously making
  great political capital, if you will, out of this tragedy.
Anyone who does not acknowledge that either has no idea of the facts or just
  wants to make cheap political capital.

This phrase is literal and apt when it depicts a situation in which something like capital—a commodity with storable value—is gained, as in the first example. Journalists have converted it to a catchphrase that means little more than "benefit."

move the needle   1
  ☛ *bring about a detectable change or improvement*
They're in it for the juice—the rush of energy they get when one of their blog
  items moves the needle of public awareness.
The TV ad, airing in two markets starting in June and going national next
  year if it moves the sales needle, shows tweens playing with and
  demonstrating the three-flavored sucker.
VW holds just 4 percent of the US auto market, and Apple sells just
  3 percent of personal computers. So, can a great ad campaign move the
  needle?

This newish cliché is used overwhelmingly in business writing, where it is likely to fall on ears inured to it. Those who are moved to use it will aid their readers by at least specifying which needle is the target of their interest, as the first two examples do.

enter a new era 2

herald a new era 1

Apple's iPod can be used to copy software from display computers at stores like CompUSA. Will it herald a new era of virtual shoplifting?

Just when everyone thought New Zealand politics had entered a new era, the National Party has just announced that they will reverse the new ACC bill.

The same goes for Bush: he had to win twice in order for liberals to perceive that we are entering a new era.

The use of software to help protect users from making lethal errors heralds a new era of devices with built-in safety systems that extend beyond switch guards and alarms.

These two clichés have slightly different meanings but their frequent infelicitous uses arise from the same motive: to suggest revolutionary change when none is actually present. In ordinary usage *era* has strayed considerably from its core meaning—a long and distinct period of history—but no reader or listener is helped by the designation of something as a new era when it may well be retrospectively indistinct after only a short time. See also *dawn of a new era* and *end of an era* in the noun clichés.

play fast and loose 1

One director may view the script as being open ended and therefore play it fast and loose. Others are strict and refuse to veer from the written word.

Microsoft plays fast and loose with HTML and it doesn't properly support XML.

To presume that the picture might embody Christ's eternal presence, however, allows the inference that a man-made representation of Christ might incarnate his presence, and now we are playing rather fast and loose with the Second Commandment.

This predicate accounts for about two-thirds of the use of the modifier "fast and loose," which without the verb is partially compositional. In writing about the arts, *playing fast and loose* seems to partake of the notion of artistic license and is often regarded appreciatively. Not so in most other contexts, making the cliché possibly troublesome to interpret. The core meaning is "take liberties" or "act irresponsibly."

play the race card 3

Today it is the race relations lobby and particularly New Labour that finds it difficult to avoid the temptation of playing the race card. By treating routine conflict as racially motivated, they are racialising everyday life.

Playing the race card has become legitimate in Australian politics as a
strategy of appeasing the racist One Nation Party, and competing for
votes in the next federal election.

Racial tension in our society seems to be growing, not decreasing, despite
almost four decades of affirmative action. One reason is that some people
are playing the race card in order to exploit racial division.

There is perhaps an underlying cliché here, *play the* _____ *card*, where
the blank is filled by a trope that is often beset by strife and controversy:
gender, nationalist, victim are examples. The *race card* is ten times more frequent than even the *trump card*. The expression is certainly more economical than "use the matter of race to gain unfair advantage" and if that is the
only thing it meant the expression would not be a cliché. The first example
helpfully contextualizes the expression. The other examples show the loose
application of the phrase, sometimes to mean no more than "mention race,"
that contribute to its being perceived as a cliché.

moan/groan with pleasure   2
He stopped for a moment, while I moaned with pleasure, my eyes closed.

The brevity of the illustration and the lack of others to support it is testament
to the difficulty of finding examples of this dreadful cliché that conform to standards of decency. Nearly all examples of moaning and groaning with pleasure
are from romantic and "adult" fiction, both of which have fairly low standards
of editorial quality. Those who should avoid using the cliché probably cannot
be persuaded. Those who would avoid exposure to it will know what to do.

point the finger (of blame)   5
☞ *accuse someone of something; apportion blame*
We are not pointing the finger of blame for a growing culture of caution at
any one group, but individuals and organisations have an important role
in making play exciting.

They point their fingers at the local midwives—the Dais who are instructed
to ensure that if the newborn is a female, she shouldn't live.

I don't see the world in those black and white terms, so it was really
important that the finger couldn't be pointed at any particular person,
and if so, it would be done with utmost empathy.

The several minor variations of this cliché seem to exist so that speakers will
not have to use *blame* as a verb. Though found preponderantly in news
journalism, finger-pointing is popular across all genres, perhaps because it

provides a milder variation of the strong and irrevocable speech act implied when *blame* is the verb in a sentence. The meaning of *point the finger* is well established and it needn't ever be followed by *of blame*.

pull out all the stops   5

☞ *make a great or extravagant effort; do everything possible*

We are pulling out all the stops to make sure that we can give our members the best practical advice.

Big Cola is pulling out all the stops in a desperate fight to halt state legislatures from enacting tough new nutrition standards for public schools.

Context often spells out more literally the idea that this cliché expresses and that fact, combined with the great frequency of the cliché, renders it ineffective or unnecessary most of the time.

pull the wool over sb's eyes   3

☞ *deceive by subterfuge; hoodwink*

They try to pull the wool over his eyes about the real value of items they want sold.

I always thought we had pulled the wool over the eyes of the committee until I was speaking to a member years later.

I feel like television is trying to pull wool over my eyes, which is both frustrating and dangerous, considering my wool allergy.

This cliché of disputed and speculative origin maintains a connotation of playfulness in many contexts, much like its near synonym *hoodwink*, which does the same job adequately. The third example adds an original note to the cliché that revives it.

push the boundaries   5

The project pushes the boundaries of cinema design and far exceeds a first-time visitor's expectations.

If a woman can conceive naturally when she is this age, how far should other women be assisted in pushing the boundaries of fertility?

Gaytime TV has given her a chance to see how quickly and easily gay and lesbian celebrities can push the boundaries of what's acceptable.

Today there are more recorded instances of boundaries being pushed than there are of boundaries being crossed, set, or defined, thanks to this cliché. In writing about the arts, where boundary-pushing is most frequent, the cliché is usually used appreciatively with the implicit notion that it is part of art's mission to do this. In other genres *push the boundaries* is more likely to mean "exceed a limit," usually with positive or negative and rarely with neutral connotation. A similar pattern applies with *play fast and loose*.

put your (own) personal stamp on something   1
☞ *add a personal dimension to something*
Prominent American country singer Mark Chesnut recorded the number
  originally and Maria Boyle has put a nice personal stamp on it.
He now puts his personal stamp on custom picture framing with a new
  collection on cotton RagMat.
The buyer will have the opportunity to specify how the interior and formal
  gardens are laid out and will be able to put their own, personal stamp on
  the property.

This cliché does not seem out of place in the first example above since personal style and creativity are things we associate with artists. *Personal stamps* cease to be personal, however, when integrated into mass-produced items, as in the second example, and they cease to be stamps when they mean no more than *personalize*, as in the third example.

raise the specter/spectre of _____   4
For Nancy Zirkin, director of public policy for the American Association of
  University Women, the new rules on single-sex education raised the
  specter of racial segregation.
The 2004 election has raised the spectre of the religious right and evangelical
  rednecks in the imagination of Democrats.
In the 1860s, the Fenian rebellion in Ireland and subsequent bombings in
  England raised the spectre of an Irish threat to social order in the colonies.

It's a spooky world indeed in which various abstractions are constantly in the habit of evoking other abstractions of a spectral nature, but that's what happens for readers of a wide swath of genres including news, soft journalism, and scholarly papers in the humanities. *Specter* seems to be shorthand for something between "intangible fear" and "undesirable possibility." It has the benefit of fewer syllables than these but the disadvantage of vagueness.

reach a crescendo   3
The Coffee Week reaches its crescendo on Saturday with a grand event
  organised by Prasad Bidappa Associates at The Club on Mysore Road.
Beginning with a murder plot conceived during a railway journey, the
  suspense of Alfred Hitchcock's Strangers on a Train reaches a crescendo

when a carousel, its operator having been struck by a stray bullet, races
out of control.
Dramatic background music reached a stirring crescendo with the star's
close-up.

This common phrase fell into the teeming vat of cliché in the early twentieth century and still swirls there, rising to the surface frequently where it is plucked by writers who deem a *crescendo* to be a climactic moment, rather than a progression. It is by far most common in the past tense, where it is a favorite with journalists to characterize a climax. Quasiliteral instances of use involving sound or music, as in the third example, are common. Writers drawn to the phrase might consider first whether what they mean is *reach a climax*. It's also possible that the verb *crescendo* would do the job they have in mind or that *begin a crescendo*, a more sensible phrase, will work in the context.

reach a tipping point   1

Forty-eight percent said that security is viewed as essential to business as
opposed to an overhead cost, up from 25 percent in 2004. Perhaps this
new, improved senior management view of security reached a tipping
point in the past year.
I still do think that we will reach a tipping point where this looks very
different than the way it looks today.
We're reaching a tipping point. The higher education establishment will
either open itself back up to the full marketplace of ideas, or it will see its
ivy-covered walls battered down by force, whether class action litigation
or extreme legislation.

Tipping points first came to light in considerable numbers in the 1960s and today people and situations reach them all the time. It's hard to know what happened before this—perhaps there were more straws breaking camels' backs. The phrase is apt when applied to a clear, stark, and probably irreversible change (whether or not it has passed) as in the third example, but it does not rise above cliché to characterize gradual change. I have not deemed *tipping point* alone to be a cliché, but those who wish to can assign it a frequency of "4."

(so) richly deserve   4

The acting on CSI is so uniformly great that time and space would fail me if
I were to try to give everyone the mention they so richly deserve.
The offender got what he richly deserved and it is a shame more people like
that are not liquidated by security guards.

Their defeat was richly deserved, and there is more than enough blame to go around.

The adverb *richly* collocates far more frequently with some form of *deserve* than with any other single word and *so richly deserve(d)*, accounting for about one-third of the instances of this union, is now the unthinking solution for anyone who wants to strengthen the idea of *deserve*. Sincere and ironic uses are both frequent and it is the reader's job to decide which is intended.

rise (phoenix-like) from the ashes   3

☛ *make a surprising or startling comeback*

There I was describing Duncan as a failure in Finland, and thousands of miles away at Everton he rises like a phoenix from the ashes to score against Manchester United.

Plans are afoot for a benefit gig to raise funds so the Mecca Café can make a phoenix-like rise from the ashes.

The image of the phoenix from Greek myth is now used widely and with highly variable forms to characterize the return of anyone or anything after even a minor setback. This overapplication is responsible for the weariness of the expression. The trope is familiar enough that mention of the phoenix or rising from the ashes alone is enough to evoke it. It is a challenge for writers to use it in an original way that justifies its many syllables in place of "comeback."

run the gamut   4

His interests run the gamut: Old Master paintings, vintage posters, nineteenth-century prints, abstracts, bronzes, and stone sculpture from Zimbabwe.

The program includes vocal music by Tschaikowsky, Borodin, Dvorak, Bartok, Smetana, and Arvo Pärt. The selections run the gamut from folk song through musical theatre to grand opera.

Her selection of gowns ran the gamut from a white floor-length jersey cowl neck design with an asymmetrical hem ($342) to a strapless silk yellow hand-beaded gown ($1,283).

This cliché supplies an alternative of possible value to expressions that use the more ordinary noun or verb *range* and is most effective when there is an eclectic or unexpected range to report, as in the first two examples. It has no obvious advantage to characterize an expected range, or only the nominal endpoints of one where the reader has no basis on which to surmise the middle.

run the gauntlet 3

Sports books run the gauntlet from manure-shovelling exposé to cheesy soul-
searcher and everything in between.

Like everyone else, I woke up this morning to the shocking images of semi-
naked and bloody Russian school children running the gauntlet through a
haze of bullets.

This phrase is a failed cliché (first example) for the minority of users who confuse it with *run the gamut* (above). For others (second example), it is a convenient characterization for anyone undertaking tribulations.

---

run riot 4

Damiano Quintieri bagged a brace for the visitors but they never looked like
making a comeback as Plzen ran riot.

The kids are just running riot, and their parents don't know what they are up to.

He manages not to be upstaged by the garish set design, which places rotary
phones alongside palm pilots, and lets colors run riot.

This cliché has slightly different meanings depending on whether its subject is an agent or not, and its effectiveness often varies accordingly. "Kids running riot" concisely evokes a distinct and effective image. Athletes and sports teams constantly run riot (judging by those who write about them) but it is rarely clear from context just what this amounts to. See also *let/ allow your imagination (to) run riot*, above.

---

rush to sb's side 1

Geneva and Annabelle both rushed to his side and interrogated him with
news of the child.

"Miss Westcott, you are unwell?" the Colonel asked as he rushed to her side.

Although Lawford was concerned about Marilyn, he did not rush to her side.

Why is it always someone's side? It may be that the image is intended to depict the rusher aiming at a position from which help can be provided, or it may simply be a precaution against the many collisions that would occur if the many rushers we hear about aimed more centrally. In any case, writers have a number of alternative if prosaic means of expressing the same idea, and this one has lost its poignancy. Online fiction is the fullest repository of this expression.

---

save the world 5

Kicking Bush out of the White House may well be the first step toward
humanizing America and saving the world from destruction.

The aim of the Allied leaders was to save the world from unimaginable tyranny. I believe that, at its best, architecture can save the world.

Talk of saving the world has persisted in speech and writing for centuries and those credited with doing the saving surely deserve recognition, for here we are. This cliché enjoyed two very noticeable spikes in frequency in the twentieth century, coinciding with the last years of the two world wars. These were perhaps the finest hours of the cliché. Convincing uses of it today are harder to find, and ironic uses are not very effective.

send a clear/strong/powerful message   5
By making a list of the points you want to make, you are more likely to send a clear message and help prevent the family from becoming defensive.
The overwhelming vote sends a strong message that the United States will continue to lead in the WTO.
Making an example of one who had abused his authority would send a powerful message to other backward regimes in the region.

Setting aside the numerous cases where *send a message* describes an actual event involving a sender, a message, and a recipient, this cliché is the first resort for writers, especially journalists, who wish to add emphasis to the idea of "indicate" or "show." In some cases the phrase can be omitted altogether without any loss to the text. In others, it is not obvious that the phrase accomplishes more than a simple verb would do.

shatter the record   2
His 60 goals in 1999 shattered the world record of Paul Litjens (58 goals) and national record of Hassan Sardar (50 goals) in one calendar year.
This year's event shattered previous records with 13,000 participants attending over 260 seminars and workshops led by industry professionals from around the United States.

This cliché would be more effective if it were used sparingly, to characterize new records that are significantly more impressive than standing ones. When this is not the case, it would usually suffice to simply say "set a new record," though writers, particularly sportswriters, do not avail themselves of this opportunity.

shift into high gear   1
For Faye, the conference is a busy time of shifting into high gear.
While the GSEs and marketable securities slowed markedly, the banking system shifted into high gear.

As the campaign shifts into high gear, we are counting on your continued
support and involvement.

Users of this cliché seem intent on conveying any of a number of related ideas, including "go faster," "work harder," and "become more active." While it may seem preferable to any of these ordinary descriptions, *shift into high gear* carries the disadvantage of leaving no obvious superlative to go beyond it. High gear does, however, prepare those who have shifted into it to *cross the finish line* (see above).

breathe/heave a (huge) sigh of relief 5

Perhaps we are all breathing a sigh of relief on the close of what was a
difficult year for our country's economy.
Presently he became aware of the choking sound of the engine starting up,
and breathed an audible sigh of relief.
If you cup your ear you could hear Republicans all over the country heaving a
sigh of relief.

The minor variations in sighs of relief that may be *breathed, given,* or *heaved*—that is, *the huge, the small, the great, the collective,* and perhaps worst of all, *the audible*—may give writers the impression that such sighs are always available for employment. In fact, "express relief" does the same work adequately. The third example above succeeds in reviving the cliché somewhat by completing the metaphor.

sound the death knell 3

Many exchanges sounded their own death knell by charging transaction fees.
The reforms they've implemented promise not only to remake the corporation
but also to sound the death knell for the imperial CEO.
Light promotes life, but now artificial light has sounded a death knell for
nocturnal animals.

This standard journalistic flourish for signaling the end or failure of something provides one-third of the work for poor little *knell* today. Its frequency could be reduced somewhat, and perhaps some of its vitality restored, if it were used definitively in the past tense for things that actually ended, and not so much for things that alarmist writers fear the disappearance of.

spearhead a campaign/effort 4

As president-elect, I volunteered to spearhead these efforts with the
assistance of the other board members.

Now the sixty-year-old is spearheading a campaign for more access to the
treatment for the country's other 120,000 Parkinson's disease sufferers.

No actual spearheads are used in modern spearheading efforts, though one can imagine an effective campaign in which spearheads were directed at the writers—overwhelmingly journalists—who mindlessly invoke this phrase when "lead" is all they mean to say.

spell the end 4

They exist with the permanent threat that Bourne's past may one day catch
up with him. And then one day the appearance of a ruthless assassin
spells the end of their happiness with alarming swiftness.
But would the Kosovar Albanians' calls for independence, or Belgrade's call
for ethnic partition, really spell an end to these problems?

This cliché is more efficient than *signify the end* or *indicate the end* and makes an acceptable substitute for those phrases. It doesn't require a specific event in the way that *sound the death knell* (which has similar meaning) does. *Spell the end*, however, doesn't have an advantage over the simple verb *end* or the unobtrusive *put an end*, though writers (overwhelmingly journalists) often use it to mean this.

stand shoulder to shoulder (with sb/sth) 3

☞ *show mutual support, or bear comparison with sb/sth*
Cigarette makers stood shoulder to shoulder against all attacks.
We are confident standing shoulder to shoulder across party lines today that the
differences that come up in the debate on this legislation will not be partisan.
In my view she stands shoulder to shoulder with them as a writerly equal.
He designed a classic, a game that can stand shoulder to shoulder with the
likes of El Grande *or* Tigris & Euphrates.

The first two examples above show the more usual meaning of this cliché, which evokes an image of strength in numbers, typically in a situation of adversity or defense. Its effectiveness in this role may be slightly compromised by frequency. A newer meaning of the cliché, which often has abstractions or inanimate objects as subject and object, is less convincing, as in the last two examples above.

stand the test of time 5

Neither of these buildings is designed like a kitchen toaster, or even a
multiplex theater. But which of them will stand the test of time: and
I mean centuries, not just a few years.

I can't think of any one clever American boardroom that could come up with a
*   better defence against takeover than that. But they cannot stand the test*
*   of time in terms of market reality.*
None of these claims has stood the test of time, especially the alleged "Stars &
*   Stripes" photos.*

The first example illustrates an apt use of this phrase, in which time is actually required for a judgment to be made. It is in fact often buildings and other enduring works of art or literature that are the subject of this phrase. Other examples might do as well with *prove worthy* or *prove true*.

stay the course   5

☛ *persist; persevere*

Effective leaders are those who have learned when to stay the course in their
*   opinions and decisions and when to be flexible.*
Last week he said that staying the course had never been his strategy.
He still has a legion of lawyers who will stay the course of justice to the limit
*   with appeals and other delaying tactics.*

Users of this cliché seem to think it will impart a notion loftier than "persist" but its extreme frequency mitigates against this. In many contexts there is no path or direction obvious that corresponds to the notion of "course," which further weakens the effect. Finally, as can be seen in the third example above, the phrase has nearly the opposite meaning when it is followed by an *of* prepositional phrase because it instantiates a different meaning of *stay*.

stem the tide   4

They effectively stemmed the tide of middle-class, largely white, families
*   flowing away from the public schools, making these schools an acceptable*
*   alternative for any parent.*
You can't run a party whose only reason for existence is to just try and stem
*   the tide of conservatism in this country.*
Unable to make even one shot to stem the rising Lakers' tide, the Blazers
*   joined the 1986 Boston Red Sox and Greg Norman, in epic-collapse infamy.*

When describing something whose movement, rise, or flow is forceful and undesirable, this idiom presents an apt and succinct image, as in the first example. In other cases it is less suitable, as in the second example, where it seems to mean "stop the increase." *Stem the tide* is popular in sports writing, where its use is perhaps the most general and unclear.

strike a balance   5

☞ *find or achieve a balance*

We must strike a balance between instilling a work ethic and commonsense
caution.

It is hard to strike a balance between the rights of newspapers on the one
hand and the rights of individuals on the other.

In its nearly five-hundred-year history in English this cliché has evolved
from having a specific meaning (determine the difference between two sets
of accounts) to having a very general one. Writers today, especially journalists, seem to feel that all balances must be struck. *Strike* is in fact a more
striking verb than *find, achieve, create,* or a few others that might be used,
but it has lost its striking qualities in this cliché.

---

stun the (_____) world   2

Pope Francis stunned the world when he indicated a softening of the Catholic
Church's views on homosexuality.

Jones Jr. stunned the world with his move up to heavyweight and the
big-money draws lie in that division.

Germany's art world was stunned by the scandal, which came to light when
officials from Xian said they were unaware that they had lent any of
their figures to Germany.

Whether a subworld or the entire world, this cliché provides journalists
(especially sportswriters) a firmly affixed hook from which to suspend stories whose central feature is surprise or unexpectedness—a not uncommon
feature of news generally.

---

sweep into power   1

☞ *take or gain authority suddenly*

Thaksin swept into power on a populist platform that promised big spending
for health care and rural development.

New Labour was swept into power on a tide of community but exists now in
a bubble of competition, choice, and citizens as consumers.

This cliché is used with the same meaning whether the verb is active or
passive. It may once have added a note of drama to the idea of a power transition but it is now only journalese for "came to power" or "was elected."
It's possible that those who are *swept into power* will assume *sweeping new*
powers (q.v. in the noun clichés).

---

sweeten the deal   1

Even just a long, dramatic pause or asking, "Is that the best you can do?" may prompt the other party to sweeten the deal.

The extra modes of play somewhat sweeten the deal but tend to feel like they were added in at the end of the development cycle.

A Collection of Dancehall Favorites *gathers together a fat CD of the man's hit songs, and sweetens the deal with a DVD of videos and a documentary.*

This cliché is standard in business parlance for "make a better offer" and if it were found there alone its numbers would probably not merit notice. Now it is frequently and not very effectively used with reference to retail products (the "deal") to describe their features.

---

take a back seat   5

It is tempting to suggest that the managers and ratings-watchers at the BBC should take a back seat and let the journalists get on with what they are good at.

Conservation was not on the radar and the development of clean and efficient public transport took a back seat to building roads.

Norton's interest in bowling took a back seat to other sports such as basketball, tennis, and her first love, softball.

About half the instances of this cliché take the form *take a back seat to* _____, where the meaning is "become less important than." In other instances, and especially where there is a human subject, the meaning is closer to "refrain from being assertive or controlling" (first example). In either case, the cliché's popularity is probably due to its being more efficient than its plodding, literal expansions and it is widely distributed across genres and registers of writing.

---

take sth/sb by storm   4

    ☞ *take possession by attack; defeat or win over forcefully and quickly*

Following up its 2002 success with the Weight Watchers giant round ice cream sandwich, the brand took 2003 by storm with a giant sundae cone.

Allie Brosh took the Internet by storm with her web comic, Hyperbole and a Half.

Yang Yimou, arguably China's most famous director, had taken China by storm and in the same breath replaced Hong Kong with Beijing as the martial arts film center.

This seventeenth-century phrase has outgrown its original confines (first gloss above) to become an unsatisfying cliché indicating sudden success. The impossibility of parsing it in any sensible way mitigates against its effectiveness. In what sense can a year, the Internet, or a country be deemed to be taken? Hundreds of thousands of items are reported to have taken the Internet by storm, most of which average readers will never have heard of. It is also a common claim to take a particular "world" by storm. Judging by statistics, the worlds most regularly taken by storm are the fashion world and the music world, both of which are taken so regularly as to give the impression that they simply stand by, waiting for this to happen.

take the cake   3
take the biscuit   1
☛ *surpass all others; be an extreme example*

Management's commitment to stinginess and by-the-book mania really took the cake.

If that takes the cake as the most absurd question of the day, a close second came from a representative of Fox Sports, who asked both Belichick and John Fox what they preferred, Levitra or Viagra.

The song that takes the biscuit is surely "Freebird"—giving words to any aspect of this song would be close to committing sacrilegious injustice.

This cliché offers both rhyme and a compact means of expressing an idea that couldn't otherwise be pressed into three syllables. There is nearly always irony present—the surpassing example reported is rarely an admirable one. The less frequent British variant *take the biscuit* is losing ground to the North American version.

take sth to heart   4

Ice cream has taken product innovation to heart: innovation is constant in the ice cream business.

The best advice a freelancer can take to heart is to always deliver what you said you'd deliver.

Does the queen represent some kind of values that the British people take to heart?

Take to heart is syllabically very economical for the range of meanings it represents. That has contributed to its great popularity and use for an expanding range of meanings, some of which might be better expressed more literally. A prevailing meaning today is "act on, rather than merely think about," which is the case in the first two examples above.

take it/sth/sb to the next level 3

Maybe Mariucci wasn't the guy who was going to take them to the next level,
but who among the candidates really makes your eyes pop?

If you enjoy your nights out and want to take hosting to the next level,
consider these accessories to adorn your bar.

Five years after founding my software company, I'm ready to take it to the
next level.

Judging by the preponderance of this cliché in sports writing, you cannot maintain your chops as an athlete unless you regularly *take it to the next level*. Writers on business and the people they quote are also fond of the admirable progress that this cliché suggests. Its popularity may be due to its ability to imply significant advancement without any indication of what the progress would actually consist of. Those who *take it to the next level* can then enjoy the impressive vista from the *whole new level* (q.v. in "Modifier Fatigue") they have ascended to.

take sth with a grain of salt 4

☛ *question the veracity of something*

Considering how many people have come out and denied bits and pieces of
what appears in the book, its important to take everything Biskind says
with a large grain of salt.

It's well known now that the reported on-die CPU temperature should be
taken with a large grain of salt as it can vary from motherboard to
motherboard.

I am not an expert on the substantive legal issues addressed by the report
and ask you to take the following comments with that necessary grain of
salt.

Though composed of monosyllables this cliché is in many cases not a better choice, and considerably less efficient, than the verb *question*. It has long been fashionable to enlarge the grain of salt as a way of emphasizing the dubiousness of some claim; this simply weighs down the cliché further. Bloggers, perhaps today's chief gadflies, use the cliché proportionally more than other writers, though it is also popular in tech journalism.

think outside the box 3

☛ *develop an unconventional or unusual strategy or solution*

Consumers are really watching their carb intake, and we need to think outside
the box as far as how to entice Atkins dieters to consume dairy products.

He has been criticised by some for failing to think outside the box but,
nevertheless, Woods is still seen as a reformer.
Where would civilisation be now if it were not for the intellectuals, those
individuals who thought outside the box, who dared to challenge the norm?

The use of this cliché in the imperative and infinitive outnumbers use in the past tense by about 20 to 1, suggesting that many are encouraged and adjured to do it while few are actually given credit for it retrospectively. When the phrase was new, around 1990, it seems to have captured the imagination of nearly every writer and it is still on a sharp upward trajectory in frequency, even as it loses potency with every implementation: a clear sign that it is now time to think outside the box about "think outside the box."

throw caution to the wind   3

Spectators lined the city streets to watch the thrills and spills as these
daredevils threw caution to the wind.
I ran further and found a door ajar and entered it, throwing caution to the
wind.
There were no giggles in New York last week when a local radio station
decided to throw caution to the wind and make merry with human misery.

The continuing popularity of this phrase may derive from the refreshing originality with which it must have impressed its first hearers and readers, well over a hundred years ago. It is used now to suggest careless, bold, or irresponsible behavior that is often spelled out in adjoining text. Many sentences in which it now appears do as well without it.

tighten one's belt   3

There is no alternative for citizens, mostly in the middle- and low-income
brackets, but to have to tighten their belts further.
Under the protracted economic downtown, people are tightening their belts.
When there's a drop-off in sales of items that are bunched around the cash
register, it's a sure sign that consumers are tightening their belts.

This euphemistic cliché may derive its popularity from a notion, hard to justify, that it is undesirable to be more blunt with words like *economize* or *spend less*, or that the image that belt-tightening adds interest to an otherwise dull predicate. This might be the case if the cliché were not so frequent. It is found mainly in news and business journalism. The derived noun *belt-tightening* shows a similar usage pattern.

tilt at windmills 1

☛ *contend against imaginary opponents*

*Instead of tilting at windmills, these people could concede that the logistics of
language support are unworkable.*

*Rather than tilt at windmills, let us seek to address the real problem
together, in a spirit of caring and sharing.*

*I'm not interested in tilting at windmills while the power-crazed modern
Republicans turn the country into a functional one-party state.*

The survival of this colorful and useful idiom depends on the continuation of
the popularity of its source, *Don Quixote*. Nearly 10 percent of current citations mention the source in a plodding way, suggesting perhaps that writers
are not sure that readers will get the allusion. It's a very compact and effective
expression, and a cliché only when not supported by surrounding context—
an exercise that is probably required for readers who may not be familiar
with the novel or its spinoffs. Typical usage (first two examples) involves
criticizing unproductive behavior and sometimes suggesting an alternative.

tip the scale/scales 4

*Because of the greater weight of the diesel power unit, the latest model tips
the scales at a more substantial 990 kgs.*

*The National league race isn't close in my opinion, although a run up to
twenty-three wins by Schilling and a failure to get to twenty wins by
Johnson would probably tip the scales.*

*Joe Contreras, all of the tight television focus on the raid and the frightened
boy and so forth and the protesters and relatives didn't, in your view, tip
the scales somewhat in terms of the coverage of the story?*

This phrase has two meanings. One of them, "weigh," accounting for about
one-third of its usage, is a cliché in every conceivable context. The other
meaning, "be a deciding or critical factor," is used to characterize something
that will favor, or less often work against, someone or something. In this
meaning the phrase is fairly economical, if somewhat overused, and is problematic only when it is not clear who or what benefits from the metaphor-
ical tipping—as in the third example above. Does *tipping the scales* imply
moving the needle? The jury is probably still out on that one.

toe the line 4

☛ *accept or conform to a rigorous standard*

*The named individuals face up to five years behind bars if they don't start
toeing the line.*

He is also a bit of a maverick who is unlikely to slavishly toe the Murdoch line
on all matters.
Bloggers are also free to give their own opinions, rather than toe the party
line in the way that some journalists have to.

Despite its great frequency, *toe the line* remains a popular and effective way to convey the idea of coerced conformity, especially where it is resented or resisted. *Toe the party line* is frequent enough to merit treatment as a separate cliché. It is still used mainly with reference to political parties but sometimes steps beyond them, as in the third example above. In these cases a slur on the demanding authority, whether intentional or not, is implicit.

---

touch base   3

☞ *make contact for a purpose; address a topic*

I left for JFK Friday night, intent on getting to our production company's
office in Paris Saturday, to touch base with the equipment and sound folks.
Parents and guardians play a crucial part as role models; touching base with
them on a regular basis will keep them current on their children's
progress.
While we have you, very, very briefly, I just want to touch base on this
patients' bill of rights.
I want to touch another base with you. The army chief of staff is proposing
outfitting all of the service's 1.3 million troops in black berets, previously
worn exclusively only by the Rangers. What do you make of that idea?

There's not much to criticize in a two-syllable cliché whose meanings can't be so succinctly conveyed by any other form of words. The phrase has left its origins in baseball far behind and is used frequently in both of the two senses above. *Touch base with* someone (first and second examples) is the more common and established meaning. A newer and less syntactically straightforward sense (third and fourth examples) involves raising or addressing a topic of conversation, which may or may not be the "base."

---

ultimately lead to sth   5

This claim placed me in irretrievable default of my mortgages that ultimately
led to my bankruptcy last year.
When damage to mtDNA is not repaired, it can result in a cascade of events
ultimately leading to a number of diseases.
Social security of this nature will be about the most profitable long-term
investment the country could make. It will ultimately lead to a higher
efficiency among workers and a lowering of production costs.

This handy formula is used to indicate to a reader that a causal event of an eventual result is being identified. It is frequent in legal, scholarly, and all varieties of scientific writing, where it is typically followed by an unpacking of the intermediate steps. It only smacks of cliché when the accompanying narrative has little or no account of steps in a process, and thus appears to be a lazy writer's attempt to make an argument without supporting facts.

unleash a wave/torrent of _____ 3

They funded paramilitary groups who unleashed a wave of massacres in rural villages intended to target guerrilla members.

Religious leaders threatened to unleash a wave of suicide bombers unless Pakistan's President Pervez Musharraf reversed his decision.

Japan's approval of the textbooks prompted South Korea, China, and other Asian countries to unleash a torrent of condemnation for what they say are distorted descriptions of historical facts.

This cliché is a darling of journalists, who use it to mean "cause" or "activate." *Waves* and *torrents*, though not in fact amenable to leashing, conjure images of overwhelming force and so the cliché finds apt use when there is a desire to portray a situation as being unstoppable or out of control.

usher in a new era of _____ 3

Al Jazeera editorialized as follows: "This flag ushers in the new Iraqi era. Everything that happens will now have an American flavor and smell."

Whether he wins or loses in November, Joe Lieberman has ushered in a new era in American Jewish life.

PlayStation went from questionable hardware to a household name that ushered in a new era of console gaming.

Of the three examples above, the first has a respectable claim to the use of this cliché, describing a situation that does justice to the main constituents of the phrase: *usher*, *new*, and *era*. In many other uses, the cliché is a hapless servant of writers who wish to make something seem more important or influential than it is. See also *enter a new era* and *herald a new era*, above.

wear many hats 2

☛ *perform multiple functions or jobs*

These six categories summarize the many hats we wear: Motivator, Fitness Pro, Customer Relations Specialist, Comedian, Choreographer, and Sound Technician.

He has created a practice based on the principle of wearing as many hats as
possible in the construction of a building, serving as developer, designer,
long-term owner, and property manager.
One of the many hats that Marty wore was that of a community news and
sports correspondent for the Sligo Weekender.

This cliché conveys its meaning economically and those intent on using it should probably consider only whether different hats are even required for someone who simply does different things. Hats, after all, do not usually merit attention unless they are quite elaborate. Lifestyle journalism and business writing are the main homes of multiple hat wearers.

weave a (rich) tapestry 1

Haggis weaves his tapestry with infinite skill, aided by exquisite
performances.
The dancers embellish with shades of folk, acrobatics, and the like, weaving a
rich tapestry of rhythm, colour, expression, movement, and sheer joy.
The architects have woven a rich tapestry of restrained luxury into the
constrained fabric of an early-nineteenth-century neoclassical seminary.

The first two examples above illustrate this cliché at its worst: a boilerplate component of jaded art criticism. The third example injects some life into the phrase by extending the metaphor with the mention of fabric to create a much more specific image. Rich tapestries are also available without the weaving; see *a rich tapestry* in the noun clichés.

wend your way 3

Fred, uninvited, wends his way through a misty landscape singing "A Foggy
Day in London Town."
Isn't magic something about wending our way to finding each of our unique
roles in the bigger whole?
The hours passed and the conversation wended its way through talk of
weddings, funerals, and salmon fishing.

Hundreds of English verbs of motion can be complemented with "your way" but *wend* is the most popular candidate for this, because of alliteration. In fact *wend* has little to do in English today outside of this expression, having long ago given up its past tense form *went*, which we use for *go*. Users of *wend your way* seem to wish to convey a nuance—of leisure or indirectness, for example—that is not available in a simple verb. This use has a good chance of continuing to succeed if other writers will refrain from using *wend your way* when all they mean is "go."

work around the clock 4

We have volunteers working pretty much around the clock for three days to get each patient's information entered into our system.

A small air load team worked around the clock to help deliver aid into tsunami-devastated Sumatra.

These workers have been working basically around the clock to fill that area with sand bags to prevent more water from flowing towards this area.

This cliché is the thematic sister of *a race against time* (in the noun clichés) and the two are often found together. *Working around the clock* is equally frequent in news reports and military writing, both of which contain proportionally far more appearances than in other genres. The cliché is often adorned with modifiers *almost, virtually, basically*, and, of course, *literally*.

wreak havoc 5

Organisms like Salmonella *and* E. coli *can hitch a ride on dust particles and wreak havoc in a poultry house or layer room.*

Understanding exogenous triggers in development can help identify which synthetic compounds are likely to wreak havoc on humans when released into the environment.

Customers come to expect regular price cuts, which can wreak havoc with the bottom line.

The two components of this cliché keep company with each other more frequently than they do with any other word. That, combined with the cliché's extreme frequency, serves to weaken rather than strengthen their meaning. This concise cliché is most effective when used to characterize a situation in which something like havoc (widespread devastation) actually occurs, as in the first example above. The last example has little to do with havoc in any usual sense and might be expressed better with a different form of words.

The following predicate clichés are treated in later chapters in this book. Please consult the index for their location.

believe passionately/passionately believe
categorically deny

dramatically increase/reduce/improve/change
freely admit
generally tend/tend generally
have absolutely no/nothing . . .
personally think/believe
quite agree
vary tremendously

6
Framing
Devices

I use framing devices to describe set forms of words that introduce or follow a clause and serve to put it in a context. Some framing devices also serve to direct the course of conversation or argument or to make some comment on what has been or is about to be said. Neither conversation nor written discourse would flow smoothly without these devices and it is not desirable— probably not even possible—to remove them from natural language. Much would be lost from the exchange of information if people did not have the option, for example, of beginning some sentences with *sure enough* and others with *strangely enough*. Even more common are *fortunately* and *unfortunately*, which are necessary for putting many sentences in a required context.

Many such framing devices are viewed as so valuable that they are abbreviated in places where verbosity is not possible, such as in texting and tweets. BTW (by the way) and AFAIK (as far as I know) are both common framing devices that I do not consider to be clichés because of the specific functions they perform. IMHO (in my humble opinion) and FWIW (for what it's worth), on the other hand, are framing devices with high cliché risk and are treated below.

Depending on their placement in a sentence, framing devices can fulfill any of several different grammatical roles covered in different chapters of this book. Most of them are adverbials, which have their own chapter. Most framing devices that are adverbials are of the kind that grammarians call *disjuncts*—adverbials that apply to an entire sentence or clause to contextualize it or to express the author's attitude and thus are not syntactically dependent on a single item in the sentence.

Framing devices become clichés when they are used inappropriately (as they often are), as when they are tacked onto the beginning or end of a clause without there being a good reason for doing so. Many framing devices in English consist of single words and while frequent, these do not generally grate in the way that phrases viewed as clichés do. Such uses of single-word framing devices are normally covered in dictionaries. A number of hackneyed framing devices are semantically merely multiword expansions of single words that, if substituted, would not draw attention to themselves so glaringly. Consider, for example, *honestly* as opposed to *To be perfectly honest* (which is treated below).

Like most clichés, most framing devices are far more common in spoken than in written language. In addition to their semantic and pragmatic functions, these clichés also give speakers a few milliseconds of thinking time while the tongue rattles off syllables that do not require engagement with the intellect. The framing devices below as a class are used far more frequently than the other types of clichés in this book. Framing devices that are most frequent at the beginning of a sentence—a few are found there exclusively—begin with a capital letter in the entries below.

(But) after/when all is said and done   4

"When all is said and done, StarLink will represent a hiccup for biotech seed,"
    says Busboom.
After all is said and done, Bush will have been a much better president than
    Clinton ever was.
We saw some of the wildest games play out during the regular season. But
    when all is said and done, the Bucs are your world champs.

Like *at the end of the day* and *all things considered*, this cliché is used to signify a speaker's arrival at a summary or essential point. It is used often, though not consistently, to characterize an imagined or hoped-for future state of affairs, often one in which the speaker's views will be vindicated. It is left for listeners to interpret whether the more generic or pointed meaning is intended.

all things considered 2

All things considered, the post-1945 alliance with the United States was a
  good bargain for Italy.
They do not even have access to clean drinking water which, all things
  considered, puts my smelly armpits into perspective.
If I had the privilege to vote at the coming congress based on what is
  known about the candidates. Hamutenya scores highest, all things
  considered.

This common phrase is widely and fairly evenly distributed across all genres of writing and is even more common in speech to signal a summary statement. The first and last examples above show typical and unobjectionable use. The second only amounts to surplus verbiage.

I would argue that . . . 5
One could argue that . . . 5
It is arguable that . . . 2

I would argue that the life of unwanted embryos would be inhumane to be
  frozen or sold for desperate couples to adopt.
One could argue that the state of Louisiana had already practiced economic
  affirmative action by declaring the area a state enterprise zone.
It is arguable that the claimant ought to have got his costs up to and
  including 13th January 1999.

These formulas and variations of them are the refuge of what writer Thomas Frank calls the commentator class, members of which are employed by media outlets to translate the events of the day into digestible clichés and commonplaces. The devices have the effect of distancing the speaker or writer from the putative argument, suggesting by the use of modal verbs that conditions do not currently prevail for the argument to be made or that the speaker, in any case, is not actually making it. *It is arguable* is far more frequent in legal language than elsewhere and may have a more formulaic use there, to telegraph that there is a legal foundation for an argument. Those so given to spotting the possibility of argument would do their listeners a service by simply owning their opinions in clearer language and supporting them with facts.

Believe me 1

Believe me, I've been watching it for two hours, and it's too, too bad. I'm
  never going to get this time back—do they realise that?

Believe me, the information we have received about all of the places he has
  hidden weapons is enough for the whole world to be busy searching.

Under normal circumstances we extend the courtesy of belief, at least provisionally, to all speakers and writers, so those who ask you for it before they begin raise a red flag on whatever follows. Unless it is your grandmother speaking, the presence of this imprecation before a sentence is often a good reason that you should not believe. In many cases it simply belies the speaker's ability to make a convincing case of what they would have you believe on the basis of the information they provide.

Believe me is far more common in spoken than in written language and while it is sometimes used merely for emphasis—a speaker's device for calling attention to a summary observation—its many uses in desperate discourse make it a poor choice for anyone whose object is to persuade. Better to let your observations and opinions speak for themselves without suspicious bolstering.

broadly speaking   2
All those who are engaged in settling out of court the many thousands of
  claims that never reach the stage of litigation at all or, if they do, do not
  proceed as far as trial will know very broadly speaking what the claim is
  likely to be worth if 100 percent liability is established.
In the existing literature, there are, broadly speaking, two competing
  approaches to the interpretation of foreign labor deployment, both of
  which can be useful in eliciting facts and asking relevant questions.
The present publication is broadly speaking a companion volume to its
  predecessor, both in the style of its layout and the organisation of the text.

This phrase is many times more frequent in legal writing than elsewhere and is also more likely to smack of cliché in legalese. Its job there is usually to provide a hedge for a statement with known or imagined exceptions (first example). In other writing it can serve to helpfully focus a discussion (second example) or serve no discernible purpose (third example).

But hey   5
That's what the commander of the 3rd Infantry Division said himself. But
  hey, maybe he's biased.
Where should I begin? My husband would say to begin at the beginning. So here
  goes. This may get very long, but hey, I have forty-three years to cover here.

This combo might not constitute an actual suit if you work in a strictly suit-
and-tie environment. But hey, it is a viable option for a night on the town,
for the more avant-garde fellas.

Bloggers and writers of soft journalism use this ingratiating device to coerce familiarity with their readers in contexts where *but* or *however* would usually do the job less obtrusively. It is conversational in tone and so perhaps is not objectionable in blogs where the writer imagines community with his or her readers. Its frequency in journalism suggests either that it is compatible with a tone that publishers now find suitable for their audiences or that copyediting can no longer be afforded.

Call it _____ 4

Call it synchronicity. But it's more likely that an established connection
paved the way, with plenty of help from a group of scientists and
international affairs specialists.
Williamsburg's Chickenbone Café features some of the best regional products
around—the region being its native borough. The result? Call it "Brooklyn
global cuisine."
Anyone can use the name Emmental and run ramshod over the recipe. Call it
the "Open Source" cheese, if you will.

This device is favored most by breezy lifestyle journalists as a way into a story or out of a paragraph. Whether the term that fills the blank is an ordinary lexical item or a nonce coinage, the cleverness of which the writer wishes to draw your attention to, there is rarely a need to *Call it* anything. The imperative form is presumably also aimed at drawing in the reader's attention but it is so overused as to be off-putting rather than inviting.

Call me _____, but ... 4

Call me old-fashioned, but a little time apart is an essential component of any
lasting relationship; the intention was to find love anew after a trial
separation.
Call me naive, but I always thought our courts looked at the facts, not the
emotional impact, of a case.
Call me cynical, but I read this quote to be an invitation into a dog-eat-dog
world of winners creating losers and to hell with enjoying the game.

This formula for introducing a label that is notionally undesirable to own is used as an egoistic device to distinguish the writer's point of view and to invalidate another that is perceived to prevail. The fill-in labels, in descending order of frequency, are *old-fashioned*, *crazy*, *cynical*, *naïve*, and *paranoid*. Not surprisingly, the cliché is proportionally more frequent in blogs than elsewhere, with soft journalism taking second place.

Let me be (perfectly) clear   4
I want to be perfectly clear   3
I want/I'd like to make one thing perfectly clear   1

Before we begin, I'd like to make one thing perfectly clear. I absolutely despise
   Star Wars, *and anything associated with it.*

Let me be very clear about my position on this. I strongly support the
   cockfighting industry in Louisiana. I am adamantly opposed to this piece
   of legislation and I will vote against it.

Send me all of the file this time, not just bits and pieces of it, sonny, or
   you'll be looking for another line of work. Do I make myself perfectly
   clear?

I will just make one thing perfectly clear. I have ruled on the point of order
   from Mr Sowry. He is quite wrong.

The several variants of these clichés arise from speakers who take it upon themselves to package up the solemn responsibility of perfect clarity and make a gift of it to their listeners. It is common—indeed, sometimes obligatory—in political rhetoric and its absence there may suggest a leader who lacks grit and commitment. In other contexts it's merely pompous.

dare I say (it)   2

The exhibition serves as an ideal opportunity for the Tate to promote the
   crafted, creative, and dare I say sculptural qualities of architecture.

It's hard for these groups to find someone that understands the substantive
   area, understands the ethical area, can blend them together and be, dare I
   say, entertaining at the same time.

I know I'm not the only fan in North America who is, dare I say it?, freakin'
   tired of them.

Users of this cliché intend to warn their audience that they are taking some risk or liberty in what they are about to say, but in fact it's usually just a setup for a letdown. At most, the cliché signals a minor departure from what might be expected in the context and most sentences read just as well without it.

Where it is the writer's intention to draw special attention to what follows, there are many more straightforward ways of doing it.

The/Webster's dictionary defines ... 1

Webster's dictionary defines "oxymoron" as a figure of speech in which
opposite or contradictory terms are combined. Jumbo shrimp. Light rock.
Microsoft Works. Many would also add tax simplification to the list.
Interestingly enough, the dictionary defines a gift as simply "a thing given."
It says nothing about cost, appropriateness, or presentation—only the
condition of the heart. One person giving to another. That's all.

The first example justifies the use of this well-trodden path into a subject by gently introducing a term that may be unfamiliar to readers and then demonstrating the usefulness of their knowing it. The second example is of a kind that makes lexicographers, and perhaps others, want to throttle the writer, by invoking "the dictionary"—the rather generic one known to the writer—without the least need for doing so or of understanding what it says.

at the end of the day 5

My sons are two grown men, and they were at the end of the day the ones
who sacrificed the most, who were sacrificed in the first round of my
political life.
But at the end of the day, just like any job, employees have to be civil with
other employees for the betterment of the organization they work for.
At the end of the day I've made my decision to leave my contract to the end of
the season, and that's the way it stands.

Originally far more common in British than in American English, this mindless phrase is now found equally in both varieties, where it is a sure marker of a speaker or writer whose main immediate need is to fill up airtime or column inches. The phrase appears typically to introduce, and less commonly to end, an observation that emphasizes, summarizes, or encapsulates an overall message. English offers unlimited ways of doing this without the hazardous deployment of such phrases as this one, and it will never be missed if you leave it out. Examine any of the many thousands of instances of it that you will find in an online news search; you'll rarely find an example of it that contributes meaningfully. If *at the end of the day* is part of your standing repertoire you will be doing yourself and your audience a favor by banishing it.

in actual fact   5
in point of fact   1

People might think it sounds horribly self-important, turgid, avant-garde, and inaccessible. But in actual fact, it's a lot lighter and more palatable than you'd think if you saw the synopsis.

In actual fact we may actually have to lay some of the blame for this at the feet of ACL for continually delaying the CVA meeting.

I saw Nick Park's short, "Creature Comforts," which has plasticine animals explaining what life is like in a zoo. The voices are in point of fact real voices of people talking about their homes.

In fact is indispensable in English. Embellishments to it often signal the writer's or speaker's vehemence, sense of self-importance, or desperation to have you accept what follows. Both clichés are far more common in speech than in written text and it is challenging to imagine any context where they are necessary.

The fact of the matter is (that) ...   1

The fact of the matter is that what was alleged here could not be a government matter and no factual inquiry would be needed.

The fact of the matter is that I have hurt myself trying to save two people who were riding double-seated on a bicycle.

The fact of the matter is that black-owned companies need financial injection from the government so that their businesses are financially sound until they reach a level of self sustainability.

Lawyers, editorialists, and soft journalists are in the vanguard of keeping this cliché standing feebly on its zombie legs. It often prefaces the main point of a text and can be a useful device in that regard—nearly always preferable to *Let's face it*. When placed before a trivial or personal fact, as in the second example, it is merely petulant.

Generally speaking   5

Thereafter he seems to have done reasonably well, but for the occasional episodes of coughing in 1986, 1990, and 1994, and generally speaking his respiratory history has been relatively uneventful until 1996.

Generally speaking, most companies will have specific goals of one sort or another when they put together their marketing plan.

Generally speaking, the more firsthand and directly relevant a source of information, the more useful it is to painting a picture of what happened.

The motive behind this extremely frequent device is often a brief acknowledgment of the awareness of contrary cases or information that the speaker will not address or that will be introduced as a contrast to the general case. *Generally speaking* is far more common in legal writing than in other genres, a fact that may serve as a red flag for its use. It can often be given a rest by replacing it with a formula that more specifically answers the intended meaning, such as *In most situations* or by simply eliminating it.

it/that goes without saying   1

I've been going to the ROH one or two nights a week to rehearse with the Royal Ballet dancers for my next piece with them—but that almost goes without saying.

I think it goes without saying that you should visit sites, local historical societies, museums, and should also track descendants.

It goes without saying that if nearly a year goes by before the claim is reported to the defendant, she will be at a disadvantage when no proper explanation has been made as to why there has been inactivity for that year.

This cliché contends with *needless to say*, also a framing device, for a distinction in irony, since it is mainly used to preface something that is, in fact, said. When not used to express the speaker's idea that his observation is obvious, *It goes without saying* often has concessive force. The cliché is particularly beloved by lawyers, judging by its frequency in legal writing. It is not saved from clichédom by prefacing it with some qualifier like "almost" or "I think." Writers who are inclined to use it might ask themselves first: if it goes without saying, does it really need to be said, and if so, does it need to be prefaced?

Having said that,   1

Any utility such as these that enable you to remove all traces of an application can also allow abuse of the demo system by artificially prolonging the demo period. Having said that, however, using the utilities in this way while possible, quickly becomes annoying (yes I have tried it) and longer-term quickly becomes impractical or just too much bother.

This is very sad and I hope that she makes a full recovery. Having said that, I bet that she is getting all the stops pulled out, and receiving better treatment than someone else would.

*With Motorola being a Google-owned company, it would make sense for the
company to work on the next Nexus phone as sharing resources would be
easy. Having said that, Google would also be careful about the signals
that it's giving to other Android handset makers.*

Users of this cliché are usually at pains to backtrack in what follows it
from some of the implications of what precedes it. So at the very least,
what precedes the phrase should have some seizable note of clarity,
which is not the case in the first example above. There is sometimes a
positive-negative contrast between the statements that *having said
that* divides, as in the second example. In general not much is accomplished by this self-evident participial clause that *However* or *But* cannot do.
Using the phrase along with either of these adverbs (as in the first example) is a sure signal that no competent editor has reviewed the text
issuing from no competent writer. In speech, *having said that* may serve
as a slightly innocuous filler while the speaker moves onto his or her
contrasting idea, but in writing it is usually replaceable with something
simpler.

I (would) hasten to add that . . .   1
Let me hasten to add that . . .   1

*The fact that that building is one of the most appalling pieces of architecture
ever to blot the London skyline, and that disgraceful sums were spent on
it, is a separate matter. I hasten to add that I have a great respect for the
excellent architect, even if it is one of his worst buildings.*

*I am comfortable with Morgan's assessment of the conditions of Jews in
America today. I hasten to add that I am not so comfortable with the
challenges we face as modern Jews in America.*

*Lest this read like a school essay, let me hasten to add that the Kashmir issue
is very much alive and kicking.*

This framing device serves little obvious purpose that *But* and *However* are
not capable of. It appears more in writing than in speech, and it seems to
indicate the writer's anxiety that the reader may consider the first idea apart
from the second if not specifically notified of their connection. This would
always be unlikely, given their juxtaposition, so the phrase is largely superfluous.

---

in my humble opinion   2
What we just saw in my humble opinion didn't help the clarity of this story at all.

In my humble opinion, I'd offer Sir Bobby the suggestion that the midfield is as much to blame as the back four.

Jasmine is one of the best Chinese restaurants in the UK in my humble opinion.

Whether inserted at the front, back, or in the middle of a sentence, this tiresome cliché never has anything of humility about it and rarely accomplishes anything more than the verb *think* would do if quietly inserted to show that an opinion is being expressed: for example, *I think Jasmine is one of the best Chinese restaurants in the UK.* This cliché directs attention away from the subject and toward the writer or speaker—which is perhaps the intention of those who use it frequently.

if you ask me   5

It's said that everyone who heard that album formed a band, that's how important it was. So if you ask me, do I value a work of art for its intrinsic value? Yes I do.

But if you ask me I would say they were delicious kebabs.

Are we now to permit anyone to get away with threats and deception if they cover themselves in the mantle of the so-called paranormal? It sounds something like a twenty-first-century "benefit of clergy," if you ask me.

The extreme frequency of this cliché in conversation derives mainly from its use to signal that an opinion—obviously one not solicited—is being put forth. At four syllables it's hard to find it offensive (even though "I think" contains only two) and it's firmly fixed as a colloquialism. In writing other than in letters or to capture speech, it doesn't have a justifiable role and is better avoided.

let's be honest   3

Let's be honest here—when last did Os really perform to a standard that's good enough to match the likes of the English, All Blacks, or French front rows, for that matter?

Tim Burton's Batman *was crap. Yeah we know it's bordering on sacrilege to say so but let's be honest.*

Men opt for the shaved style because it looks sharp, intimidating, and it's practical, easy to maintain, and let's be honest, knocks another step off one's daily grooming routine.

The rhetorical thrust behind this cliché, a standard tool of lifestyle journalists and perky motivational speakers, is to soften the audience for an inconvenient or uncomfortable truth (as perceived by the author) and to bring the audience into conspiratorial sympathy with the author's point of view. It raises the interesting question, never addressed in the context of its use, of who was not being honest before. Does the cliché work? Probably not so well, because its frequency mitigates anyone actually paying attention to it.

let's face it 5
let's face facts/the fact 1

Every company needs to develop a unified wireless strategy, encompassing every type of wireless device or connection you can envisage ever affecting your network. Because let's face it, they're coming.

But let's face it: the image of an accountant with his hand in the client's pocket will never fade unless lawmakers erase it.

Let's face facts, when it comes to a "Lifetime" warranty, very few things last forever and vinyl fencing is not the exception.

The standard use of this cliché, somewhat like *let's be honest*, is to preface an inconvenient or unfortunate fact, as perceived by the writer or speaker, and perhaps to hold the listener's hand for the revelation of it. The overwhelming numbers of the main form push it deep into cliché territory, and examples show it to be used to preface facts that are neither really surprising nor earth-shattering. Most texts read as well without the introduction.

lo and behold 3

I just have to adjust how I enter text when writing an entry. I edited the existing posts below and, lo and behold, they look right now.

This disc was my biggest surprise of the year. I was incredibly reluctant to even buy this album until, lo and behold, I found it at Target for 6.98.

Since then, the industry itself has hired scientists to do studies that—lo and behold!—found no safety problems.

This interjection is used to signal wonderment or surprise, now nearly always jocularly or ironically. It appears proportionally more often in blogs today than in any other genre, where it contributes four syllables but nothing of obvious value to the subject at hand.

make no mistake 5

Bulluck may still get lost in the media buzz that surrounds players like Steve McNair, Jevon Kearse, and Eddie George. But make no mistake, he is regarded as one of the most valuable defensive players in the league by those who step between the lines.

Representative Carolyn Maloney said that the bill's definition of a fetus was "so broad it would cover three cells." She continued, "Make no mistake: this is an attack on a woman's right to choose."

This introduction to what the writer or speaker would have you believe is an enduring truth is dear to politicians and, perhaps surprisingly, sports writers: *Make no mistake* is proportionally more frequent in sports writing than elsewhere. It frequently introduces matters of opinion rather than fact and for that reason is not obviously respectful of listeners. In most cases, any of the dozens of other formulas that English makes available to preface an emphatic statement will do as well or better.

(as a) matter of fact   1

It is trivially true that as a matter of empirical fact, property in the hands of owners and income-earners is what is left to them after the levying of these taxes.

No, as matter of fact, it's not open to interpretation, Wolf. The law says that every bag must be screened, meaning one of several ways.

I trained for about seven months prior to shooting Con Games *to get in good shape for the film. Matter of fact I was trained by Lou Ferrigno on several occasions prior to shooting the film.*

This versatile phrase has many uses that may or may not constitute clichés. The phrase's origin is in law, where it is still more frequent than in any other genre and has a technical meaning: *There was not enough found as matters of primary fact nor such an analysis of causation to justify the holding.* As a cliché it is sometimes a slightly emphasized substitute for *in fact* to contradict an earlier suggestion (second example) or to introduce an extra piece of information (third example). It is pointless filler (first example) as an emphatic preface to bolster a declarative sentence.

The miracle is that/It is a miracle that   1

For Augustine, the miracle is that recollection of sin is not always a renewal or repetition of that sin.

It's nothing short of a miracle that Carson, a thirty-seven-year-old, two-term Congressman, is running neck-and-neck with his Republican rival.

We're talking about a movie that's so suspenseful for so long, it must be a miracle that this witless, talentless director made it, right?

The shortage of genuine miracles in the world is perhaps what prompts people to find them everywhere and introduce them with this well-worn cliché. Hyperbole is a common way to draw attention to a subject, but clear, engaging, and original use of language does this even better. Miracles of this exaggerated variety are surprisingly common among writers on religion, who would presumably have a better grip on actual miracles than the rest of us do and might do well to avoid the phrase since they more than others would be expected to report on miracles factually.

I must admit   5
I must confess   2

For all the shortcomings I perceive about my homeland these days, I must admit it has allowed me to function freely in my vocation, which is saying a lot.

Hendrix's version is the one I know and love, however I must admit that the ominous tension created by Plant and crew is imminently more germane with the lyrical content.

I must admit my surprise that a progressive Afrocentric sister can travel to Utah for a ski vacation, have a fabulous time, and stand ready to try it again.

Sometimes, I must confess, I do still harbour doubts and wonder if that is exactly what I should be doing.

There's been many a time when my own burdened heart has been lifted by thinking of Christ's suffering—a meditation that is helped, I must confess, by contemplating an image of that suffering.

When a genuine admission or confession is made or when the context provides for some concession (as in the first example), these extremely overworked clichés have a small job to do in framing what follows for the listener. Without these introductions, however, it is not likely that the admission or confession would be misconstrued. Both phrases are regularly pressed into service as stand-ins for *I think, In fact, it is surprising,* or any number of other meanings, many of which do not require specific expression because the implication is clear from the context. Both clichés are evenly distributed across many genres, with blogs having a slight edge.

Needless to say   1

Hellenic Paganism is a reconstruction of the ancient Greek religion. Needless to say, it is not an eclectic path.

And then there was that day I walked to Dancing Grounds and took pictures of the neighborhood flowering trees along the way. Needless to say, the page loaded slowly.

I've heard that the folks who attend usually get to see grown men and women
puking into the gutter and/or urinating off the top of parking structures,
etc. Needless to say, I don't go anywhere near this parade.

Logic would suggest that either this phrase or what follows it is superfluous but the cliché persists as a way of introducing something self-evident or expected. Bloggers find many opportunities to use it. In speech it is a harmless contextualizer with several synonyms such as *as you would expect* or even *so*. It can seem a bit jarring and petulant in more formal contexts and anyone tempted to put it in writing might first reflect on its literal implication before proceeding with the "needless" realization. Less frequent variants are *needless to add* and *needless to mention*.

No offense, but ... 1

James, no offense, but I'm not ready to be any man's wife, much less yours. I
barely know you.
There is such a thing as bad poetry, and, no offense, but I've read a fair
amount of it on here.
I went from a size 12 to a size 18. Women would come up to me in M&S and
say, "no offence, but I'm so glad you're fat."

This formula abounds in fictional dialogue of a certain quality (see first example) and it is to be hoped that invented people use it more than real ones: those who embark on intentional offense should preface it less cavalierly than this if civil discourse is to be maintained. When the formula is used to provide criticism or feedback its intention is sometimes polite, but it is often unnecessary here as well or could be more suitably replaced by something less formulaic.

pardon the expression 1

... Gatorade, and things that are owned by companies like Pepsi Cola that are
just, pardon the expression, kicking Coke's butt.
If you'll pardon the expression, it takes, er, balls to take on such a challenge
and carry it off with such aplomb.
As time goes on, I wonder whether I'm just an old slapper. If you'll pardon the
expression.

Some uses of this phrase have the same meaning as *pardon/excuse the pun*, q.v. below. Others, as illustrated above, signal either the writer's intentional and usually regrettable crossing of a line of decorum or the writer's imagining that he or she has done this. In most cases the reader is better served by the withdrawal of the cliché and perhaps by what follows it as well.

to be perfectly honest (with you)   1

When we travel outside of Baghdad, we do so in convoy. And to be perfectly
*   honest, we've faced very, very little hostility in any of our dealings with*
*   the Iraqi people.*
I think it is a badge of honour to be attacked by people like David Aaronovitch
*   to be perfectly honest.*
No, I think being perfectly honest, if I was his adviser, which I'm not, I'd tell
*   him to go knock Hillary out of the box.*

This cliché rarely has any literal force, which is a comfort: if it did, the suggestion would be that perfect honesty had not prevailed in what preceded it. People use it with some concessionary force, to bring to light an uncomfortable fact, or to set up a statement to be interpreted as a confession or the revelation of a secret. Aside from drawing particular attention to the statement it frames (and English has dozens of ways of doing this), it has no particular function and there is nearly always a better choice. Some other clichéd uses of *perfectly* as a modifier are examined in chapter 7, "Modifier Fatigue."

pardon/excuse the pun   2

Satan comes to earth and takes the body of Gabriel Byrne and apparently
*   he's a horny devil (pardon the pun) as he hits on or sleeps with any*
*   woman striking his fancy.*
We first called into a Jade Factory and the ladies ran amok buying all they
*   could lay hand on leaving the men in their lives looking very Jaded, if you*
*   will excuse the pun.*
The Alaskan wilderness did not have the same resonance for me as the upstate
*   romance of the Appalachian mountains. Alaska, excuse the pun, left me cold.*

Do puns need excuses? The ones that accompany this cliché very often do, because they tend to be forced and unnecessary, which further contributes to the perception of the phrase as a cliché. The plea for a pun to be excused often has roughly the same effect as explaining a joke, quickly removing any opportunity for mirth that may be present or, worse, signaling the writer's insecurity that readers will even notice a double entendre if it is not pointed out. Blogs and soft journalism are the chief outlets for these devices.

The real question is . . .   3

The real question to me isn't whether magick can be used as a tool of
*   insurrection, as it clearly has great potential to be one. The real question*
*   is, will it be used as one?*

The real question is: how did this mild-mannered, gifted researcher end up at the centre of one of the most extraordinary scientific furores of our time?

For America today, the real question is only whether there will be a short, sharp downturn, or a more prolonged, but shallower, slowdown.

About 1 percent of writers who begin a sentence with *The real question is...* are actually contrasting it with some other question already mentioned, as in the first example. The 99 percent divert their listeners or readers from the actual meaning; all that users of this formula usually mean is "an important or interesting question is..."

relatively speaking   2

Americans are paying an enormous amount of attention to gasoline prices, even though economists will tell you, relatively speaking, they're cheaper than they were back in 1980 or 1979.

Qatar has been a very progressive country, relatively speaking, throughout the entire Arab world, as a country that works together with the United States.

Edano said the Fukushima Daiichi Nuclear Power Station is in a stable situation, relatively speaking, but that much work remains before the damaged reactors are fully under control.

In contexts where an explicit comparison is made—often indicated by the presence of a "than" clause—*relatively speaking* has a particular and not necessarily clichéd job to do, as in the first example. In many other cases, where *relatively speaking* is present merely to add some limitation of scope without reference to a framework for it, it's a needlessly prolix variant for "somewhat" or some other scalar adverb.

It's (probably) safe to say (that) ...   4

While it is probably safe to say that there have been incidences [sic] *of excessive executive pay, we are not able to generalize from these cases about whether the average level of executive compensation is excessive.*

Even if the Steelers lose to the Eagles, it's safe to say Bill Cowher has another Super Bowl contender in his thirteenth season as Pittsburgh's coach.

Although it's safe to say that body waxes are generally more popular among gay men than heterosexual males, waxing your body hair has nothing to do with your sexuality.

This cliché is often used as a hedging device, especially when prefaced by *probably*, but it is nearly always inapt and unnecessary. Any of English's many one-word concessives will do the job as well, without puzzlingly introducing the notion of safety into the discourse where it has no obvious application.

By the same token   4

☛ *for the same reason or in the same way*

A public body is in principle liable for torts in the same way as a private person. It is submitted that, by the same token, a public body cannot be under a greater liability at common law than a private person would be.

Children need a lot of love. By the same token they also need discipline to give them an understanding of what is right and wrong.

Brutality is wrong, in all cases, no matter what cause it is alleged to serve. By the same token, we should not let our recognition of the brutality of communism to serve as an excuse for what our own government did either.

This cliché is an exact syllabic substitute for its most common literal meaning ("for the same reason") and if used only for that meaning, as in the first example, it would be deemed merely an idiom and not a cliché. But writers and speakers have flattened its meaning by using it where *furthermore* or *in addition* is what they mean (second example) or to dodge the work of finding a more accurate way of joining the ideas of two sentences whose meanings have a related but not straightforward relationship (third example).

to say the least   5

The chances of a patient at this stage becoming pregnant are negligible, to say the least.

The returns from savings, shares, and pension plans have been disappointing to say the least in recent years.

The experience was enlightening to say the least but after a heated argument between myself and the teacher I was no longer welcome.

The most typical use of this cliché is to suggest that a person, event, or situation is not adequately described by the adjective that precedes the cliché. The three adjectives most likely to occupy this slot are all common (*interesting, disappointing, strange*), so the cliché might as well be considered an excuse for the writer's failure to find a more compelling characterization. The cliché is not effective with adjectives that are not typically gradable (first example). Many instances of *to say the least* are vehement in tone, making it generally a poor choice unless this is the tone intended.

Say what you will (about sth)   1

Say what you will about Robert De Niro—slave to mannerisms, caricature of
   himself, awkward in comedy—there can be no doubt that when he puts
   his mind to it, he delivers.
Say what you will, but I can't knock Martha. She may be a bit stiff and stuffy,
   but she does a damn fine party.
Say what you will about Carr and his progress as a quarterback, but even his
   most vocal critics can't deny this: He's one tough customer.

This cliché is mainly used to concede that there are grounds for criticism of
someone or something before going on to praise them. It is most frequent
where it seems to be least effective, in sports journalism, and also occurs
frequently in lifestyle journalism. The first example above is a good use of
the formula, laying out the points of censure rather than leaving them to
the imagination of the reader.

so to speak   5

Imitation involves being able to appreciate not just what an act looks like but
   also what it is like to do that act oneself. Children must be able to put
   themselves in another person's shoes, so to speak.
I was, so to speak, in the right places at the right times to help organize this
   memorial column.
Because my father moved far away, they never had anything good to say
   about each other and I felt they were playing each other, using me as a
   pawn so to speak.

So to speak is typically used to signal that the expression or word immediately
preceding is used in some figurative or nonstandard sense. It can be used
humorously to introduce double entendre, as in the following examples:

> *That quote has been up for a long time and we suspect that they're just*
>   *trying to get it removed now because he doesn't want to upset the*
>   *dairy industry. It's utterly ridiculous, so to speak.*
> *In fact if you could swap the current cannabis laws for the current*
>   *alcohol laws then maybe the violence in every town centre on a*
>   *Saturday night would disappear into a puff of smoke (so to speak).*

In the three examples at the top of the entry, however, the speakers unac-
countably give warning of the figurative use of an expression whose figurative use is already well established. These uses rarely appear in edited text.

To tell the truth   4
Truth be told   4

Truth be told, it doesn't take an industry analyst or a sideshow soothsayer to
   notice that cottage cheese isn't exactly jumping off the shelves these days.
To tell the truth, I don't know much about it, but I have heard there's a field
   called "evolutionary epistemology."
Covering the Astor trial was a swift education for a twenty-six-year-old
   dreadlocked black guy who has been in the city for only four years and,
   truth be told, did not know who Brooke Astor was until she died.

These similar clichés may serve as colloquial alternatives to the prosaic *The
fact is* in many instances of its usage. They are up to ten times more frequent
in speech than in edited text. In other contexts, they share some qualities
with *Believe me*: their presence should alert the reader or listener to the possibility of departure from rather than adherence to truth. For many speakers, they serve merely as a thoughtless device to isolate what follows for
particular attention.

There comes/will come a time/day   3

There comes a time in every woman's life when the only thing that helps is a
   glass of champagne.
There comes a day in the life of every pastor when it is time to face the music
   and preach the dreaded stewardship sermon.
There will come a time when every team will need a pinch-hitter in a crucial
   playoff situation, either because of injuries, matchups, or percentages.
By reason of his condition there will come a time when the claimant will be
   entirely dependent on others for his care and indeed for his very survival.

The two main uses of this cliché are distinguished by tense. In the future it
is used to express a prediction of some fact or condition that will prevail. In
the present it expresses what the writer would put forward as a general
truth. The formality of the subject-verb inversion is sometimes exploited
for comic effect in the present tense, with dubious results.

There is (a) real concern ...   1

There is real concern that when patients are commenced on high-dose
   steroids for any reason the dose is not reduced once control is achieved.
You have spent the vast majority of your adult life in custody and there is a
   real concern about your ability to cope with the stresses of life after release.
There are real concerns that Ireland is falling behind in the broadband race.

This cliché is most common in journalism as a means of suggesting the newsworthiness of the subject being reported on. It also serves a convenient purpose for the expression of a concern that the writer or speaker would emphasize without having to attribute it to anyone in particular.

For what it's worth   1

For what it's worth, the advertising on your site has paid off handsomely for me and is still doing so in terms of tours done and booked.

For what it's worth, Doctor Jackson, I and every other member of this facility agreed with you.

The two examples given are poor usages of a cliché that, when used properly is really not an offender against intelligent language at all; its cliché credentials stem merely from inapt use. *For what it's worth* is a sensible way to introduce an opinion, concession, or fact to a conversation in a humble way that indicates a speaker's acceptance of some uncertainty as to the value of the contribution. When no such doubt reasonably exists, the faux humility that this phrase conveys does not serve the speaker well.

With all due respect   4

With all due respect, sir, when I came home from Vietnam, there were no parades, no parties, no sense of accomplishment and I was indistinguishable from anyone else that came home from Vietnam.

However, with all due respect to Crowe's performance, one cannot help but imagine how much better Mel Gibson would have done had he not declined the offer.

With all due respect, what planet are you guys on? You pick an All-Time Milwaukee Bucks franchise team but leave Sidney Moncrief off the team entirely.

This fixed formula, in a minority of uses, politely introduces a point that represents conflict or contrast with what has gone before, as in the first example. In most uses, however, it is merely a formulaic cliché that involves no respect and implies at the same time that little is due anyway.

In a world where …   1

In a world where every product is marked and inexorably linked to the conglomerate that backs it, factions develop, and brand loyalty reaches quasi-religious levels.

In a world where 98 percent of religious teaching consists of fantasy and lies and 2 percent might be true for you, this could be the safest approach.

In a world where men and women still claim to want to find a soul mate to spend their life with, what role can and should we afford technology?

This cliché seems to be indispensable, and perhaps excusable, in tendentious movie trailers. Its use in mainstream discourse does not seem warranted in cases where it begins a sentence. It can often be replaced with *given that*, or the same idea can be couched in an *if* or *when* sentence, without loss of effect. The frequency of *In a world where...* mitigates against people actually pausing to consider whether the world described really exists or is worth imagining.

7
Modifier
Fatigue

All of the clichés in this chapter share the element of a modifier that is used automatically, merely in imitation of the frequently encountered and familiar model that the cliché represents. These clichés could also be classified under a different chapter in this book—adverbials, noun clichés, or predicate clichés, for example—but are collected here because of this shared element and indexed at the ends of those chapters as appropriate. These phrases normally consist of two words: adjective + noun, adverb + verb, or adverb + adjective. They become clichés via the lockstep fashion in which speakers and some writers insert the modifier before or after its referent in preference to any other that might go there, or in preference to no modifier at all. The modifier's meaning is thus diluted, eventually to the point of meaninglessness. Nigel Rees, in his *Dictionary of Clichés*, calls these "inevitable pairings."

The collocations I have included here are mainly those that far outnumbered other collocations of the same modifiers in the Oxford English Corpus. A telling symptom of such overused collocations is sometimes the absence in English of an expression of the opposite idea. Have you ever encountered an indistinct possibility or advantage? Probably not, even though *distinct possibilities* and *advantages* are the most frequent collocations with the two nouns. There are, of course, *vague possibilities* though they are far less frequently noted than the distinct kind. By way of contrast, *distinct impression* is also a frequent collocation but I have not included it here because it does not smack of cliché: it has a clear literal meaning, as well as an opposite expression that is nearly as frequent in the form of *vague/indistinct impression*.

In a few cases corpus data showed some collocations involving modifiers that appear in the entries below in equal or greater frequencies with other words than in the phrases that I have included. For example, *eminently qualified* (which I do not consider a cliché) is as frequent as *eminently reasonable*, which is noted below. The former, to my mind, escapes the sentence of cliché by having a distinct meaning that suits the modifying word.

Some of the clichés in this chapter consist of adverb + adjective (or adjective + adverb), where the adverb functions as a submodifier—in other words, a modifier of a modifier. Submodifiers are typically intensives, of which the busiest in English is *very*. It might be suitable, though it would hardly be tempting, to consider many *very* + *adjective* collocations as clichés. It is probably not very productive to do this since for many speakers, especially of British English, *very* without a previous negation is effectively a filler, not a content word, and seems to be used without apparent motive: for the five most frequent such collocations in English (namely, *very good, very important, very different, very difficult, very hard*) usage in British English is substantially greater than in US English, sometimes nearly double. Britain, to the perception of most, is not a land of relative extremes, and so the frequent use of *very* in British English does not seem to be supportable on semantic grounds. See below for the one *very* + *adjective* combination that deadens the ears and minds of all, and which I regard as a cliché: *very real*.

Partly in an effort to provide some variety and relief for the dependable soldier *very*, writers and speakers call in replacements such as *tremendously, hugely, vastly, massively, totally*, and the like. The descent into cliché begins when the insertion of the submodifier becomes automatic, and an experience or other phenomenon that the reporter may wish to note as extraordinary is characterized by a phrase that has lost the desired accentuating force.

abject poverty   3
abject failure   3

Born into abject poverty, Henry Darger suffered a traumatic childhood before being committed to an institute for feeble-minded children at the age of twelve.

His efforts at reassuring African-American constituents in the White House of his good intentions were an abject failure.

These two collocations account for close to half the uses of *abject* before a noun. They serve mainly as variants for *extreme* or *complete*, and so in one sense they simply provide writers with an alternative to two modifiers that are themselves already very frequent. Is *abject poverty* worse than the extreme kind? If a failure is complete, does *abject* take it even a step further (or: *take it to the next level*?)? These questions are probably not scribbled by editors in the margins of writers' copy as often as they should be but writers might well put the questions to themselves.

abundantly clear   4

Against that background, it is abundantly clear that by 1992, if not earlier,
   Mr. Sarwar was aware of and raised no objection to the bank's retention
   of the Bury legal charge.
He would have had either to refuse the offer of payment in lieu or make it
   abundantly clear that his acceptance of it was without prejudice to his
   employment continuing for the remaining twelve weeks.
I would like to make it abundantly clear that somebody at Reuters wrote the
   story, not me.

Without its participation in this phrase, *abundantly* would have only half-time work in English. The cliché is spread across all genres, with the strongest concentration in legal writing. There it is often used as a battering device in argument.

believe passionately/passionately believe   3

I passionately believe that markets are incredibly inefficient, so the best way
   to make money is to get out on the road and see the companies.
As long as you believe passionately in what you are doing, others will follow.
Ambassador Bolton believes passionately in the goals of the United Nations
   charter to advance peace and liberty and human rights.

This cliché holds down one corner of a passionate triad, the other two being *feel passionate about sth* and *(be) passionate about something*, which are treated in the chapters about predicate and adjectival clichés, respectively. *Believe* is accompanied by *passionately* more than by any other adverb, which might give the impression that mere belief without emotional engagement is inadequate today. Instances of the cliché, however, merely indicate that *passionately* is undergoing continuous devaluation with each use when it is yoked to this verb. The cliché has had generally increasing usage since the late nineteenth century and a sharp increase since the 1980s.

categorically deny   3

Oakley categorically denies that 40 million alpha particle and 100,000
gamma photon hits each week, every week over a lifetime, to a fixed piece
of soft tissue in the lung can cause cancer.

I produced a detailed report, including statements, conclusions, and
recommendations from a variety of independent sources that
categorically denied what was being put forward by Messers Bush
and Blair.

I received no response at all until Feb. 28, when I received a reply from the
Justice Department categorically denying my request. The primary reason
cited was that the department had a longstanding policy of not providing
Congress with information about people who have been investigated but
not prosecuted.

About 10 percent of the time this phrase is the predicate of the pronouns *we*
or *I*, and in these cases the listener may decide how it should be interpreted.
The other 90 percent of instances involve writers deciding for their readers
that a categorical denial took place, though in many of these cases it appears
that *categorically* is simply used as an intensive and that we are experiencing modifier overreach. When used with third-person subjects it is helpful
to justify the use of the adverb with circumstantial information, as in the
third example.

---

close proximity   5

The functional group in closest proximity to the distal piperazine nitrogen is
the other nitrogen on the piperazine ring.

Despite the close proximity of the two countries, there isn't much rivalry
between France and Switzerland.

Proximity means "nearness" so it is extraordinary that in some genres of
writing it is accompanied by *close* nearly half the time. Scientific writing
(first example) often discusses multiple proximities, making the modifying
use of *close* or its inflections sensible, but this is not usually the case in journalism, where the pair of words is simply riveted together.

---

consummate professional   2
consummate skill   1

Lewis won't be able to do that as well as Ali could have done, but Lewis is a
consummate professional and if he takes good advice he could easily do a
similar job on Tyson.

Disney took their work, and the writings of numerous other authors, and
  retold their tales through animation and film with such consummate skill
  that they became the modern definitive versions.

These two collocations account for more than 10 percent of all uses of the attributive *consummate*, suggesting that writers are not feeling around extensively in the adjective jar before pulling this one out. *Consummate professional* is unusually common in sports writing to praise an already (in another sense) professional athlete. *Consummate skill* gets its most rigorous workout in writing about the arts to praise works, performers, and performances and is the less objectionable of the two in that it characterizes a domain where perfect and complete skill is most effective.

dirty/dastardly deed   1

James Bamford reveals in his latest book that US military leaders planned
  to commit terrorist acts against Americans and blame the dirty deeds on
  Castro as a pretext for invading Cuba.
Slabodkin eventually got turned off by some of the dirty deeds he was
  ordered to carry out by the unit's chief, Michael Lewis.
Eighteen of the twenty-six businesses she works with did not recycle at all
  before she met with them, despite the fact that municipal inspectors can
  fine them up to $2,000 for the dastardly deed.
If Rudy is just going to talk about what dastardly deeds Schaffel did, I don't
  think that's going to get them anywhere in tying Jackson to this conspiracy.

These noun clichés' single claim to merit is alliteration, which their users may think adds a light touch to their text. Both are nearly synonymous with *misdeed*, which is preferable in any formal context. *Dastardly deed* is frequently used ironically for minor misdeeds and transgressions; the adjective has limited circulation outside of this cliché.

deeply concerned   4
deeply rooted   4

I'm deeply concerned about the war on terrorism, and that is why I'm still
  undecided.
An atmosphere of nostalgia stemming from the impossibility of the
  immigrants' return to their homeland is deeply rooted in Argentinean
  culture, especially in its music.

The motive to use *deeply* in place of some other intensive when talking about *concern* probably stems from the frequent figurative association of depth with feeling. Its high frequency dilutes its effectiveness in this collocation. Outside of particulars in agriculture and horticulture where shallowly rooted things exist, it is the nature of things rooted to go deep, and it is thus not usually helpful for us to be reminded of it.

distinct possibility   2
distinct advantage   2

There are opportunities all around the world for a UK angler to go and combine their love of small boats with the distinct possibility of having their arms pulled off.

This technique can offer distinct advantages over the time-resolved optical techniques that have been traditionally used for this type of study.

Proclaimers of the *distinct* versions of these two abstractions seem intent to raise the odds of theirs happening or existing above what they would get by simply giving us the noun without a modifier. It works to some comic effect in the *possibility* example above. The *advantage* example is not improved by the adjective.

dramatically different   3

The slow rise is followed by a non-desensitizing phase of the response that is dramatically different from the fast desensitization observed for wt 5—HT 3AS Rs.

The biophysical behaviors of the two cpn 10 variants are dramatically different.

Since we're dealing with dramatically different stories with different characters playing in different genres, the quality can be inconsistent.

Does alliteration alone license interlocutors to wield words whose meanings do not precisely represent their intentions? This seems to be the case with *dramatically different*, an emphatic kind of difference that is often invoked even when no drama is present. Even in science writing, where it is surely desirable to keep drama to a minimum, the collocation is frequent, as illustrated in the first two examples. The third example is rendered ambiguous because of the dilution of meaning that *dramatically* receives as an intensifier: it may mean "different with regard to drama" or simply "markedly different."

dramatically increase/reduce/improve/change   5

The acquisition enabled Smith to dramatically increase its volume and expand into soft-serve and extended shelf life dairy products.

Our dramatically reduced cycle time is working to enable less reliance on standing inventories for sale.

The president is pursuing a national strategy to dramatically improve America's air quality.

These four verbs represent the favorite companions of *dramatically* as an intensifier of verb meaning. The choice of *dramatically* does not usually add drama to the kinds of change indicated, even when it may be the wish of the writer for it to do so. There are several relief adverbs that can do the job as well if not better: *greatly*, for instance.

eminently sensible 2
eminently readable 1
eminently reasonable 1

Both these reviews look eminently sensible, but we'll have to wait and see what sort of proposals they come up with.

My learned friend has tried to say that this case is one where the restraint was eminently reasonable even though restraint of trade was not mentioned in the case at all.

Although it's eminently readable and surprisingly funny, there's no mistaking that this is a true cultural guide and not travel writing.

Eminence implies a context in which prominence or superiority is distinguishable, so a collocation like *eminently qualified* has a clear meaning with the implication "more qualified than all others." The synonymous clichés *eminently reasonable* and *eminently sensible* use *eminently* merely as an intensive with no more meaning than *very*, but with more syllables. *Eminently readable*, a cliché only in British English, is in the same category except in the rare cases where the reading material is discussed in context with competitors.

entirely likely 1
entirely possible 4

Given that the Hebrew peoples were previously polytheistic, it's entirely likely that the Elohist source for Genesis chapter 1 meant the words to be literally plural.

It seems entirely likely that we will see worldwide struggles well into this new century between modernity and fundamentalism.

It's entirely possible that the qualities that make 8 Mile a brilliant movie also hold it back from greatness.

By 2006, it is entirely possible that boll weevil management will consist
of keeping the insect out of the country instead of controlling its
damage.

Studying many instances of these frequent qualifiers do not make it clear why speakers so often choose them over simpler constructions—such as *maybe, I think,* or *it's likely that,* which is all that the clichés amount to in many instances. Both expressions put some distance between the speaker and the posited scenario, framing it abstractly in a world of possibilities rather than attaching a personal point of view to it or describing it as likely, which may give speakers the hedge they are seeking.

justly/deservedly famous   1

Solti was justly famous for his Wagner interpretations and his pioneering
first studio recording of the Ring Cycle, also for Decca, has acquired cult
status.
The earliest of these vessels, the justly famous North Ferriby boat, has
recently been dated to about 1900 BC.
Leos are deservedly famous for their loyalty, and that's most obvious when
your astrological ruler, the sun, is in that persistent and solid sign,
Capricorn.

These closely synonymous collocations are not frequent by the measure of clichés in this category but they imply judgments about fame that would be more convincing if they were actually used to characterize things that most people—or at the very least, most people in a given audience—have heard of or know, as in the first example.

far-reaching implications   3
far-reaching consequences   3

These claims have very far-reaching implications and every possible effort is
being made to establish the facts surrounding them.
Most of the fighting has been on Guadalcanal but the consequences have
been far-reaching: paid jobs nationwide have all but disappeared as a
result.
The change is being seen as the country's first legal acknowledgement that it
is possible for a human being to be neither male nor female—which could
have far-reaching consequences in many legal areas.

Modifying *consequences* and *implications* accounts for a substantial portion of what *far-reaching* has to do in English and it's an apt adjective for the purpose. The reach can be spatial, temporal, or figurative, as illustrated in the examples above. The combination only falls flat when misapplied trivially. The presence of modals *could* or *might* along with these phrases is often a sign of a writer engaging in speculation of dubious value.

---

because frankly 2
frankly speaking 2

Mr. Greenspan, I always enjoy your presentation, because frankly, I wonder what world you live in.

Frankly speaking, you will need to really make a significant physical effort to remove this baby from its box: it weighs almost 20 kg.

Speaking quite frankly I am just a little disappointed with it in view of the sensational experiences you have gone through during recent months.

Mothers who are breastfeeding are sometimes forced to sit uncomfortably at a desk or stand for hours, because quite frankly some employers may not understand how a lactating woman's body works.

Frankly is used in numerous fixed phrases as an intensifier, most frequently in these two. Both are usually followed by a pause, marked by a comma, and signaling the arrival of frankness in a discourse that is already in progress. Where this is not enough, some speakers double up the cliché by inserting a *quite: because quite frankly* or *speaking quite frankly*. There's no stopping those in the habit of setting up pronouncements in this way but for those who have not developed the tendency, it is always worth considering whether a more original way of delivering emphasis might serve the purpose better. See also below at *quite*.

---

freely admit 3

Julie freely admits to feeling helpless and occasionally bursting into tears with the frustration of it all.

So here we had the Marines freely admitting they made a bad, bad mistake, that they accidentally killed these three people.

I freely admit that other factors, including cuts in taxation, have also contributed to our economic success.

Freely shows a fairly consistent pattern of following verbs of motion (*move/ flow/roam freely*) and preceding verbs of more abstract volitional actions (*freely choose/elect/express*). *Freely admit* is more than twice as common as its next *freely + verb* neighbor, suggesting that the choice to use it is perhaps not freely made but is implemented by a speaker's automatic pilot. Does the adverb contribute meaningfully to sentences in which it appears? Usually not, because no suggestion of admission under coercion or other restraint is ever present to be countered.

general consensus   5
general overview   2
general pattern   1
general trend   4

Regardless of definition, the general consensus is that American cheeses have held steady as a mainstay of the overall cheese category.

First we will give a general overview of our business history. Next, we will outline what we feel are some critical elements of success.

The general pattern is to marry kin, although families try to diversify their social assets through marriage.

While the general trend of the four lines is similar, temporal differences exist between the in situ measurements and the ex vivo quantitation by spectrofluorimetry.

The cliché value in all of these collocations is the usually meaningless use of *general* to qualify a noun that is already a generalization. *General pattern* and *general trend* are both frequent in science writing where they may be aptly used to contrast with specifics (such as in the fourth example).

generally tend/tend generally   2

Analysts generally tend to see a bright future for a company that transformed itself in the past ten years from a commodity-based un-sexy group to one of the market's blue chips.

The colour clothes I have on generally tend to reflect my mood, my view of my self etc., etc.

The schizophrenic tends generally to retreat from involvement with his environment.

Tendencies are general by their nature so unless some countertendency is mentioned, *generally* adds nothing of importance to the verb in this predicate cliché, though it may suggest a withholding of full commitment to a position by the writer. It is frequent in blogs and news.

have absolutely no/nothing ...   5

We have absolutely no doubt that maintaining credit, speculative, and spending bubble excesses are simply not going to rectify the problem.

I have absolutely no doubt whatsoever that there would also have been

criticism of witnesses had those witnesses been absolutely word
perfect.

The church says they had absolutely nothing to do with it and says that they
didn't even know that these people were there.

This is the go-to construction for those in the business of vehement denial, and since so many are in this business all the time, the construction gets no rest and *absolutely* is reduced to being a mere intensive, with little relation to its core meaning of being without qualification or limitation. Speakers and writers wishing to make a clearer expression may want to consider a less flat-footed way than this formula, which often simply has the effect of making its audience feel verbally battered.

heated argument   3
heated debate   4
heated discussion   3

After heated debate in Johannesburg on how to reconcile different international
agreements, the final documents merely call for mutual supportiveness.

A brief and heated discussion followed their testimony but changed nothing.

Siskel explained this during a heated argument with Ebert about why Free
Willy sucked, which ended with Siskel saying Ebert identified with Willy
because he's fat.

Heated debates seem to have become popular in the late nineteenth century and have been simmering since. Perhaps they are a natural outgrowth of matters *hotly debated* (see the next entry). Users of *heated* with the nouns above prefer it to any of several possible synonyms (*angry, passionate, vehement, fiery, torrid*, for example) and thus create a cliché by not stopping to consider alternatives and choose one that suits the occasion best.

hotly contested   4
hotly debated   3

After a hotly contested race, Yeo easily defeated Margaret Albright, 5,485 to
3,010, for the Ward 2 seat on the School Committee.

For the past eight years the Poetry Cup has been hotly contested by the
region's performing poets.

The merits and drawbacks of those AIDS- and HIV-prevention strategies
have been hotly debated.

These phrases both become nearly meaningless via the automatic fashion in which journalists bang their components together. Even brief reflection in most cases will bring to light a more suitable adverb, if one is needed, to illuminate a particular controversy or contest. See also *heated argument/ debate/discussion*, above.

---

invaluable resource   2
invaluable tool   2

Optical tweezers have been an invaluable tool in cell biological research: for trapping cells, measuring forces exerted by molecular motors, or the swimming forces of sperm, and for studying the polymeric properties of single DNA strands.

This is a fabulous and absolutely invaluable resource for anyone stuck with that difficult to research project or teachers faced with that perennial curly question about whose faces adorn our banknotes.

Use short bold text, for example in the form of a hyperlink, to make important information stick out from the page. Bullet lists are an invaluable tool as well.

The cliché-maker here is the adjective *invaluable*, which in fact also collocates frequently with other nouns (*experience, service, information, assistance*) but not as frequently as with these two. The implication of *invaluable* is "valuable beyond estimation" or "priceless." It is occasionally used to actually mean this and can be effective when supported with evidence, as in the first example above. *Invaluable contribution* is often used in a complimentary way that should probably not be called a cliché since its intent is to give credit. Most users of *invaluable* would do as well with *valuable* or with any of its numerous synonyms in English from among which a writer or speaker can thoughtfully choose a better alternative. Writers who settle on *invaluable* may at least be commended for not invoking *worth its weight in gold* (in the adjective clichés).

---

largely due to sth   5
largely ignored   5

The loss was largely due to accounting problems and replacement of a software program to better serve its member cooperatives.

Dodd-Frank was passed in response to the financial crisis, which resulted largely due to the bubble burst of the inflated housing market.

The unfashionable conjunction of women with parochial Christianity means that, with a few exceptions, local church women's groups are seriously underresearched . . . and largely ignored by aid organizations.

Unlike in Ireland, where Stakeknife has sold 15,000 copies since it was published a month ago, the book has been largely ignored by the British media.

Largely shares most of its semantic space with synonymous adverbials such as *mainly, primarily,* and *to a large extent.* In sentences where it can be used interchangeably with any of them it works best when there is an actual extent imaginable or where physical space (or a figurative extension of it) is involved—in *largely overshadow,* for example. The use of *largely* in the two collocations above is often the work of an automatic pilot making word selections. *Largely due to,* whatever its shortcomings, is a less dire resort than *due in large part* (in the adjectival clichés). *Largely ignored* is often a way of indicating that someone or something didn't get as much attention as the writer deemed was merited. It passes unnoticed in a lot of writing, even technical writing, but it probably shouldn't because of an explained gap between entirely ignored (not a frequent collocation) and *largely ignored.* The writer's purpose in using this cliché is usually to focus on what has been neglected rather than what has been said or done.

legendary coach/singer/producer/player/director (etc.)   4

*A death chant performed by the legendary singer Demetrio Stratos (who
    collaborated with John Cage in the 1970s) completes the piece.*

*Legendary coach Joe Gibbs and his Skins were unable to do anything,
    resulting in a 17–0 blowout.*

*One of the things that Something Weird Video is known for is its access to
    legendary players in the exploitation market.*

Like *fabulous* before it (original meaning: "resembling or suggesting a fable"), the meaning of *legendary* is now steeply discounted from "characteristic of a legend" to mean merely "well known." There is surely nothing to be gained by further diminishing the scope of *legendary* by associating it with people known only to a small circle, but this now happens regularly, particularly in journalism. Writers would do their readers a service by considering more thoughtfully what genuinely distinguishes the figure they are writing about and perhaps even pause to consider whether any legends exist. There is surely always a more appropriate adjective to distinguish a subject.

massively popular/successful/important   2

*Obviously education is a massively important part of this whole thing and
    prevention is in the end far cheaper than dealing with people who are infected.*

*What makes The Sims massively popular with female gamers, who
    traditionally don't make up a big number of gameplayers?*

*The latest film from the creators of the massively successful Bayside
    Shakedown series is titled simply Udon after the very tasty noodles that
    feature prominently in the film.*

Massively is a way station on the road to *overwhelming* and *overwhelmingly* for many writers who are not content with *very* or *extremely* and have already bypassed *hugely*, which collocates most frequently with the three adjectives above. *Massively* (unlike *hugely*) also collocates frequently with scalar verbs (*increase, decrease, reduce*, etc.) by extension of *massive* as an elegant variant of *big* and *large*. In combination with the adjectives above it may be intended to evoke the idea of "the masses" but it typically only evokes an awareness that one is being fed hyperbole.

by no means/not by any means/not by any manner of means   4

Stephenson Harwood replied saying that the sale of the Notes would not by any means satisfy Manlon's indebtedness to BCCI.

I am not by any means the first to suggest the relationship between the frustrated altarpiece program and these over-door images.

The prospect of tweaking a wine to fit a desired chemistry is still a bit more unusual there, if by no means unheard of.

By no manner of means is he perfect because he can be a moody little blighter, but on balance he is a marvellous lad.

Though this formula does not seem to have originated in law, it has a happy home there (first example), where it is often used aptly in sentences where some means might actually be involved. As a general purpose, emphatic negater in a wide range of genres, it is overused and often smacks of bluster. The older formulation, *by no manner of means*, has disappeared from all but the most purple writing.

forward/positive momentum   3

His defensive work, a combination of bone-jarring hits and last-ditch scrambling, repeatedly helped stop Australia from establishing forward momentum.

His direction provides the forward momentum the screenplay needs to build towards its multiple revelations and climaxes.

KFC and its franchisees are eager to keep the positive momentum of product promos—crucial for generating traffic and bolstering sales.

Use of these two noun clichés identifies you as a nonphysicist and a devotee of jargon. Their meanings are roughly equal—they mean "momentum"—but their distribution is surprisingly different. *Forward momentum*, the more frequent of the two, predominates in sports writing and writing about the arts. *Positive momentum* is found mainly in business writing.

personally think/believe   4

I personally believe that productivity growth will remain elevated as firms learn to make better use of the technology they purchase.

I personally think if you can only grow two plants it should be a pot of tomatoes and a pot of basil.

Do you personally think this is a more important election than some of the others?

Speakers occasionally use *personally* with these two verbs in order to mark contrast with a more generally held view that has been previously stated or implied. More often it is used, overwhelmingly with *I* as the subject, to emphasize the speaker's opinion, in the belief that it is important to do so or that someone cares. A quick review of the semantics of personal pronouns establishes that *I*, juxtaposed with nearly any verb, carries a very strong implication of *personally* that need not be further emphasized.

---

perfectly entitled/justified   3
perfectly normal/capable/possible   4

People are perfectly entitled to express their views for and against any issue, and I would in no way discourage them from doing that.

Today I was treated to not one but two precise illustrations of why my reasons for feeling that way are perfectly justified.

I recently caught my boyfriend looking at pornography. He says it's a perfectly normal thing for a grown man to do.

Schubert was perfectly capable of developing themes when he wanted to and his capacity for harmonic juxtaposition of distant keys succeeds, even in the exceedingly long piano sonatas.

It is perfectly possible to imagine a woman in her twenty-sixth week of pregnancy deciding that an abortion is the best solution for her, even though there is no fetal abnormality.

In all of these frequent collocations, *perfectly* departs from ordinary associations with perfection or completeness and acts merely as a worn-down intensifying modifier or submodifier. *Perfectly entitled* and *perfectly justified* abound in legal writing, where they sometimes address the notion of legal entitlement or justification, for example, *The Respondents were perfectly entitled to question the Tribunal decision and appeal if they were so minded.* Many of the uses even in legal writing, however, are not different from uses outside of law, where the entitlement and justification are a matter of declaration or perception, with *perfectly* added for various rhetorical motives. With the other adjectives noted above, *perfectly* is meant to impart emphatic force. The high frequency of these collocations mitigates this.

quite frankly   5
quite right   5
quite agree   2
quite simply   2
quite possibly   2

We aren't allowed to be racist—and quite right too—but being racist about body shape doesn't seem to bother anyone.

I'm just quite simply diabolical at names, and have a memory that would shame a sieve.

Some of the statistics you have quoted have quite frankly shocked me.

It is knowing, loving, kidding, and quite possibly one of the year's best films.

I quite agree that a professor who has little or no background in a particular area may be unable to provide adequate supervision in that area.

Quite is an extremely versatile submodifier that is indispensable in many constructions to convey a shade of meaning not available with other words, such as quite + noun (*That's quite a statement!*), not quite (*We're not quite ready*), and some quantifying expressions such as *quite a few* and *quite a lot*. In many cases *quite* functions like *very*—as a filler rather than a word that conveys any intention on the part of the user. I deem it a participant in cliché in the collocations noted at the top of this entry because of the disparity of their usage in different varieties of English and because of the frequencies with which these compounds occur in some varieties.

When used as an adverbial with verbs, adjectives, and other adverbs, the use of *quite* is more problematic and may convey nothing beyond the alacrity of the writer or speaker to pad out words with fixed expressions, forgoing any reflection about their usefulness. The selection noted above is certainly not the full extent of *quite*-based clichés but contains some of the worst offenders, most of which are more common in British than in American English. *Quite frankly* enjoys equal abuse on both sides of the Atlantic and is used most frequently by speakers to supply emphasis for an unimaginative declamation that follows, or less frequently, precedes it.

quite the _____   3

In older days they were quite the danger, but in the last few centuries they had quieted down in activity.

Work's Christmas party is tonight. It's quite the shindig apparently: a few big
  tents, bumper cars, snake charmers, dancing.
The official cast announcement was turned into quite the spectacle, as
  hundreds of screaming people lined the El Capitan Theatre in Los Angeles,
  waving signs and generally causing a frenzy.

Unlike the *quite* phrases noted in the previous entry, this colloquialism is harmless in conversation where it designates an exemplar. It sinks to cliché only in blogs and online fiction, where it comes to the aid of writers who bypass the search for a compelling adjective to modify their noun. *Quite the* merely shifts the responsibility to the reader to augment the features of the noun highlighted.

rather different   4
rather good   3
rather large   4

The lead-up to a mass declaration for Hinduism on this island was rather different
  to the Javanese case, in that conversions followed a clear ethnic division.
Who Wants to be a Millionaire *presenter Chris Tarrant was spotted*
  walking along Esher High Street carrying a rather large cardboard box.
Having a big house with a couple of spare rooms is not a guarantee of B&B
  success. This rather good book could change that.

These collocations are the most frequent of a list that could probably be extended. The first and last are not typical of American English but abound in British English. The common element here and with some other *rather + adj* pairings is the superfluity of *rather*. It fills the syntactic slot of a scalar adverb but nearly always without the existence of—or the need to reference—a scale, since the modified adjective can easily stand without one to give the intended meaning.

staunch conservative/Republican   1

He was a staunch conservative, a devout evangelical Christian, and a tireless
  campaigner against inhumanity.
One such backer is Lucy Billingsley, a white real estate developer from Dallas
  and a staunch Republican.

Staunch is used literally in these phrases and that argues against their being considered clichés. What is more, *staunch* collocates more frequently with many partisan-neutral words: *supporter, ally,* and *defender,* to name a few. The cliché trap here is that instances of *staunch conservatives/Republicans* outnumber *staunch liberals/Democrats* by nearly four to one, suggesting that the users of these phrases are speaking or writing formulaically—or alternatively and not very persuasively, that liberals and Democrats are less steadfast in their principles and so do not merit the *staunch* label.

thoroughly modern   2

As thoroughly modern masters of war, you comprehend the captivating
     power of television to simultaneously mesmerize and anesthetize.
The thoroughly modern spaces are assembled with sensuous materials: deep
     blue terrazzo on the entryway floor, glass mosaic tiles on the fireplace wall
     and on the wainscoting in the bathrooms.
The pages have the size and texture of an old Sunday paper comics supplement,
     but the short story they present is told in a thoroughly modern manner.

This collocation is somewhat anomalous since other adjectives that share company with *thoroughly* characterize qualities that are habitually accompanied by adverbs of degree (*enjoyable, entertaining, familiar*). The suggestion is that writers would assure us that no aspect of modernity has been overlooked, but instances of usage indicate that *thoroughly* slips in more on the basis of rote than of meaning; there is rarely any contrast with anything historical or ancient, although the cliché is justified when this is present (see third example). Some usage may echo the 1967 film *Thoroughly Modern Millie* though, interestingly, the cliché had its heyday earlier in the twentieth century.

truly amazing   3
truly great   4
truly remarkable   3

Don Weller, one of the truly great hard bop tenor sax players, will be the
     guest at The Rhythm Station, Rawtenstall on Tuesday.
A goal down, playing into the rain and wind after losing three players to
     injury in the first half, City were truly amazing.
Mammon's Music *is a magisterial delineation of a fascinating subject and*
     compelling reading, a truly remarkable achievement.

The phrases noted here are at the top of a cliché pile consisting of uses of *truly* as an intensive; there are many others, such as *truly global/unique/wonderful/awful*. There is never any intended or implied contrast with *falsely* for things described with *truly*; the writer's intent is mainly to distinguish, for example, mere greatness from *true* greatness. Most sentences do not suffer from the deletion of the intensive.

vary tremendously 1

Empirically, the prevalence of male-killing endosymbionts varies tremendously among host species.

People also vary tremendously in how they respond to the same events in their lives.

It is surely not fair to words to require that they maintain some loyalty to their origins; language might never evolve as rapidly or interestingly as it does if they had to do this. Nevertheless, it is unfortunate that *tremendously* so readily takes up company with *vary*, since the verb has mainly to do with variety and the adverb with trembling, dread, awe, power, greatness, and enormous size. Science writers, who are often more conservative than others, are great fans of tremendous variation. Despite the status of *tremendously* as a general purpose intensifying adverb, there are many better choices to characterize variety.

a veritable feast/cornucopia/smorgasbord/treasure trove 2

The author undertook a project of tremendous breadth and returned with a veritable treasure trove of vibrant detail.

Towards the centre of the island lies the Andromeda Gardens where the glorious tropical foliage is a veritable feast for the eyes.

Estonia is a veritable cornucopia of architectural history and styles.

Veritable often appears before nouns used metaphorically that typically stand for something quantifiable. Dictionaries note that the purpose of *veritable* is to emphasize the meaning of the noun, but it is nearly always used before nouns that already smack of hyperbole and usually give the same meaning without modification by *veritable*. The upshot: a veritable explosion of clichés. The collocations shown above are all frequent and roughly synonymous in use with *veritable*. They are symptomatic of the general cliché nature of *veritable* + noun.

very much _____ 5

I very much appreciated Hardy Green's book review of Rich Cohen's Machers and Rockers: Chess Records and the Business of Rock & Roll.

In spite of its significant gains, the survival of Dawhenya Irrigation Cooperative Rice Society Ltd. is very much in doubt.

They are very much aware of the double standards and perhaps this is the reason why we are not sure who to show loyalty to.

Banham's book, although it presents engineering as another culture
incompatible with architecture, is very much about architecture.
Royal Navy fighter control is still very much alive and well, and indeed
changing to meet new developments and new tactics.
I would very much like to be put in touch with any scientist, anywhere in the
world, for whom Mr. Geller performed this wonder.

Very much has many utilitarian functions in English that, despite great frequency, are not regarded as annoying or clichéd because of their literal nature: *Thank you very much! Was there very much snow? We didn't like the film very much.* It has crept into the misfortune of cliché by occupying a sentence slot that isn't well designed for it: one that precedes or interrupts a verb phrase, or that intervenes between a copula and its predicate, as in all of the examples above. Many users of the phrase even in these constructions probably regard it as harmless and fit for its task and for speakers it is probably indispensable: finding a more suitable and expressive adverbial at short notice involves a search of memory banks that the moment does not provide time for, and merely intensifying whatever expression is at hand with *very much* serves a practical if not very inspired purpose of allowing the speaker to move on—in many cases, to the next cliché, as in *very much alive and well.* Thoughtful writing draws more pointedly on the inexhaustible supply of adverbial intensives in English, rather than slotting in this all-purpose one.

very real   5

We would thus face the very real danger of this move triggering a devastating
inflationary runaway.
This matter of safely storing transferred data is a very real problem, not just
for mainframes and open systems but between open systems servers too.
Two of the three structures would not have survived more than a few years—
the degree of risk was very real.
In a very real sense individuals create themselves through their moral choices.

Real has long-standing credentials in English as an intensifying adjective, arising from one of its core meanings, "genuine." And *very* is English's most frequent intensifying adverb, so perhaps it is only natural that the two should team up to form a dire cliché. Journalists (and very serious people they quote) perpetuate this unfortunate partnership thousands of times each day, usually with the intention of adding drama, urgency, or bona fides to the phenomenon they are reporting on. It's unlikely they can be broken of the habit but it would behoove them to ask, before naming a *very real danger*, whether they simply mean "threat." *Very real problems* don't lose a great deal of importance by being characterized simply as real problems or big problems. *Very real possibility*, the most frequent misfortune brought to the attention of the reading public, is treated separately in the noun clichés.

---

virtually impossible   5
virtually identical   3
virtually nonexistent   3

Grossly inadequate yo-yo budgeting from Sacramento has made it virtually impossible to plan even one semester ahead.

In fact the bananas used in all conditions were virtually identical, as rated by five judges.

The plot is virtually nonexistent and I found myself seeking any explanation whatsoever.

When placed before any of the adjectives above, which are by far the most frequent adjective companions of *virtually*, the adverb functions as a somewhat formal synonym of *almost*—which is a suitable job in *virtually identical*, frequent in legal, scientific, and medical literature. The cliché component of these phrases emerges from a recurring desire on the part of the writer or speaker to characterize a quality as negligible.

---

a whole new _____   5

They give a whole new meaning to the term "a thinking man's music."

Whey protein fractionation is leading to a whole new generation of whey protein–based ingredients.

It's a whole new way of thinking about chronic versus sustained pain that just won't go away.

Some *a whole new _____* clichés are frequent enough to merit individual treatment and they are noted below. *A whole (new) set* is treated with the quantifying clichés at the end of the adjectival chapter. The examples here serve to point up the pointlessness of characterizing something as *a whole new* when it is merely different. Writers would do well to pause before their fingers travel to the keys that will instantiate *a whole new dimension/range/light/perspective/approach* (in addition to the nouns that appear in the examples above) and consider whether it is the best way to characterize a contrast with what has gone before. *A whole new ball game* is also a candidate for this caution and it is frequent enough to be considered a cliché unto itself—but examples of usage suggest that it is in fact a very efficient way of characterizing a situation in which a great and sudden change makes it necessary for all participants to take a new approach.

---

a whole new level 3

It's going to take a whole new level of commitment from architects like Wes, who are willing to engage communities directly.

He has achieved a whole new level in power dressing.

Turducken is a way to enjoy all three at once, bringing the holiday meal to a whole new level.

This common cliché could have some force if it were applied more sparingly to things that actually admit of discernible levels, but as hyperbole for "more" or "to a greater degree" it has used up all of its credit. Like several other of the common *a whole new* _____ clichés it is most typically found in soft journalism and news reporting. *A whole new level* typically occurs after verbs such as *bring, take, reach,* and *achieve.*

a whole new look 1

Cover crappy badges in camouflage, floral, or fishnet fabric and you have a whole new groovy look.

A light color can give your room a whole new look.

Substitute shirt 2 with the same slacks and jacket for a whole new look!

Though not as frequent as some of the other *a whole new* _____ clichés that are lumped above, *a whole new look* deserves special attention for the abandon with which it is used by writers on fashion and décor. How often are *whole new looks* necessary? It may well seem that one is required every day, judging by the frequency of this cliché in the perky articles aimed mainly at women with the implication that they are under obligation to change the way things look with exhausting regularity.

a whole new world 3

When I discovered the internet at the age of fifty-eight, a whole new world opened up to me.

The minute you stop listening to your own self-doubt, you'll be able to open up a whole new world of possibilities for yourself.

Actually talking to her could open me up to a whole new world of misery.

The characterization of an area of experience as a "world" is common, and people do regularly encounter circumstances that might seem like *a whole new world*—the first example above is a valid instance of this. But like other *whole new* clichés, it is more effective to reserve *whole new world* for something grander than "more."

8
Clichés in Tandem

This brief chapter looks at a small number of clichés that never travel alone—they are phrases that speakers and writers use to warn their audience that they are about to use or are using a cliché. Unfortunately, most of these devices qualify as clichés in their own right, and so their appearance signals an unavoidable double whammy: an insult in the form of a lifeless phrase that you have no means of escaping, following the injury inflicted by the other phrase that heralded it.

The motive of writers and speakers who use these devices may be their felt urgency to impress upon an audience their awareness of the cliché they are about to deploy. Since clichés are by their nature known generally to native speakers, it's not clear that this advance notice enhances regard for the author. A secondary motive may be an implicit or explicit apology: the writer is at a loss for an expression to convey what is usually a common situation, and so mentions the witting use of cliché:

It sounds a tired cliché but winning the competition really has been a dream come true.

*The company doesn't want to reinvent the wheel, as the old cliché goes, but
is asking key questions about what a semiconductor solution should be.*

A trope in journalism is to identify some expression as an old cliché or a tired cliché—sometimes even a tired old cliché—and then go on to explain its apt applicability to a particular case. This is a broader meaning of cliché than the one that operates in this book, but the use of cliché in this way is certainly a cliché: to identify proverbs or simple statements of fact as a cliché and then go on to say how they apply. Here are some examples from current online writing:

> *The rich are getting richer. It's an old cliché, but it also happens to be true, according to the latest data available from the census.*
> *Friends, it is but a tired cliché that beauty is in the eye of the beholder, yet isn't it the truth?*
> *Life is frequently said to begin at 40 but in the case of Aberdeen striker Scott Booth, that tired old cliché might just ring true.*

As if to ensure they are covered against accusations of cliché, some writers use this device even when no obvious cliché is present. Sportswriters are particularly fond of invoking the phantom cliché:

> *He had runners on base in every inning but one and to steal an old cliché he wasn't fooling anyone.*
> *We know it's a tired cliché to say that the game had a "playoff atmosphere," but this one really did.*

The first example may leave the reader baffled as to what cliché is being referenced. In the second example, the collocation *playoff atmosphere* is not frequent enough to register on most people's radar as a cliché, let alone a tired one, and so the identification of it as a cliché simply conveys the impression that the writer inhabits an extremely small world of limited expression that he rarely escapes from (which may, after all, be true).

Many formulaic expressions in English are productive: speakers recognize the template on which a variation of the original is based and there is a consequent freedom to play with the expression in order to characterize actors and situations that depart considerably from the original referents. Do you need to warn readers of your imminent employment of this license? Probably not, because the original template expressions are familiar and even your most plodding readers will see immediately what you've done:

> *To put a new twist on an old cliché, you can lead a salesperson to your*
> *CRM system but you can't force him or her to use it.*

In this example, the "cliché" referenced (it might be more accurately called a proverb or a chestnut) is "You can lead a horse to water but you can't make it drink." Is the writer's exploitation of the original a "new twist" that merits an introduction? Only the reader can judge.

The frequent framing device *so to speak*, treated with the framing devices, also very often functions as a paired cliché when the adjacent phrase is also a cliché, used in a typical way that usually does not require notification to the reader:

> *Lambert likes the grit, the blood, sweat and tears so to speak, that ac-*
> *companies the dreaded hill.*
> *You don't want to play the "black card," so to speak, and you almost don't*
> *want to feel what you're feeling.*
> *People like me tend to wear our political sentiments on our sleeves so to speak.*

Nothing would be lost from any of these sentences by the omission of *so to speak*.

---

as it were   5

> *Now, with the structure a reality, it seems a suitable time to test the waters,*
> *as it were, of China's rapid development with the Yangtze as good a*
> *barometer as any to do so.*
> *She was talking about the general sense of alienation, the general sense of*
> *problems, huge problems that are not being addressed. This, as it were, is*
> *the kind of oxygen that fuels something like Boko Haram.*
> *Angry, resentful, and left-out, those students who fall off the edge, as it were,*
> *will be a burden on any peace and reconciliation process.*

This three-syllable qualifier is shorthand for "as if it were so," which in expanded form sometimes brings sense to the context in which the shorter form is used, and sometimes doesn't. The phrase is a way of signaling a not strictly literal or usual interpretation of what precedes or follows, in some cases to indicate a play on words: *Pinterest Followers: Don't be afraid to go over-board, as it were—the most successful Pinterest accounts have more than two hundred different boards!* It may also telegraph a writer's coinage or nonce usage for the occasion at hand:

> *Some employers will let employees buy—and others, sell—vacation days.*
> *It sounds simply like taking unpaid vacation days, but according to the*

Associated Press, there are companies with somewhat more compli-
cated vacation day markets, as it were.

As it were can be used effectively with an idiom or cliché, as in the first example at the top of the entry, when it signals similar wordplay—in this case,
that *test the waters* is not used in ignorance of *Yangtze*. In other cases though,
and in the other examples, *as it were* merely signals to the reader that the
writer isn't entirely sure whether the cliché applies or what it means. Aside
from these usages, *as it were* qualifies as a cliché with adverbial or adjectival
function, depending upon how it is misused, by writers who insert it for no
discernible reason, as in the following examples:

> *Upper Arlington, Ohio, is a suburban town in Franklin County that*
> *shows a population of about 34,000; a rather small community that*
> *sits between the Olentangy and Scioto rivers as it were.*
> *Indiana, in particular, had been a tough sell to potential recruits as it*
> *were, playing in an outdated facility before the state-of-the-art Bart*
> *Kaufman Stadium opened on campus this season.*
> *She took a deep interest in world affairs and, typically as it were, brought*
> *out her culinary know-how at the most unexpected moments.*

There is little difference in the contexts in which writers feel impelled to use
as it were and *so to speak,* which is discussed briefly above and also in the
chapter on framing devices.

literally _____ 5

> *The filmmakers make multiple artistic statements, some so sweeping and*
> *grand that they will literally take your breath away.*
> *Well, frankly, I think nobody wants the country to literally go down the*
> *drain, and I think that there is now a huge international movement to*
> *keep the country afloat literally.*
> *In this rush to reduce populations, untested or untried contraceptives have*
> *been introduced in the Third World countries, literally making these*
> *women guinea pigs.*
> *The time was right to leave ballet because my joints were literally falling*
> *apart after dancing until the age of thirty-six.*
> *Now the state is in a huge position of power. They've literally got him by the*
> *short hairs.*

Various abuses of *literally* are a favorite subject for usage pundits and ordinary
people alike; the popular press is rarely free of revelations and observations

about it. Its frequent inapt use as an intensive is what most irritates people—for example, when it is used in ways that stretch credulity and force the listener to forgo a literal interpretation of *literally* in order to accept a statement: *I found it literally impossible to put down until I'd readjusted my life so I could keep reading it all day and deep into the night, savoring the suspense until the very last word on the final page.* At the other extreme is the attachment of *literally* to a statement that no one would find difficult to interpret literally without the adverb: *They wonder why their share of business is literally getting smaller and smaller* or *I literally get goosebumps listening to the St. Matthew Passion.* The cliché credentials of *literally* are indisputable since it seems to be used incorrectly more often than not. The examples at the top of the entry show the form pertinent to this category, in which writers and speakers attach *literally* to some tired expression in the vain hope of reinvigorating it. This literally fails in every attempt.

---

the proverbial _____ 2

We're not always implementing things the traditional way, but trying to find
*   new ways of skinning the proverbial cat.*
It quickly becomes apparent he's caught between the proverbial rock and hard
*   place: winning the game will invoke the wrath of the prison's governor,*
*   and throwing the game will double-cross the crimeboss.*
I think I have hit the proverbial brick wall with him, and I need to know if
*   I am being petty or practical in my assessment of our relationship.*
Finding items in the maze of pallets and containers was like searching for the
*   proverbial needle in a haystack.*

None of the examples above, each of which introduces a familiar idiom or cliché, are helped by *proverbial*. Removing it does not redeem the sentences from cliché but renders them somewhat less mired in it. Writers who feel compelled to use this adjectival introduction in their tired bag of tricks may do their readers a favor by either omitting part of the chestnut that follows—*80 bucks on a new sound system would be the proverbial straw*—or adding something to the cliché in order to inject some life into it: *This swindle takes the proverbial cake, icing, candles, and all.*

Occasionally it is the case that writers insert *proverbial* as a flag of surrender—to their inability to find an original way of expressing an idea that is conventionally represented by a cliché, as in these sentences:

One could hear the proverbial pin drop as the four actors related a touch-
*   ing and evocative story of human tragedy and its sequence of events*
*   unfolding with one surprise after another.*

*I know I am going to be accused of beating the proverbial dead horse, but
I think that, yet again, the dissolution of our football team is an issue
that needs to be addressed.*

*None of the delegates wants to change his or her vote so the convention
is deadlocked and representatives of the candidates meet in the proverbial smoke-filled rooms.*

Writers also use *proverbial* to bolster an expression that is too variable in
form to represent a strict verbal cliché but that is clearly a monochrome way
of expressing an idea, as in these examples:

*As 2003 dragged on, however, a new release failed to appear, and now,
like the proverbial buses, along come two at once.*

*Our modern hero and his half-witted companions must overcome endless
obstacles to reach the proverbial pot of gold at the end of the rainbow.*

*His steadfast refusal to see the proverbial glass as less than half-full is
more inspiring than cloying.*

Finally, on Nov. 7 (like the proverbial monkeys banging out Hamlet*),
the rag printed the correct information.*

*Antoine Walker has been a key contributor to Miami's rise from the
proverbial ashes.*

These sentences also do not obviously benefit from the use of *proverbial*,
even in cases where the familiar idea behind the expression may still be productive. The last example is particularly inept, since if any part of this idea
partakes of proverb, it is the absent phoenix, and not the ashes. Temptation
to use *the proverbial* should prompt any writer who wishes to rise above the
status of hack to consider whether the well-worn grooves of cliché are the
best way to express the idea at hand.

(as) the (old) saying goes   5

*The idea for the grant came to Porter from farmer folklore in Minnesota: The
saying goes that soybeans are made in August.*

*We found that more consumers go shopping with a mission and know exactly what
they want. Sound familiar? Well, it describes me to a "T" as the saying goes.*

*If John Negroponte thinks he has a tough job serving as US ambassador to
Iraq, wait until he takes over as the nation's first director of National
Intelligence. As the saying goes, he ain't seen nothing yet.*

Most of the busywork that leaves this expression so tired as to be unable
to stand on its feet could be eliminated if writers who use it would ask:

(1) is the observation that follows actually a saying?, and (2) do readers need to be warned of this? The first example helpfully contextualizes the presentation of an idea that would in fact be unfamiliar to all but a small circle and therefore uses the expression aptly. The other examples would benefit by removal of both the familiar saying and the setup for it.

to use a/the cliché   1

As much as I hate to use the cliché, form does follow function.

I hate to use the cliché, but people in glasshouses shouldn't throw stones.

What we have now is basically better than anything we've had before and that in thinking about alternatives you can't chuck the baby out with the bathwater, to use a cliché.

Not to use a cliché, but I think people were expecting to see some serious "big fish."

Sorry, but I must use a cliché to describe your June 21 issue: the best ever!

I hate to use this cliché, but we've got the elephant in the room right now, and that is, this same case is happening thousands of times a year across this country.

I would also like to try to get through my analysis without using the cliché "the grass is always greener" but I am afraid that that is not meant to be.

"It was a real family, to use a cliché," Enoch said. "It's the only real way of describing it to people who weren't there."

This means it will take you a little longer to save for the first property, but time is on your side if you are young, and to use a cliché, Rome wasn't built in a day.

A cliché aptly used does not require an apology or acknowledgment, and an apology for one misapplied does not redeem it. The examples above show some of the formulas that writers and speakers use to excuse their use of clichés or to acknowledge their awareness of their perceived descent into cliché. Is communication aided by any of these devices? Clichés will speak for themselves if they have anything to say and need not be formerly introduced or pointed to in retrospect. If all clichés were so telegraphed to their audiences, language would become far more cluttered with detritus than much of it already is.

Afterthoughts

It is not a typical reader who will have arrived at this chapter after reading everything that precedes it—in fact it would be a rather peculiar reader, given the kind of book that it is. But this place seems an appropriate one to summarize many impressions that have occurred to me about clichés over the course of the two years that I spent researching and writing this book. I preface these remarks with the caveat that these impressions, though informed deeply by my study of clichés through examining thousands of examples of them, are drawn mainly from my own instincts about English, my own *Sprachgefühl*, and that these observations may not be shared by others.

1. Idiomatic expressions with a concrete element—especially a part of the body, an animal, or a natural object—are less likely than others to be regarded as clichés, perhaps because of their strong and indelible link with sense data. Readers and listeners do not mind, and may even welcome, for example, that *root and branch* is used in place of "thorough" or "thoroughgoing" in *a root and branch assessment of the spending*, or in place of "completely" in *a system of class oppression that must be destroyed root and*

branch. Idioms that evoke images of objects not typically encountered in everyday life may have a greater chance of remaining vivid—*tip of the iceberg*, for example—and thus are not necessarily subject to the same threshold of fatigue from overuse that arises from expressions formed from more mundane words.

2. English speakers like economy of expression. If we can say it in two syllables, there's not much point in stretching it out to five or six. On this basis, many fixed figurative expressions, such as *shed light, shut up, skin the cat*, and *smackdown* (to draw only from a tiny alphabetic range), maintain their popularity and impact and avoid being perceived as tiresome.

3. English, not surprisingly, has a natural sympathy for words of native or Germanic origin and for imported words that have been conformed to the look and feel of a native English word—typically, a word that is a monosyllable with consonants or consonant clusters surrounding a vowel sound. A characterization such as *grow by leaps and bounds* is much less likely to be received as wan and lifeless than a Latinate one along the lines of *increase exponentially*. We always have the option to use a phrase like *an essential feature of* or *an integral component of*, but we're more likely to use *part and parcel*—a frequent idiom that I do not consider a cliché because it does its job better than its more formal equivalents in most contexts.

4. Somewhat in line with the previous point, expressions that offer some other attractive feature, such as alliteration or a euphonious prosodic pattern (like *part and parcel*, which offers both), enjoy a degree of immunity from being perceived as clichés because people like to say them and hear them. In a related way, some clichés serve a pragmatic purpose that supplants whatever (little) meaning they may carry and for this reason they may enjoy frequency of use far beyond what seems necessary. Examples of this are clichés such as *on a daily basis, worth its weight in gold*, and *going forward*, which are very often placed at the end of a clause and are inflected so as to inform listeners that the speaker has reached the end of his current thought and that a pause in the discourse has arrived.

5. Those several points notwithstanding, English speakers employ a num ber of needlessly wordy clichés merely from habit and the failure to consult their imaginations to find or develop shorter, more suitable expressions.

A question that arises naturally to anyone engaged in the study of clichés over a period of time is this: Why do writers continue to use them? What genuinely motivates the cliché, when there is nearly always an alternative that, if it is not a cliché, is ipso facto more original and probably a better expression of the idea at hand? Cliché-ridden prose usually gives the impression of being written or spoken thoughtlessly, if not hastily, and it is hard to find fault with the argument that a great deal of cliché results simply from language users not taking particular care about what they say. Thus, cliché finds its way to expression from language users taking the path of least resistance—where the resistance is to the effort that would be required to consult the intellect for a more original or apt way of expressing an idea.

People who are required to write—whether hastily or not—and those who write without any awareness of what separates good writing from bad, such as poorly educated students or poorly read adults, naturally write in a semiautomatic style, laying down the first words that come to mind much as the wagon wheel quickly finds the well-worn groove. Writing of this kind is bound to produce thick patches of cliché simply because of the ready availability of cliché in the lexicons of writers and speakers and the want of any compunction against using it. Taken together then, carelessness and ignorance are certainly responsible for a great deal of cliché that is expressed in speech and print. I suggest that these two causes—I hesitate to call them motives—are largely the explanation for the greatest breeding grounds for the written cliché today, journalism and online writing in the form of blogs and fiction.

I noted in the introductory chapter that journalism contains more clichés per unit of text than any other genre. Readers who have engaged with this book even casually will have noted that journalism is mentioned more frequently than any other genre of writing in the individual entries. This is because journalism is demonstrably the greatest repository of cliché in English. This is not a criticism, just a fact. Journalists are required to produce verbiage hastily most of the time. While their work is typically edited, it is not edited for clichés because cliché is a substantial part of the code of journalism, and consumers of journalism accept conventional and stereotyped ways of expressing ideas, whether consciously or unconsciously, as part of the diet. Because of the natural tendency of speakers and writers to be influenced by what they read and hear, it is also inescapable that journalists are the greatest vectors of cliché in English.

The Internet age has brought us two other genres that represent rich veins for miners of cliché: blogs and online fiction. While neither may have a comparatively large audience, they are both full of unedited writing that is shot through with clichés, which are gobbled up uncritically by the avid perusers of these genres. The world of online fiction is relatively self-contained and the virulence of clichés there is mainly a self-infecting and reinfecting phenomenon. Blogs, which reach a wider audience, are today probably second to journalism in spreading and popularizing (and thus further deadening) clichéd expressions.

Eric Partridge, in the introductory essay to his *Dictionary of Clichés*, eloquently encapsulates much of what I have said above in his account of the prevalence of clichés:

> Why are clichés so extensively used?...A half-education—that snare of the half-baked and the ready-made—accounts for many: an uncultured, little-reading person sees a stock phrase and thinks it apt and smart; he forgets that its aptness should put him on guard. The love of display often manifests itself in the adoption of foreign phrases....The use of clichés approximates to the use of proverbs, and certain proverbial phrases lie on the...No Man's Land between the forces of Style and Conscience entrenched on the one side and those of Lack of Style and Consciencelessness on the other: but proverbs are instances of racial wisdom, whereas clichés are instances of racial inanition.

YOU, TOO, CAN PREVENT THE SPREAD OF CLICHÉS

In editing and rereading the manuscript of this book before releasing it to the publisher, I have noted my own prejudice throughout that is effectively the book's leitmotif: words work best when they are specifically chosen for the job you wish them to do. This will not be the case with an expression that you use because it was the first compatible one that came into your mind for the syntactic slot you needed to fill and so you let it fall in, Tetris-like, without really examining its features. This is an obvious point that deserves emphasis because there is so much writing and speech that has clearly been done with no clear thought given to the purpose of the words that compose it. If all writing was entirely of this kind, it seems likely that people would be put off reading and clichés would live in a rather small, moribund world that would eventually extinguish itself. But we all must read, whether for entertainment, vital communication, or acquiring new information; and all of the writing we read is bound to contain some portion of cliché. Because of these factors we cannot help exposing ourselves to cliché and being infected by it. Whether we become active vectors of cliché ourselves is a matter of choice. All that is required for clichés to flourish is for good writers to disengage their attention from what they are doing.

This is not to say that a cliché, when it comes to mind, should be rejected simply because it is a cliché. Every cliché has the potential to bring light or provoke thought if it is used in a way that does not simply deaden the reader's sensibility, which is what unexamined cliché always does. Consider, for example, the nominal clichés highlighted in the following sentences.

1. A theory of turnaround is lacking because of a wide separation between empirical findings (based either on large samples or on case descriptions) and work done toward systematically uncovering the causal structure of events from the onset of a firm's decline to its ultimate recovery or death. Using Meyer's comment in reference to the bankruptcy of US businesses in the 1980s, it can be concluded that turnaround researchers are "*a long way up the empirical creek without a theoretical paddle*" (from the *Canadian Journal of Administrative Sciences*).

2. Who could possibly *tilt at windmills*? In the federal election, almost every party had a billion-dollar wind-power plank in their platform (from *The Tyee*).

These, and many other examples that I have highlighted throughout the book, show that clichés are not incapable of resuscitation, but the fact remains that they are dormant by their nature. A cliché in itself and by definition has no element of originality and if a cliché is to be used, it places greater demands on a thoughtful writer to justify its use in preference to a more straightforward or succinct expression. Requiring a cliché to do more than it normally does by extending its meaning, application, or reference is one way to do this. If the effort is only minimal, there is always the chance that the result will be merely groan-inducing: *Researchers weigh in on the body fat versus BMI debate*.

I will have failed in my mission with any reader who, after perusing this book for minutes, hours, or days, feels at liberty to dismiss me as a usage curmudgeon. I have no agenda to reform English. I embrace the whole mansion of it, from the dankest corner of promotional blurb to the grandest auditorium of epic poetry. It is out of love and respect for it that I write about it. It is a tall order to suggest to speakers and writers that they choose their words more carefully and that they be more circumspect about using words whose presence does not add meaningfully to what they are saying, but I fully own that there is a respect in which this book urges that advice. It takes only a little more time, but considerably more effort, to write mindfully than it does to write mindlessly. You have to engage your intellect and examine the requirements of what you mean to express, and the words available to do it for you. But writing mindfully can be developed to become a habit with some effort, just as writing mindlessly becomes a habit with no effort. To quote George Orwell again, from the same source as I did in the introductory chapter: "Modern English, especially written English, is full of bad habits which spread by imitation and which can be avoided if one is willing to take the necessary trouble."

If you've arrived at this chapter in the book after spending a considerable amount of time in other parts of it, or in the index, it may have occurred to you at some point: "_____ is a cliché but I can't find it in this book." Such an observation may arise from three possible causes: (1) you and I disagree about the status of a particular expression and whether it constitutes a cliché; (2) I agree that your expression is a cliché in some contexts but it is generally used felicitously and does not constitute any sort of usage or semantic problem; (3) I agree that the phrase that peeves you is a cliché and if I had come across it in my research I would surely have treated it here.

I have only documented in detail a fraction—albeit a rather large fraction—of the phrases I originally gathered in a spreadsheet for consideration as clichés. I have examined many frequent phrases and idioms and concluded that they are not usually clichés according to the criteria that I set out in the beginning of the book. The main reason for rejecting the label of *cliché* for a given familiar expression is that I do not find that it is ineffective in the majority of cases where it is used. Is this a personal judgment? Undeniably it is; there is no other means by which to determine the effectiveness of language. In a few cases I have provided details about an expression whose use is not really problematic—such as *take a backseat* or *every nook and cranny* as opposed to *nooks and crannies*—because I find that the meaning and usage are broader than are accounted for in dictionaries. But for their inferior treatment elsewhere, a few such expressions would not have been included in this book.

As I stated very early in the book, it has not been my intention to catalog all the clichés in English in order to arm the speakers and writers who wish to avoid using them and thus also avoid the aspersions that might be directed at them. All speakers, and most writers, use clichés, and language would be a very different vehicle for communication from the one we know if we were all required to purge it of clichés. But at the same time, the concept of *cliché*, with its attendant negative associations, only exists because people consistently employ fixed expressions in ways that their audiences find to be uninspired, unoriginal, ineffective, and even irritating. If you have used this book in any sequential or systematic fashion, I hope that by now you have a better understanding of clichés and why they are problematic.

I hope even more that you have given some thought to how you wish to deal with them in your own use of language.

Even the most unhurried writer rarely has the leisure to examine and research every phrase that comes to mind as a candidate for expressing an idea and deciding, part-of-speech by part-of-speech, whether the chosen candidate is the best one and thereby avoids an unwanted rendezvous with cliché. Most of the time we all write with a goal in mind—to finish the task at hand—and this motive presumably drives the stream of words onto the page or screen. The best way to ensure that your writing is as good as you can make it without needlessly interrupting this process is simply to consult your imagination and judgment as you write and take note of whether you are using an expression that has found its way into the stream simply because it's always there, swirling lifelessly in an eddy, where it was recently deposited by some other writer you have read.

For writers with the time to devote to a more empirical approach for determining the cliché risk of a particular expression, resources are freely available: anyone can do armchair investigation of the status of fixed expressions, their frequencies, and facts about their usage. I have enjoyed the benefit of using several corpora, particularly the Oxford English Corpus, in assembling this treatment of clichés. I have surely also benefited from my training, and my many years of working as a lexicographer, in arriving at the judgments I have made about the use of clichés. But as I stated early on, it has not been my intention to provide an exhaustive catalog of clichés, and I am sure that many more still exist in the wild, ripe for harvesting. So I leave you with tools to determine for yourself whether a given form of words constitutes a cliché in a given context—particularly some common form of words that you do not find in the index of this book.

None of us has much of an opportunity to edit our extemporaneous speech. Those who would avoid the use of clichés there would do so in vain, and in any case, there is rarely a need to: clichés are an expected part of most kinds of verbal communication and you would probably sound stilted and peculiar if you trained yourself to speak extemporaneously without the use of clichés. Public speakers very often rely on clichés to provide the glue connecting the elements of their discourse: to connect them otherwise while also remaining grammatically coherent would probably exhaust nearly all the resources of short-term memory and hardly allow the speaker to organize the next topic, let alone finish the one at hand without lapsing into anacoluthon.

Speech aside, however, all of us have an opportunity to edit our writing, and it is in writing that we have the greatest opportunity to communicate effectively, efficiently, and meaningfully—while also diminishing the generally unhelpful contagion of English with pointless clichés. The function of clichés in writing is much more limited and focused than in speech, and if you have questions about the effective use of some familiar phrase that comes to your mind and that you do not find in this book, there are tools readily available for you to decide whether it is a phrase that suits your purpose. The questions you may ask are as follows:

1. Who uses this phrase, and in what contexts?
2. Is the phrase effectively and appropriately used in contexts where you find it? Does it convey the meaning intended in a way that is helpful to readers? Are there equivalent and less frequent expressions that do the job better or more efficiently?
3. Does your intended use for this phrase align well with the apt uses of it that you have found?

There are many corpora online that you can use to examine usage of a phrase in the same way that I did. For American English, a good and easily accessible corpus is the Corpus of Contemporary American English, found at http://corpus.byu.edu/coca/. An older but still useful corpus for British English is the British National Corpus, found at http://corpus.byu.edu/bnc/. After a short learning curve with the corpus's querying interface you will be able to call up multiple instances of an expression in a format that enables you to see at a glance where, how, and by whom your target expression is used.

You can also simply use the web as your corpus. Search engines—notably, Google—enable you to limit your search to particular genres of text so that you can, for example, look only at text from scholarly journals, blogs, news, or books. The format in which the text is returned will not be as helpfully presented as it would be if you used a corpus but you will be able to examine a sample of sentences containing the expression of interest and also get an idea of its frequency. From this, it soon should be obvious whether the phrase you are questioning has already had its day in the sun or whether it offers the opportunity for you to say exactly what you mean to say.

Index

This is a machine-sorted index in which only parentheses and blanks (_____) are ignored, reflecting the form of the cliché that appears in the body of the book and that in most cases is the canonical or most frequently encountered form. Clichés that have variability at the beginning (such as *lull sb into a false sense of security* and *be lulled into a false sense of security*) are indexed twice to facilitate finding them; those with variability at the middle or end (*cannot be overstated/overemphasized/underestimated*) are usually lumped in a single index entry.

give sb/sth a wide berth, 132
go (the) whole hog, 133
go back to (the) basics, 115
go from strength to strength, 133
go the extra mile, 132
go through the motions, 133
going forward, 101
grand old dame/woman/lady, 36
grand old man, 36
grave concern, 37
grind to a halt, 134
grip the country/nation, 134
grist to the mill, 37
groan with pleasure, 143

hale and hearty, 73
half the battle, 73
hang in the balance, 134
hard-fought battle, 38
hard-pressed to do sth, 73
has seen better days, 74
have absolutely no/nothing…, 195
have another think/thing coming, 135
have one's ducks in a row, 127
have the bandwidth (to do sth), 135
Having said that, 172
head and shoulder above _____, 102
hear the pin drop, 136
heated debate/discussion/argument, 196
heave a (huge) sign of relief, 150
heavy lifting, 38
herald a new era, 142
high and mighty, 74
hit a/the wall, 136
hit your head against a (brick) wall, 136
hop, skip and a jump, 39
hot-button issue, 39
hotly contested/debated, 196

I must admit, 177
I must confess, 177
I want to be perfectly clear, 168
I want to make one thing perfectly clear, 168
I would argue that, 166
I (would) hasten to add that…, 173
iconic image, 40
I'd like to make one thing perfectly clear, 168
if ever there was one, 75
if the truth be told, 183
if you ask me, 174
if you like, 103

if you will, 103
impact negatively (on sb/sth), 137
in a nutshell, 106
In a world where…, 184
in actual fact, 90
in all conscience, 91
in an ideal world, 102
in and of itself, 75
in any way, shape, or form, 92
in effect, 97
in high dudgeon, 102
in large part due to _____, 69
in my humble opinion, 173
in no small part/measure, 105
in no uncertain terms, 106
in point of fact, 171
in the affirmative, 90
in the extreme, 98
in the true/truest sense of the word, 109
in this day and age, 96
ins and outs of sth, 41
invaluable resource, 197
invaluable tool, 197
It is arguable that, 166
It goes without saying, 172
It's (probably) safe to say (that), 180
it's a miracle that, 176

jump the shark, 138
justly famous, 193

keep your head above water, 138
kith and kin, 41
know for a fact, 139
know full well, 139

largely due to sth, 197
largely ignored, 197
lay down the law, 139
leading light, 42
leafy suburb, 42
leave a/an aching/empty/huge void, 140
leave no stone unturned, 140
leave sth/much/a lot to be desired, 140
legendary player/coach/singer/producer, 198
Let me hasten to add that, 173
let your imagination run riot, 137
let's be honest, 174
let's face facts/the fact, 175
let's face it, 175
light at the end of the tunnel, 43